U.S. History
Through
Children's Literature

U.S. History Through Children's Literature

From the Colonial Period to World War II

WANDA J. MILLER

1997
TEACHER IDEAS PRESS
A Division of
Libraries Unlimited, Inc.
Englewood, Colorado

To my husband, Randy
and our children, Randy and Kari

📖

TEACHER IDEAS PRESS
A Division of
Libraries Unlimited, Inc.
P.O. Box 6633
Englewood, CO 80155-6633
1-800-237-6124

Production Editor: Kevin W. Perizzolo
Copy Editor: Jan Krygier
Proofreader: Jason Cook
Indexer: Linda Running Bentley
Typesetter: Kay Minnis

Library of Congress Cataloging-in-Publication Data

Miller, Wanda Jansen, 1959-
    U.S. history through children's literature : from the colonial
period to World War II / Wanda J. Miller.
      xiv, 229 p. 22x28 cm.
      Includes bibliographical references and index.
      ISBN 1-56308-440-6
      1. United States--History--Study and teaching (Elementary)
2. Children's literature--Study and teaching--United States.
I. Title.
LB1582.U6M49   1997
973'.071--dc20   96-38234
                                                                   CIP

Contents

Acknowledgments

I'd like to thank my husband and children for their support throughout the writing of this book. It couldn't have been done without their patience and help.

Cheryl Gravelle from the Williamson Public Library was a whiz at locating materials.

Colleagues from Williamson Middle and Elementary Schools were full of ideas, literature recommendations, and much encouragement!

Without encouragement from John Robbins and Noreen Mascle, I may never have started writing in the first place.

Finally, I'd like to thank my late parents, Arnold Jacob Jansen and Marjorie Lookup Jansen, for their encouragement to always do my best and keep trying.

The following permissions were obtained to reprint materials that appear in this book.

The Certificate of Arrival Document for Aarnout Jansen, is reprinted with permission of the document's owner, Wanda J. Miller.

The Declaration of Intention Document for Aarnout Jacobus Jansen, is reprinted with permission of the document's owner, Wanda J. Miller.

The *Literature Response Guide* (see fig. 10.1), is reprinted with permission from Leslie Wood, Williamson Elementary School, Williamson, NY.

The *Medical Release from Military Duty Document* for Franklin S. Dean, from the town of Marion in Wayne County, New York, dated August 12, 1864, is reprinted with permission of the document's owner, Wanda J. Miller.

The Oath of Allegiance Document for Arnold Jacob Jansen, is reprinted with permission of the document's owner, Wanda J. Miller.

The Petition for Naturalization Document for Aarnout Jansen, is reprinted with permission of the document's owner, Wanda J. Miller.

The poem "Pioneers" is from *Patriotic Plays and Programs* by Aileen Fisher and Olive Rabe. Copyright (c) 1956 by Plays, Inc., Boston, MA.

The recipes for Butter, Maple Syrup Candy, Cornmeal Spoonbread, Indian Pudding, Virginia Pound Cake, Corn Fritters, Baked Beans, Hardtack, and Appleade, and The Indian Diet and A Soldier's Daily Camp Ration, are used with permission from *Cooking Up U.S. History: Recipes and Research to Share with Children* by Suzanne I. Barchers and Patricia C. Marden. Copyright (c) 1991, Teacher Ideas Press, a division of Libraries Unlimited.

The *Surgeon's Exemption from Military Duty* form from Wayne County, New York, is reprinted with permission of the document's owner, Wanda J. Miller.

The poem "There Is Power in a Union," attributed to Joe Hill (pp. 87-89), is reprinted with the permission of Simon & Schuster Books for Young Readers from *Hand in Hand: An American History Through Poetry,* collected by Lee Bennett Hopkins. Text copyright (c) 1994 Lee Bennett Hopkins.

The poem "A Visitor" by Sarah Smith Caldwell, is reprinted with permission from Wanda J. Miller, great-great-great niece of the author.

Introduction

Purpose

U.S. History Through Children's Literature was written for use by teachers in grades four through eight. The purpose of this book is to provide teachers with information to begin or expand their use of quality children's literature in the teaching of United States history. Teachers who have already begun teaching history in this format have been forced to purchase their own materials and create their own questions, activities, vocabulary exercises, and lessons to supplement the trade books that they are using. With the many demands on their time, including regular teaching duties, parent conferences, staff meetings, committee meetings, and paperwork, teachers do not have the time or energy to build a literature-based history program from the ground up. *U.S. History Through Children's Literature* was written to help fill this need.

The core of any good literature-based curriculum is a collection of quality trade books. The trade books recommended for inclusion in this book were selected based on teacher recommendations, book reviews, and recommendations from librarians.

Teachers often have to purchase numerous trade book guides, as what is currently available, while often good, may only cover a certain time period, or a small sampling of books dealing with various time periods. In addition, many guides may have excellent activities, but do not include discussion questions or vocabulary, or vice versa.

Advantages

The advantages of using children's literature to supplement your United States history lessons are numerous. The greatest advantage is having historical literature at your fingertips when teaching about a certain historic time period.

Nothing brings history more alive than reading quality literature about what life was like during that time. Although the facts learned in textbooks are very important, students more easily grasp a true understanding of the time period and hardships through a historical character's dilemmas, thoughts, and feelings.

Students forget facts and details learned strictly from textbooks more easily than those learned through immersion in literature based on the time period. Because a lasting impression and understanding of history is our ultimate goal for our students, use of historical literature in addition to textbook teaching is a must, whether it be in social studies class, English, or reading.

To immerse your students in quality historical literature, you should have available a classroom set of a novel to be read as a whole group (approximately 30 copies), several small group sets (4-5 copies) of other titles to use in cooperative learning groups, and many individual titles for read-alouds, extra-credit opportunities, and research. In addition to recommending titles, this book also includes ideas for the teacher in the development of the theme, including activities, writing ideas, and summaries of each large and small group title. Research topics are suggested for each chapter as well.

Although reading one historical novel or nonfiction trade book is beneficial, reading two or more is even better. This is the reason for having a class set of a novel to read, as well as several small group sets. This way, students can share information with each other. After sharing a variety of books about a certain time period, it becomes clearer that any single event in history is not a single story but several stories told from differing points of view. Reading a second or third story reinforces background information and fosters critical thinking through the comparison of different points of view. It is highly recommended that you read the trade books first to decide if they are appropriate for use in your classroom. Whole group titles may be interchanged with any of the small group titles. Decisions may be made based on the availability of books, teacher preference, or students' needs. If class set quantities are not available, the book may be used as a read-aloud.

Finally, having these books available is a hassle-free way to incorporate quality literature with U.S. history. Using this book as a guide, teachers—be they history teachers, English teachers, or reading teachers—can build United States history libraries to use in their classrooms. The trend toward interdisciplinary teaching makes such collection building even more important.

Author Information

It is my belief that it is important for student readers and writers to learn about the lives of authors. Therefore, where possible, information about the authors of the whole group and small group titles has been included for your use.

Vocabulary

Vocabulary words for each of the whole group and small group titles are listed and defined. They are to be used in whatever way you feel is most appropriate. These vocabulary words were not necessarily provided for use in testing students but as a resource to help them better understand what they are reading. It has been my experience when working with small groups of students that teachers sometimes take for granted that all students know the more commonplace vocabulary in a novel. This is often not the case. Therefore, to provide a better understanding for all students, many of these more common words have been included.

Page numbers for the vocabulary words have been included for your reference. It is possible that these page numbers might be incorrect if you were to acquire different editions of any of the titles. If this occurs, I would suggest enlisting the help of a parent volunteer or teacher aide to locate the appropriate page numbers to correspond with your edition.

Grade Levels of Trade Books

Although the focus of this book is on middle-grade students, trade books encompassing a wide range of reading levels have been included. As we all know, our students do not all read at the same level. Some students may need materials at a lower level for independent reading and/or small group reading, while others may need more challenging materials.

Also, regardless of independent reading level, the use of picture books as read-alouds with middle-grade students is an excellent way to introduce or expand on a theme. Picture books provide a visual stimulus for capturing students' interest in a subject.

Building the Trade Book Collection

In a time of tighter budgets, we often need to find creative ways to fund projects such as this. If possible, ask your school's governing body to set aside at least $100 in your school's reading, social studies, and English budgets for this purpose. It would be wise to focus on one or two historical time periods in your proposal the first year, and add more in later years as funds become available. You could also purchase as many materials for a historical time period as your budget allows and add to it each year.

Often, school parent-teacher associations or parent-teacher organizations hold fund raisers to help with programs. Try contacting the organization in your district to see if it would also be willing to help fund your U.S. history library.

Book clubs, such as Scholastic, Trumpet, Troll, and Carnival, often offer selections that would be appropriate for your collection at a reduced cost. These savings, along with bonus points earned toward free books, can help stretch your budget.

Make use of the resources that are already available to you. Your school and public libraries most likely will have many of the titles you wish to use. Another possibility would be to inform parents and community members about your literature-based program. You could solicit donations by sending out a wish list of books for your library.

It may take a few years to have in place the books that you would find most suitable for your use, but the payoff will make the initial investment in time, effort, and money worthwhile.

How to Use This Book

Chapters 1-9 in this book contains the following sections: a suggested trade book for whole group reading, several suggested trade books for use in small groups, a bibliography of individual titles, theme resources, and an end-of-unit celebration. Chapter 10 provides a list of supplemental resources.

After reading a novel with your whole class, divide your class into cooperative learning groups of three to five students for small group reading. Books with summaries, author information, discussion questions, and activities are included for use by these groups. Choose from the activities listed in this book those that best fit the learning styles of your students and the time frame you have to complete the unit. Use these activities in reading, English, or social studies classes at the upper grades. In many classrooms today, there are times when remedial teachers, whether they are Title I teachers or special education teachers, work with classroom teachers and students in their classrooms, rather than in pull-out settings. An optimum time for these cooperative learning groups would be when other support personnel "push-in" to the room. The classroom teacher and resource person should rotate among the reading groups to provide guidance and direction when needed.

This book lists and summarizes many titles for independent reading and research by your students. These titles can be used in several different ways: for further research for a project; for extra credit toward their reading, social studies, or English grades; or as an independent reading assignment during your unit. In addition, chapter 10 of this book includes a general response guide for journal writing for students to use.

A section on theme resources in each chapter includes commercial resources, as well as some computer resources and videos.

Each end-of-unit celebration includes suggested research topics for you to use as a starting point for a culminating research project with your class. Some chapters also include recipes and reproducibles for use with your students. I encourage you to expand these celebrations to fit the needs of your students. The recipes included may be prepared by you or by parent volunteers before your final day studying a particular time in U.S. history. Should you decide to prepare them in class with your students, strict safety precautions should be presented to your students ahead of time. Before cooking day, arrangements need to be made with your cafeteria staff so you can use the kitchen facilities. Check out school safety regulations and get permission in writing. Also, it is highly recommended that you enlist the help of two or three parent volunteers or other staff members when cooking with students.

Chapter 1

Native Americans

Introduction

Native Americans settled in America long before anyone else. From the names of cities, rivers, and streets to foods such as corn, potatoes, and squash, Native Americans have left their mark on history.

The trade books selected in this chapter are recommended to help students understand the relationships between the Native Americans and the early European settlers. Many of the individual titles are included for further study of Native Americans and for research purposes.

Read and discuss the following poem with your class to begin your study of Native Americans:

Indian Names

Ye say they all have passed away,
That noble race and brave;
That their light canoes have vanished
From off the crested wave;
That, mid the forest where they roamed,
There rings no hunters' shout;
But their name is on your waters,
Ye may not wash it out.

'Tis where Ontario's billow
Like ocean's surge is curled,
Where strong Niagara's thunders wake
The echo of the world,
Where red Missouri bringeth
Rich tribute from the west,
And Rappahannock sweetly sleeps
On green Virginia's breast.

Ye say their conelike cabins,
That clustered o'er the vale,
Have disappeared, as withered leaves
Before the autumn's gale;
But their memory liveth on your hills,
Their baptism on your shore,
Your everlasting rivers speak
Their dialect of yore.

Old Massachusetts wears it
Within her lordly crown,
And broad Ohio bears it
Amid his young renown.
Connecticut hath wreathed it
Where her quiet foliage waves,
And bold Kentucky breathes it hoarse
Through all her ancient caves.

Wachusett hides its lingering voice
Within its rocky heart,
And Allegheny graves its tone
Throughout his lofty chart.
Monadnock, on his forehead hoar,
Doth seal the sacred trust,
Your mountains build their monument,
Though ye destroy their dust.

Lydia Huntley Sigourney

1

Whole Group Reading

Richter, Conrad. *The Light in the Forest*. New York: Bantam Books, 1990. Reprint.

A young white boy is captured by Indians and, after becoming a true tribe member, is suddenly returned to his parents. *Country of Strangers* is a companion volume. *The Light in the Forest* is a good book to read as a class because it highlights the feelings of the Native Americans and the early settlers toward each other. This book is a classic. Grades 6-8.

Author Information

Conrad Richter was born on October 13, 1890 in Pine Grove, Pennsylvania.

From the age of fifteen, Richter worked at many jobs, including clerk, teamster, farmhand, bank teller, timberman, and subscription salesperson before becoming editor of the Patton, Pennsylvania weekly *Courier*. During his career as a writer, he had many books published, some of which were made into movies.

According to Richter, one of the purposes of his novel *The Light in the Forest* was "to point out that in the pride of our American liberties we're apt to forget that already we've lost a good many to civilization." He believed that "perhaps if we understood how those first Americans (the Indians) felt toward us even then and toward our white way of life, we might better understand the adverse, if perverted, view of us by some African, European, and Asian peoples today."

He died on October 30, 1968.

Activities

1. On a map of the United States, have students locate the following:

    Allegheny River   Ohio River

    Lancaster, PA   Susquehanna River

2. Throughout *The Light in the Forest*, white people view the Indians as barbaric and uncivilized, and themselves as peaceful and righteous. Have students write essays to persuade the white settlers of the time period to change their view. Have them use examples from the book as well as information researched in the library to support their position.

3. Have students act out the tribal council meeting described at the end of the novel and decide the fate of True Son. Following the mock tribal council meeting, allow them to share their own feelings about what True Son's fate will be.

4. Have students write diary entries as True Son describing his feelings when he is returned to his birth family, and the strange ways (to him) of the white people.

5. Have students write an epilogue taking place twenty years after *The Light in the Forest*, telling what has become of True Son, his white family, and his Indian family.

Discussion

Give the class the following instruction: As we read this book we will be discussing the following questions. Write down your ideas about the questions and add to them as needed.

1. Why is True Son being given to the white man?

2. What did Del tell the colonel and why?

3. Why were the white captives ungrateful to be rescued?

4. What did True Son plan to do to keep from being taken to Pennsylvania?

5. Discuss True Son's feelings when Half Arrow found him.

6. What did Half Arrow give to True Son?

7. What did Little Crane say about why the white people are so foolish and troublesome?

8. What advice did True Son's Indian father send to him?

9. How does True Son feel about the white man's land?

10. How did True Son react to being reunited with his white father?

11. Discuss the feelings of True Son's white father since finding his son.

12. Why did True Son feel at home in the basket-maker's cabin?

13. What does Harry Butler feel guilty about?

14. What do you think is making True Son so sick?

15. What do you think will become of True Son now that Half Arrow has come?

16. What is True Son's only regret about leaving his white home?

17. Why did Half Arrow and True Son spend so much time at the prepared place?

18. What was Half Arrow's and True Son's welcome like when they finally reached their village?

19. How is True Son feeling about the Indians' quest for revenge against the white man?

20. Why did True Son decide to warn the white people on the boat of the ambush?

21. What did Cuyloga tell True Son about what their future would now be like?

Vocabulary

redoubt (p2)
a small fort, enclosed all around, often standing alone to defend a hill or pass

aversion (p2)
extreme dislike

affront (p4)
an insult or a rude, public act

plumb (p5)
completely; entirely

savage (p5)
a person living in a wild or primitive condition

palavering (p5)
empty talking, especially intended to flatter or deceive

bandy (p6)
to give and take; exchange

doughty (p6)
strong and brave; now rarely used except humorously

truss (p7)
to tie or bind; to fasten

dignity (p8)
proper pride in one's worth or position

forsake (p10)
to leave completely; to desert; to give up

earnest (p13)
very serious, determined, or sincere

wigwam (p15)
a hut in the shape of a cone or dome built by Native American Indians, consisting of a framework of poles covered by bark, hides, or other materials

ominous (p16)
threatening or foreboding

disposition (p17)
a person's usual mood or spirit; nature; temperament

cumbersome (p17)
hard to move or manage

impassive (p21)
not affected by emotion; showing no feeling

persimmon (p21)
the reddish, plumlike fruit from a native American tree, which puckers the mouth when green but is sweet to eat when ripe

turncoat (p23)
a person who goes over to the opposing side or party; a traitor

exile (p23)
to banish an individual from his or her native land

desolate (p23)
dreary; barren

barbarous (p24)
uncivilized

ostentation (p24)
   an excessive or uncalled-for display of something to attract attention or admiration

cloak (p25)
   a loose outer garment, usually without sleeves

pallid (p26)
   pale in appearance; lacking in color or strength; weak

presumptuous (p27)
   too confident or bold

squadron (p29)
   a unit of cavalry

scow (p30)
   a large boat having a flat bottom and square ends, usually towed

heathen (p34)
   a person who is regarded as irreligious, uncivilized, or unenlightened

pestilence (p38)
   any contagious, often fatal disease that spreads rapidly, such as cholera or plague

abhorrence (p39)
   a feeling of disgust, repulsion, or loathing

debase (p40)
   to lower in character or worth

derision (p42)
   mocking laughter; ridicule

pagan (p44)
   a person who has no religion

languish (p48)
   to become weak or feeble

odious (p48)
   arousing hate or disgust; offensive

bower (p48)
   a bedroom or other private room

cooper (p54)
   a person who makes or mends such things as barrels and casks

militia (p59)
   a body of citizens given military training outside the regular armed forces and called up in emergencies

lithe (p59)
   supple; limber

dram (p61)
   a small drink

condone (p61)
   to forgive or pass over

fervent (p63)
   very eager and earnest

seraph (p64)
   an angel of the highest rank, having three pairs of wings

brusque (p65)
   blunt and abrupt in manner; curt

miasma (p65)
   a heavy vapor rising from the earth, especially from decaying matter in swamps, formerly thought to cause disease

aboriginal (p65)
   of or having to do with aborigines; one of the earliest people, plants, or animals known to have lived in a particular area

antagonism (p66)
   mutual opposition, especially with hostile feelings

oration (p70)
   a serious public speech, usually given at a formal occasion

insidious (p72)
   slyly treacherous, evil, or deceitful

alacrity (p85)
   willingness or promptness

exultation (p102)
   great joy and jubilation

meritorious (p106)
   having merit; worthy; commendable

imperial (p108)
   superior, as in size or quality; magnificent

Small Group Reading

Dalgliesh, Alice. *The Courage of Sarah Noble*. New York: Charles Scribner's Sons, 1954.
   Young Sarah travels with her father to Connecticut, helping him while he builds a house for the family. They are befriended by Indians, and Sarah is left in the care of an Indian family when her father leaves to collect the rest of the family. This is a 1955 Newbery Honor Book. Grades 1-5.

Author Information

Alice Dalgliesh was born October 7, 1893 in Trinidad, British West Indies. She was an elementary school teacher for almost seventeen years and later taught a course in children's literature at Columbia University. She served as a children's book editor for Charles Scribner's Sons from 1934 to 1960. She wrote more than forty books for children and served as the first president of the Children's Book Council.

In the resource *Something About the Author*, Dalgliesh is quoted as saying, "Children are my major interest; they come first; and second, books in relation to children; never just books . . . I write different kinds of stories for different kinds of children."

She died on June 11, 1979 in Connecticut.

Activities

1. Have students illustrate the beautiful scene Sarah saw from the clearing, described on pages 15 through 17.

2. Have students write diary entries from Sarah's point of view. They should tell how she feels and what happens while her father is gone.

3. On a map of the United States, have students trace the journey that Sarah and her father made from their village in Massachusetts to the settlement in Connecticut.

4. Have the small group share their reading of this book with the class in the form of a debate. One student can be Sarah and another her mother. Sarah should attempt to convince her mother that the Indians are friendly and that she has nothing to fear. The rest of the group should be divided in half. One group should help Sarah by reminding her of the kind things the Indians have done. The other group should help Sarah's mother by giving her suggestions regarding why Sarah should be afraid of the Indians.

Discussion

Give the small group the following instruction: As your group reads this book, discuss the following questions.

1. Why did Sarah's mother tell her to keep up her courage?

2. Why did Sarah travel with her father to their new home?

3. What did the Robinson children tell Sarah about Indians?

4. How do Sarah and her father tell how their home will be different from Mistress Robinson's?

5. How did Sarah make friends with the Indian children?

6. What did Sarah and the Indian children teach each other?

7. Where did Sarah stay while her father left to get the rest of their family?

8. What did Sarah mean about friends having ways of speaking without words? Do you agree?

9. What were Sarah and Tall John afraid of?

10. Discuss Sarah's feelings when her father returns with her mother, her brothers, and her sisters.

11. What did Sarah tell her mother that she wants to do when she is a grown woman?

12. What did Sarah's cloak mean to her? Why didn't she need it any longer?

Vocabulary

cloak (p1)
  a loose outer garment, usually without sleeves

musket (p3)
  an old type of firearm, replaced by the rifle

heathen (p10)
  a person who is regarded as irreligious, uncivilized, or unenlightened

savage (p10)
  wild, untamed, and often fierce

solemn (p14)
  serious

porridge (p20)
  a soft food made by boiling oatmeal or some other grain in water, milk, or other liquid

palisade (p25)
  a fence of strong stakes set in the ground as a barrier against attack

scarlet (p33)
  brilliant red with a bit of orange

mush (p36)
  a porridge made with cornmeal

outlandish (p50)
  strange or unfamiliar

wigwam (p52)
  a hut in the shape of a cone or dome built by North American Indians, consisting of a framework of poles covered by bark, hides, or other materials

Small Group Reading

Keehn, Sally M. *I Am Regina*. New York: Philomel Books, 1991.
  In this book, based on a true story, a ten-year-old Pennsylvanian girl is kidnapped in 1755 by Native Americans and raised as an Allegheny Indian. Grades 4-7.

Author Information

Sally M. Keehn has a degree in library science and continues to work in that field.
  While doing research for a travel book she was writing with her husband, Keehn discovered the record of Regina's capture.
  Keehn is married and has two daughters and various pets.

Activities

1. Have students write a letter from Barbara to Regina, telling what may have happened to her in captivity after the two were separated.

2. On a map of the United States, have students locate the following:
    Allegheny Mountains   Stouchsburg, PA
    Ohio River   Susquehanna River
    Philadelphia, PA   Tuscarora River
    Selinsgrove, PA

3. Have students compare Regina's experiences after being captured by Indians with True Son's experiences in *The Light in the Forest*. What feelings and experiences did they share? How were they treated differently?

4. Have students create a newspaper that deals exclusively with Regina's capture, her captivity, and her return home. Students can then share it with the rest of the class. Some headlines about which students could write stories might be:
    Ten-Year-Old Captured by Indians: My Life with Indians by Regina
      Town in Uproar   Home at Last

    Also include letters to the editor with responses to Regina's capture.

Discussion

Give the small group the following instruction: As your group reads this book, discuss the following questions.

1. Why does Barbara think they have no reason to fear an Indian attack?

2. Why doesn't Regina want her mother to go to the mill?

3. What was Regina's family's journey from Germany to Pennsylvania like?

4. Discuss Regina's feelings about the encounter that she, Barbara, her father, and her brother had with the Allegheny Indians.

5. What do you think the Indians will do with Barbara and Regina?

6. What did Peter Lick tell Regina about what the Indians will do with them?

7. Why does Regina think that she and Barbara will be separated?

8. How did Galasko help Barbara and why?

9. Do you think Regina can survive without Barbara?

10. Where did Tiger Claw take Sarah and Regina?

11. Why did it anger Tiger Claw when Regina spoke like a white man?

12. How is Nonschetto's hut different from Woelfin's?

13. Why does Nonschetto want Regina to teach her the white man's words?

14. What makes Regina feel that part of her has died?

15. Describe Regina's feelings when she catches the trout.

16. What did Nonschetto tell Regina about the white man that troubled her?

17. What happened to Nonschetto? What effect did it have on Regina?

18. What did Woelfin tell Regina about what the white man has done to the Indian and why there cannot be peace? How did Regina feel?

19. What happened to Tiger Claw and many others in the village?

20. When the white man came to rescue the white prisoners, how did Regina feel?

21. Now that what she had wished for for so long has come true, why is Regina so sad?

22. Discuss your feelings at the end of novel.

Vocabulary

roost (p11)
a place where birds rest at night

venison (p12)
the flesh of the deer, used as food

reap (p12)
to cut down or gather in (grain); to harvest (a crop)

smokehouse (p12)
a building or closed room where foods and other things such as hides, are hung and treated with smoke to preserve them

johnnycake (p13)
a flat cornmeal cake baked on a griddle

remnant (p13)
a remaining trace

heathen (p13)
a person who is regarded as irreligious, uncivilized, or unenlightened

solitude (p15)
a deserted or lonely place

homespun (p18)
cloth made of homespun yarn or a strong, loose fabric

partial (p19)
having a special liking

idle (p19)
of no worth or importance; useless; meaningless

lye (p20)
a strong, alkaline solution, now usually sodium hydroxide, used for several purposes, including making soap and refining oil

dally (p21)
to treat lightly or playfully

savage (p24)
a brutal, fierce, or vicious person or animal

brandish (p30)
> to wave triumphantly or threateningly

sough (p35)
> a rustling sound, as of wind through trees

stoic (p36)
> unaffected by pleasure or pain

docile (p37)
> easy to teach, manage, or handle; obedient

yoke (p37)
> a device or frame fitted to a person's shoulders for carrying a bucket at each end

recount (p39)
> to tell in great detail, as a story or event

disband (p42)
> to break up as an organization; to scatter or become scattered

arid (p42)
> without rainfall to grow things

spit (p60)
> a rod on which meat is speared and roasted

fathom (p62)
> to understand

halloo (p64)
> a loud call or shout

gauntlet (p66)
> a punishment in which the victim runs between and is hit by two lines of people with clubs

dank (p68)
> unpleasantly cold and wet

sinew (p74)
> a band of tough, fibrous tissue attaching a muscle to some other bodily part, such as a bone; a tendon

permeate (p79)
> to spread itself or spread through

solace (p82)
> comfort in times of unhappiness or trouble

shard (p83)
> a broken piece of a brittle substance, such as a clay pot

saucy (p93)
> lively with a dash of daring

compassion (p98)
> pity for the suffering or distress of another and the desire to help

contrary (p101)
> stubbornly determined to oppose or contradict

cache (p103)
> a place for concealing or storing something

admonition (p112)
> a mild criticism, warning, or reminder

garrison (p114)
> the troops stationed in a fort or town

mortar (p122)
> a bowl in which materials are crushed with a pestle (a grinding or pounding implement)

pottage (p123)
> a thick soup or stew

vermilion (p124)
> a brilliant red pigment

cloak (p126)
> a loose outer garment, usually without sleeves

wampum (p127)
> small beads made of polished shells, usually cylindrical in shape, often worked into belts and bracelets, and once used as money or ceremonial pledges by North American Indians

crone (p140)
> a withered, old, witchlike person

sampler (p143)
> a piece of cloth covered with designs, mottoes, or words, done in fancy needlework

tedious (p146)
> long, dull, and tiresome

talon (p147)
> the claw of a bird or animal, especially of a bird that feeds on other animals

pillage (p149)
> to rob openly and destructively, as in war

grandeur (p168)
> nobility of character

smallpox (p188)
> a highly contagious viral disease causing a high fever and skin eruptions that usually leave permanent scars

herald (p193)
> a person or thing that announces something to come

gaunt (p195)
> very thin and bony, as from illness or malnourishment

musket (p208)
> an old type of firearm, replaced by the rifle

palisade (p210)
> a fence of strong stakes set in the ground as a barrier against attack

sentinel (p216)
> a watcher or guard

talisman (p220)
> an object, such as a ring or a stone, bearing symbols believed to bring good luck

Small Group Reading

📖 Kudlinski, Kathleen V. *Night Bird: A Story of the Seminole Indians.* New York: Scholastic, 1993. Night Bird will someday be the leader of her clan . . . if it survives. The Seminoles must hide to avoid capture. They are offered land in Oklahoma by the white men. Night Bird must decide whether to stay in the Everglades or go to Oklahoma. Grades 2-5.

Author Information

Kathleen V. Kudlinski is the author of biographies of Rachel Carson, Juliette Gordon Low, and Helen Keller for the Women of Our Time series. She lives in Guilford, Connecticut.

Activities

1. On a map of the United States, have students locate the Florida Everglades and Oklahoma.

2. Have students draw illustrations of the Everglades, including hummocks, chickees (huts), saw-grass, the cooking fire, frogs, and dragonflies.

3. Seminole Indians have told stories and passed them down for generations. Have students ask their parents or grandparents to tell them a family story. In turn, students can share these stories with their group.

4. Have students write a diary entry from Night Bird's point of view. They should include her feelings about the tribe having to move deeper into the Everglades and the reason for the move. They should also include her reasons for deciding to stay with her grandmother and her feelings about being separated from her family. Students can share these entries with the rest of the class.

Discussion

Give the small group the following instruction: As your group reads this book, discuss the following questions.

1. Why did Night Bird go to the edge of the island?

2. Why was Night Bird's grandmother hiding also?

3. What did Grandmother mean about the water turning hard?

4. How does Grandmother feel about the white men, and why?

5. Why was Night Bird so happy to see Little Mouse and her family?

6. What did Little Mouse and her family say that worried Night Bird's father so much?

7. How did Grandmother manage to calm everyone in the village?

8. What did Night Bird and Little Mouse awaken to the next morning?

9. Why are some of the Seminoles thinking about going to Oklahoma?

10. Do you think Night Bird will stay with her grandmother in the Everglades?

11. Discuss why Night Bird made the decision that she did. What would you have done?

12. Why were so few Seminoles left in the Southeast by 1858?

13. How did the Seminoles help the slaves?

14. What do Seminoles celebrate during the Green Corn ceremony?

15. What is the Seminole way of learning?

Vocabulary

hummock (p3)
a low mound

clan (p3)
a group of families claiming descent from a common ancestor

moccasins (p5)
shoes or slippers with soft soles and no heels

sacred (p7)
of, having to do with, or intended for religion or religious use

chickee (p12)
hut

shrill (p21)
having or making a high-pitched, piercing sound

chant (p24)
any monotonous, rhythmic singing or shouting

horrid (p27)
frightful; horrible

heron (p28)
any of several wading birds having a long bill, a long neck, and long legs

twilight (p28)
the light in the sky just after sunset or just before sunrise

flint (p36)
a hard, dark stone that produces sparks when struck against steel

distant (p42)
far off or remote in space or time

powwow (p54)
a conference with or of North American Indians

Small Group Reading

Speare, Elizabeth George. *Calico Captive*. Boston: Houghton Mifflin, 1957.
This story follows the fate of Miriam Willard after she is captured by Indians in 1754 and forced to march from her home in New Hampshire to Montreal, where she and others are sold to the French. It is based on an actual narrative written by Miriam's older sister when she was an elderly woman. Grades 7-9.

Author Information

Elizabeth George Speare received her bachelor's and master's degrees from Boston University and began teaching high school English in Massachusetts in the mid-1930s.

After marrying and raising a family, Speare began writing novels for children. She was successful immediately. Her first novel, *Calico Captive*, was named an American Library Association Notable Book, and her next two novels, *The Witch of Blackbird Pond* and *The Bronze Bow*, were Newbery Medal winners. Her last novel, *The Sign of the Beaver*, was a Newbery Honor Book. In 1989, Speare was awarded the Laura Ingalls Wilder Award, an honor given every three years to an author for his or her distinguished and lasting contribution to children's literature. Speare died November 15, 1994, at the age of eighty-five.

Activities

1. On a map of the United States and Canada, have students locate the following:

   Boston, MA
   Charlestown, NH
   Connecticut River
   Crown Point
   Lake Champlain

   Montreal
   Quebec
   St. Francis
   St. Lawrence River

2. Have students compare Miriam's experiences after being captured by Indians with True Son's experiences in *The Light in the Forest*. What similar feelings and experiences did they have? How were they treated differently?

3. Have students create a time line of major events that took place in *Calico Captive*, beginning with Miriam and the others being taken prisoner by the Indians. They can then display it in your classroom.

4. Have students write letters from Miriam to Phineas Whitney, telling him what she has gone through since being captured by Indians. These can be read aloud to the rest of the class.

Discussion

Give the small group the following instruction: As your group reads this book, discuss the following questions.

1. Why is Miriam so excited?

2. Why were the women and children staying at the fort?

3. Why do you think the Indians took Miriam and the others as prisoners?

4. In what ways do the Indians seem to be acting thoughtfully toward their hostages?

5. What do James and Peter think the Indians will do with them?

6. How does Sylvanus feel about the Indians?

7. Why doesn't Miriam know how to swim?

8. What happened that brought Miriam and Susanna closer than they had ever been?

9. Why was everyone afraid to go to Saint Francis?

10. How were Miriam and the others treated in the Indian village?

11. Why is Susanna worried about Vanus?

12. Why was ruining her calico dress so traumatic for Miriam?

13. Discuss Miriam's feelings about going to Montreal.

14. What happened to James, Miriam, and the children when they reached Montreal?

15. Why does Miriam have mixed feelings about her new life in Montreal?

16. Why was Miriam surprised to discover that there were Indian children who went to school in Montreal?

17. Compare how Polly and Sue are doing in their new homes.

18. How and why did Miriam and Susanna's lives change when James was paroled?

19. Why were Madame and her daughter so angry with Miriam the morning after the ball?

20. What did Hortense do to help Miriam, Susanna, and Captive when they were forced to leave the Du Quesnes's?

21. Why do the people of Montreal hate the English?

22. How did Miriam plan to work to support herself, Susanna, and Captive?

23. How did Susanna get Polly back from the Mayor's wife?

24. Discuss the difference between Pierre's and Miriam's feelings about Indians.

25. Why didn't Miriam tell Susanna about seeing Sylvanus?

26. Why do you think Miriam felt confused when she read the letter from Phineas Whitney?

27. Why did Miriam send a note to Pierre?

28. If you were Miriam, would you have made the dress for Hortense as a wedding gift?

29. Do you think Miriam will marry Pierre?

30. What made Miriam realize what she really wanted?

Vocabulary

boisterous (p1)
  noisy and wild

musket (p1)
  an old type of firearm, replaced by the rifle

lintel (p1)
  the horizontal part above the opening of a door or window, supporting the wall above it

banter (p2)
  playful teasing; good-natured joking

calico (p6)
  cotton cloth printed with a figured design

homespun (p7)
  cloth made from homespun yarn or a strong, loose fabric

stout (p10)
  strong or firm in structure or material

incessant (p10)
  unceasing; continuing without letup

palisade (p11)
  a fence of strong stakes set in the ground as a barrier against attack

abstracted (p11)
  not paying attention

menace (p11)
  to threaten with evil or harm

emboldened (p11)
  to make bold or bolder; encouraged

plunder (p16)
  goods taken by force

plight (p20)
  a condition or situation, usually bad

savage (p20)
  wild, untamed, and often fierce

pilfer (p22)
  to steal by taking a little at a time

porridge (p23)
  a soft food made by boiling oatmeal or some other grain in water, milk, or other liquid

horde (p23)
  a great crowd of people

mortification (p25)
  a feeling of loss of self-respect or pride; humiliation

vex (p27)
  to irritate or annoy

gruel (p27)
  a thin, liquid food made by boiling cereal in water or milk

quiescent (p27)
  in a state of rest; inactive; quiet

stolid (p28)
  having or showing little or no feeling

prattle (p28)
  foolish or childish talk

derision (p28)
  mocking laughter; ridicule

retaliate (p29)
  to do something to get even, as for an injury or wrong

anguish (p30)
  great suffering of mind or body; agony

sinewy (p38)
  strong, firm, or tough

arrogant (p39)
  prideful and disdainful of others

swagger (p39)
  to walk with a proud or insolent air; to strut

papoose (p47)
  a North American Indian baby or small child

barbarian (p49)
  a crude or brutal person

scrupulous (p49)
  giving strict attention to what is right

relish (p53)
  to have an appetite for; to like or enjoy

vermilion (p53)
  a bright red pigment

apparition (p53)
  a ghost or spirit

sagamore (p61)
  a North American Indian chief

squalor (p63)
  filth, poverty, or degradation

incongruous (p65)
  not suitable or appropriate

catechism (p67)
  a short book in the form of questions and answers for teaching the principles of a religion

wampum (p69)
  small beads made of polished shells, usually cylindrical in shape and often worked into belts and bracelets, that were once used as money or ceremonial pledges by North American Indians

convent (p83)
> a house or building occupied by a group of nuns who live together, following set religious rules

portage (p85)
> the carrying of boats and goods overland between two bodies of water

haughty (p86)
> satisfied with oneself and scornful of others; arrogant

malice (p88)
> an intention or desire to hurt or injure someone

formidable (p95)
> causing fear or dread because of strength or size

rebuke (p105)
> a strong statement of disapproval; a sharp scolding

sustenance (p107)
> something that maintains life or strength; nourishment; food

chagrin (p115)
> a feeling of embarrassment or distress caused by a disappointment or failure

genteel (p125)
> polite or well-bred; refined

idolatrous (p130)
> having to do with the worshipping of idols

indulgent (p133)
> very kind and lenient; not strict or critical

parole (p135)
> the release of a prisoner from part of a prison or jail sentence on the conditions that he or she observes certain rules and behaves according to the law

affable (p136)
> very pleasant, friendly, and courteous

damask (p136)
> a rich, reversible silk fabric with an elaborate woven design

capricious (p138)
> likely to change without warning

surreptitious (p142)
> acting or doing secretly

enmity (p167)
> deep hatred, mistrust, or dislike

caterwaul (p174)
> a sound like that of cats fighting

impertinence (p180)
> deliberate disrespect

nonchalant (p183)
> not excited or concerned

coiffure (p189)
> a hairstyle

militia (p212)
> a body of citizens given military training outside the regular armed forces and called up in emergencies

fracas (p259)
> a noisy fight or quarrel

wharf (p265)
> a structure, usually a platform, built along or out from a shore, alongside which ships or boats may dock to load or unload

poach (p267)
> to trespass on another's property, especially to hunt or fish

supremacy (p274)
> supreme power or authority

Small Group Reading

Speare, Elizabeth George. *The Sign of the Beaver*. New York: Dell, 1983.

Twelve-year-old Matt is left alone in a wilderness cabin while his father leaves to get the rest of their family. Matt becomes friends with an Indian named Attean. Attean teaches Matt many things to help him survive during the long wait for the return of his family. This is a truly moving story of companionship, acceptance, and survival. *The Sign of the Beaver* was chosen as a Newbery Honor Book. Grades 5-8.

Author Information

See page 10.

Activities

1. Write a diary entry from Matt's point of view, telling what it was like to meet Attean's family.

2. Have students create a time line of events in the story, starting in July when Matt's father left. Display the time line on a wall in your classroom and have the students in the group explain it to the rest of the class.

3. Have students compare and contrast their own lives to Matt's. This could be done in chart form on a poster and shared with the class. Include the following in the comparisons: food, shelter, family activities, school, and transportation.

4. Encourage students interested in reading more survival stories to read any or all of these:

   O'Dell, Scott. *Island of the Blue Dolphins.* Boston: Houghton Mifflin, 1960.

   Paulsen, Gary. *Hatchet.* New York: Bradbury Press, 1987.

   ———. *The River.* New York: Delacorte Press, 1991.

5. Have students write a new ending for *The Sign of the Beaver*, in which Matt leaves with Attean and his family.

6. On a map of the United States, have students locate the following:
   Massachusetts
   Maine
   Penobscot River

Discussion

Give the small group the following instruction: As your group reads this book, discuss the following questions.

1. Why is Matt alone in the wilderness?

2. What chores does Matt have to do?

3. What advice did Matt's father give him about Indians?

4. What happened to Matt's rifle? What does it mean to Matt?

5. Discuss Matt's mistake when he went fishing and what he found when he returned to the cabin.

6. What happened to Matt at the pond? Who helped him?

7. Why does the Indian want Matt to teach Attean to read?

8. How does Attean feel about being taught to read?

9. What is Attean teaching Matt?

10. How is Matt and Attean's relationship changing?

11. Why does Attean's grandmother hate the white man?

12. What made Attean's grandmother change her mind about Matt?

13. What offer did Attean's grandfather make to Matt? Why did he refuse it?

14. What gift did Attean give Matt before leaving to hunt?

15. How did Matt feel after the Indians left?

16. Why did it take Matt's father so long to return with their family?

17. Discuss Matt's feelings upon the return of his family.

Vocabulary

surveyor (p2)
a person whose profession is measuring and mapping land

puncheon table (p3)
a table made from a piece of roughly finished timber with one flat side

blunderbuss (p4)
a short gun with a wide muzzle for scattering shot at close range, no longer used

rueful (p5)
feeling or expressing sorrow, regret, or pity

johnnycake (p5)
a flat cornmeal cake baked on a griddle

proprietor (p9)
the legal owner of something, such as a store or business

deacon (p10)
a clergyman who is next below a priest in rank

passel (p13)
a large number or amount

lingo (p15)
a language or talk that seems outlandish or is not understood

captive (p16)
a person or thing captured and held in confinement; a prisoner

earnest (p28)
very serious, determined, or sincere

treaty (p30)
a formal agreement between two or more nations related to an issue such as peace or commerce

defiance (p31)
bold opposition to power or authority; refusal to submit or obey

savage (p32)
a person living in a wild or primitive condition

primer (p32)
a textbook for teaching children to read

heathen (p32)
a person who is regarded as irreligious, uncivilized, or unenlightened

disdain (p33)
scorn or haughty contempt, especially toward someone or something considered inferior

adz (p38)
a tool like a broad chisel or an ax, whose blade is set crosswise to the handle

snare (p40)
a noose that jerks tight, for catching small animals

nonchalant (p41)
showing a coolness; not excited or concerned

contemptuous (p41)
full of scorn

horrid (p42)
frightful; horrible

halloo (p42)
a loud call or shout

mangy (p52)
having mange; a skin disease of animals marked by itching and loss of hair

cascade (p55)
a small waterfall

chagrin (p60)
a feeling of embarrassment or distress caused by a disappointment or failure

sinew (p62)
a band of tough fibrous tissue attaching a muscle to some other body part, such as a bone; a tendon

indignant (p64)
angry because of something that is not right, just, or fair

stern (p77)
the rear part of a ship or boat

pungent (p78)
sharp or piercing to the taste or smell

boisterous (p80)
noisy and wild

contortion (p81)
a twisted shape or position, such as one taken by an acrobat

typhus (p131)
an acute, contagious disease, caused by a germ carried by certain body lice or fleas, that is marked by high fever, skin eruptions, and extreme physical weakness

musket (p133)
an old type of firearm, replaced by the rifle

Bibliography

Individual Titles

Adler, David A. *A Picture Book of Sitting Bull.* New York: Holiday House, 1993.

This is a short biography of the Sioux chief who worked to maintain the rights of Native American people and who led the defeat of General Custer at the Little Big Horn in 1876. Grades 2-5.

Armer, Laura Adams. *Waterless Mountain.* New York: David McKay, 1963.

In this reprint of the 1931 Newbery Medal book, the authentic and moving story of a Navaho boy's spiritual journey that chronicles his coming of age as a medicine man is told. Grades 5-9.

Baker, Betty. *The Shaman's Last Raid.* New York: Harper & Row, 1963.

Two modern Apache children try to ignore the old Indian ways. Grades 6-9.

Baker, Olaf. *Where the Buffaloes Begin.* New York: Warne, 1981.

This is an American Indian story about Little Wolf, who finds the fabled Buffalo Lake and saves his people from a marauding tribe. Grades 3-6.

Baylor, Bird. *When Clay Sings.* New York: Charles Scribner's Sons, 1972.

This book tells of the lives and thoughts of the ancient people whose pottery can still be found in the desert of the American Southwest. Grades PreK-3.

Bierhorst, John, selector. *On the Road of Stars: Native American Night Poems and Sleepcharms.* New York: Macmillan, 1994.

This is a collection of fifty-one poems and sleepcharms in a large-format picture book. The selections come from a wide range of Native peoples, from an Inuit "Comforting Song" to a Navajo "Song to Straighten a Bad Dream." Grades 2 and up.

Bruchac, Joseph. *The Boy Who Lived with the Bears: And Other Iroquois Stories.* New York: HarperCollins, 1995.

This is a collection of traditional Iroquois tales in which animals learn the importance of caring and responsibility and the dangers of selfishness and pride. Grades 3-6.

———. *Iroquois Stories: Heroes and Heroines, Monsters and Magic.* Trumansburg, NY: Crossing Press, 1985.

Bruchac tells his own versions of stories of the Iroquois people. They are based on original stories of long ago, long before Europeans came to this earth on Turtle's back. This is an essential book for a study of Native Americans. Grades 3-6.

———. *Native American Animal Stories.* Golden, CO: Fulcrum, 1992.

This is a collection of Native American stories that illustrate the power and importance of animals in Native American life and culture. A map is included that shows the cultural areas and tribal locations of Native American groups. Grades K-6.

Bruchac, Joseph, reteller. *The First Strawberries: A Cherokee Story.* New York: Dial Books for Young Readers, 1993.

This Cherokee tale is accompanied by beautiful watercolors and tells how strawberries first came into the world. Grades 1-4.

———. *Flying with the Eagle, Racing the Great Bear: Stories from Native North America.* Mahwah, NJ: BridgeWater Books, 1993.

Included are sixteen thought-provoking Native American tales from a variety of tribal nations associated with rites of passage. Grades 5-8.

———. *Gluskabe and the Four Wishes.* New York: Cobblehill Books, 1995.

Four Abenaki men set out on a difficult journey to ask the great hero Gluskabe to grant each his fondest wish. Grades 2-4.

———. *The Great Ball Game.* New York: Dial Books for Young Readers, 1994.

Bat, who has both wings and teeth, plays an important role in a game between the Birds and the Animals to decide which team is better. Grades K-3.

Bruchac, Joseph, and Gale Ross. *The Girl Who Married the Moon: Tales from Native North America.* Mahwah, NJ: BridgeWater Books, 1994.

Sixteen legends, each from a different Native American tribe, center on the experiences of young women. Coauthor Gale Ross is a descendent of John Ross, the principal chief of the Cherokee nation during the Trail of Tears. Grades 6-9.

Bruchac, Joseph, and Jonathan London. *Thirteen Moons on Turtle's Back: A Native American Year of Moons.* New York: Philomel, 1992.

This book celebrates the seasons of the year through poems from the legends of such Native American tribes as the Cherokee, Cree, and Sioux. Grades 1-5.

Bruchac, Joseph, and Thomas Locker. *The Earth Under Sky Bear's Feet: Native American Poems of the Land.* New York: Philomel, 1995.

This is a collection of tales about the Big Dipper from various North American Indian Cultures. Grades K-5.

Campbell, Maria. *People of the Buffalo: How the Plains Indians Lived*. Buffalo, NY: Firefly Books, 1995.
This book tells how the Plains Indians hunted buffalo and made their teepees, clothing, and tools. It also explains their beliefs, ceremonies, and philosophy of family life. Grades 3-7.

Crompton, Anne Eliot. *The Ice Trail*. New York: Methuen, 1980.
Two outcasts from an Indian tribe survive a hard winter. Grades 4-7.

Curtis, Edward S., collector, and John Bierhorst, ed. *The Girl Who Married a Ghost: And Other Tales from the North American Indian*. New York: Four Winds Press, 1978.
This is a collection of nine Native American tales. Grades 7 and up.

Dorris, Michael. *Guests*. New York: Hyperion Books for Children, 1994.
This story about Thanksgiving is told from the point of view of a young Native American who flees to the forest because he resents his father's invitation to the white men to join them at their festivities. Grades 2-5.

Edmonds, Walter. *The Matchlock Gun*. New York: Dodd, Mead, 1941.
To ten-year-old Edmond, the huge gun is a magnificent reminder of his Dutch grandfather. But it becomes much more than that when he is forced to defend the family against Indians in his father's absence. Winner of the 1942 Newbery Medal. Grades 3-6.

Esbensen, Barbara Juster, reteller. *The Star Maiden: An Ojibway Tale*. Boston: Little, Brown, 1988.
A glowing star, tired of wandering across the sky, longs to live among the people as a flower, which is how water lilies came to be. Grades 2-5.

Ferris, Jeri. *Native American Doctor: The Story of Susan LaFlesche Picotte*. Minneapolis, MN: Carolrhoda Books, 1991.
This is a biography of a young Omaha Indian woman who became the first Native American woman to graduate from medical school. Grades 4-8.

Freedman, Russell. *Buffalo Hunt*. New York: Holiday House, 1988.
The author describes the Plains Indians' hunt and uses of buffalo until the white man's conquest during the 1880s. Grades 5-6.

——— . *Children of the Wild West*. New York: Clarion Books, 1983.
The book's many black-and-white photographs help to tell the stories of the children who came West with their families. A chapter is devoted to Native American children. Grades 4 and up.

——— . *Indian Chiefs*. New York: Scholastic, 1987.
This book contains profiles of six Indian chiefs who led their people in a historic crisis. It also includes photos, a map, and an index. Grades 4 and up.

——— . *An Indian Winter*. New York: Holiday House, 1992.
This is an account of two Europeans on a historic journey up the Missouri River and the Native Americans who befriended them. Grades 3-7.

Fritz, Jean. *The Double Life of Pocahontas*. New York: Trumpet, 1983.
This is a biography and a recounting of Pocahantas's life among the early Jamestown settlers, covering the events from 1607 to her death in 1617 in England at age twenty-one. Grades 4-6.

Gardiner, John Reynolds. *Stone Fox*. New York: HarperCollins, 1980.
An American Indian who is trying to reclaim lost land and a boy who is trying to save his grandfather's farm are adversaries in a dogsled race. Grades 3-6.

Glassman, Bruce. *Wilma Mankiller: Chief of the Cherokee Nation*. New York: Blackbirch Press, 1992.
Glassman discusses the life and career of the first female to be chief of the Cherokee Nation. Grades 4-7.

Goble, Paul. *Buffalo Woman*. Scarsdale, NY: Bradbury Press, 1984.
In spite of his tribe's disapproval, a young man bravely follows his wife and child to her Buffalo Nation people. He becomes one of them by demonstrating his love and courage. Grades 2-6.

——— . *Her Seven Brothers*. New York: Bradbury Press, 1988.
This is a Cheyenne legend of the girl who sews clothes for her adopted brother, and, to escape the Buffalo People, becomes part of the Big Dipper in the northern sky. Grades 3-6.

Gregory, Kristina. *Jenny of the Tetons*. San Diego, CA: Harcourt Brace Jovanovich, 1989.
Two stories make up this book. One is the fictionalized tale of Carrie Hill, a fifteen-year-old girl who is left wounded and alone after an Indian attack. The other is a factual account of the family life of trapper Beaver Dick and his wife Jenny. Carrie hates the Indians who killed her parents and goes to live with Beaver Dick and Jenny. She is horrified to learn that Jenny is an Indian, but comes to love her. This book received a "Notable Children's Trade Book in the Field of Social Studies" citation awarded by the National Council for the Social Studies. Grades 6 and up.

Highwater, Jamake. *Eyes of Darkness: A Novel*. New York: Lothrop, Lee & Shepard, 1985.
Yesa, an Indian boy, studies the white man's medicine and becomes a doctor. He returns to his people and is caught between two worlds. Grades 6 and up.

———. *Many Smokes, Many Moons: A Chronology of American Indian History Through Indian Art.* New York: J. B. Lippincott, 1978.

Highwater uses the art and artifacts of various Indian cultures to illustrate events affecting their history, from earliest times through 1973. Grades 6-9.

Hirschfelder, Arlene. *Happily May I Walk: American Indians and Alaska Natives Today.* New York: Charles Scribner's Sons, 1986.

Hirschfelder provides a wealth of information and descriptions of Native American lives today. Grades 6-9.

Hirschfelder, Arlene, and Martha Kreipe de Montaño. *The Native American Almanac: A Portrait of Native America Today.* New York: Prentice Hall, 1993.

This wonderful sourcebook provides information on every part of Native American life, from tribes, treaties, and government, to language, literature, religion, and art. It also includes maps of tribal areas, a chronology of significant events, and a listing of landmarks, museums, and cultural centers. Grades 6 and up.

Hoyt-Goldsmith, Diane. *Arctic Hunter.* New York: Holiday House, 1992.

This book documents the contemporary lifestyle of a Native family. Reggie, an Inupiat who lives above the Arctic Circle in Alaska, tells of the activities of his family's hunting and fishing camp. Grades 2-6.

———. *Pueblo Storyteller.* New York: Holiday House, 1991.

Young April learns about the traditions of her people, the Cochiti Indians. This book was named a "Notable Children's Trade Book in the Field of Social Studies" by the National Council for the Social Studies. Grades 3-7.

———. *Totem Pole.* New York: Holiday House, 1990.

David, a young member of the Tsimshian tribe, helps his wood-carver father fashion a forty-foot pole from a cedar tree. Grades 4-8.

Hudson, Jan. *Sweetgrass.* New York: Philomel, 1989.

Living on the western Canadian prairie in the nineteenth century, Sweetgrass, a fifteen-year-old Blackfoot Indian girl, saves her family from a smallpox epidemic and proves her maturity to her father. Grades 6 and up.

Jacobs, Francine. *The Tainos: The People Who Welcomed Columbus.* New York: G. P. Putnam's Sons, 1992.

This book describes the history, culture, and mysterious fate of the first Native Americans to welcome Columbus in 1492. Grades 5 and up.

Johnson, Dolores. *Seminole Diary: Remembrances of a Slave.* New York: Macmillan, 1994.

This book is written in diary form by Libbie, a young slave. It tells of her family's escape from slavery in 1834. *Seminole Diary* reveals a seldom told story of slaves who escaped and joined Native American groups, where they found safety and acceptance. Grades K-3.

Keegan, Marcia. *Pueblo Boy: Growing up in Two Worlds.* New York: Cobblehill Books, 1991.

This photo documentary illustrates the life of Timmy Roybal, a ten-year-old boy who lives at San Ildefonso Pueblo. The text explains some of the pueblos, which are still important in their lives today. Grades 3-6.

King, Sandra. *Shannon: An Ojibway Dancer.* Minneapolis, MN: Lerner, 1993.

Thirteen-year-old Shannon readies herself for her dance at a powwow in Minnesota. Her grandmother tells her about the traditional costumes of their tribe. Grades 2-5.

Lampman, Evelyn Sibley. *White Captives.* New York: Atheneum, 1975.

This is a fictional story of Olive Oatman's five years as a captive, first of the Apaches and later the Mohaves. Grades 5-6.

La Pierre, Yvette. *Native American Rock Art: Messages from the Past.* Charlottesville, VA: Thomasson-Grant, 1994.

This is a fascinating look at pictographs and petroglyphs and the people who painted and engraved them. Grades 4-9.

Lenski, Lois. *Indian Captive: The Story of Mary Jemison.* New York: HarperCollins, 1961.

This is the fascinating story of Mary Jemison's capture, flight, and early years with the Indians. Grades 5 and up.

Manitonquat (Medicine Story). *The Children of the Morning Light: Wampanoag Tales.* New York: Macmillan, 1994.

This is a collection of traditional stories that describe the creation of the world and the early history of the Wampanoag Indians in southeastern Massachusetts. Grades 3-6.

Martin, Rafe. *The Rough-Face Girl.* New York: G. P. Putnam's Sons, 1992.

This is a haunting version of the Cinderella tale from Algonquin Indian folklore. Grades 1-4.

McConkey, Lois. *Sea and Cedar: How the Northwest Coast Indians Lived.* Vancouver, BC: Douglas & McIntyre, 1990.

This book explores how the Northwest Coast Indians made canoes and huge houses from cedar logs, how they lived off salmon, how they wove rainproof hats and blankets, what their beliefs were, and why they carved and erected totem poles. Grades 3-7.

Meyer, Carolyn. *Where the Broken Heart Still Beats: The Story of Cynthia Ann Parker.* San Diego, CA: Harcourt Brace Jovanovich, 1992.

This novel is set in Texas in the 1860s. It is an example of the continuing conflicts that arose between white settlers and Native Americans during the westward movement. Grades 6-9.

Morrow, Mary Frances. *Sarah Winnemucca*. Milwaukee, WI: Raintree, 1990.
This biography recounts the life story of the influential Paiute woman who fought for justice and a better life for her people. Grades 2-5.

Naylor, Phyllis Reynolds. *To Walk the Sky Path*. New York: Dell, 1973.
Ten-year-old Billie Tomie, a Seminole Indian, lives with his family in the Florida Everglades. Billie's grandfather has taught him the legends, stories, and rituals that are important to the Seminole people, and he says that an honest man who lives a good life will walk the path to the city in the sky when he dies. Grades 4-7.

O'Dell, Scott. *Sing Down the Moon*. Boston: Houghton Mifflin, 1970.
The tragic forced march of the Indians to Fort Sumner in 1864 is told by a young Navajo girl. Grades 5-8.

———. *Streams to the River, River to the Sea: A Novel of Sacagawea*. Boston: Houghton Mifflin, 1986.
A young Indian woman, accompanied by her infant and cruel husband, experiences joy and heartbreak when she joins the Lewis and Clark Expedition seeking a way to the Pacific. Grades 5 and up.

O'Dell, Scott, and Elizabeth Hall. *Thunder Rolling in the Mountains*. Boston: Houghton Mifflin, 1992.
In the late nineteenth century, a young Nez Percé girl relates how her people were driven off their land by the U.S. Army and forced to retreat north until their eventual surrender. Grades 5-8.

Ortiz, Simon. *The People Shall Continue*. San Francisco: Children's Book Press, 1977.
This is a picture book presenting American history from a Native American point of view. Grades 2-6.

Osborne, Chester G. *The Memory String*. New York: Atheneum, 1984.
This novel discusses how the Native Americans might have moved from Siberia to Alaska 30,000 years ago. Grades 5-8.

Peters, Russell M. *Clambake: A Wampanoag Tradition*. Minneapolis, MN: Lerner, 1992.
A twelve-year-old Wampanoag Indian in Massachusetts learns from his grandmother how to prepare a clambake in the tradition of his people. Grades 2-5.

Richter, Conrad. *A Country of Strangers*. New York: Alfred A. Knopf, 1966.
Richter chronicles the captivity of a white girl by Indians. Stone Girl was adopted into an Indian family and married early to an Indian. Stone Girl and her son were returned to her white family, only to be rejected by them. This is a companion novel to *The Light in the Forest*. Grades 6-8.

Ridington, Jillian, and Robin Ridington. *People of the Longhouse: How the Iroquoian Tribes Lived*. Vancouver, BC: Douglas & McIntyre, 1992.
This book describes in detail every aspect of the Iroquoian way of life, as well as the effect of contact with Europeans. Grades 3-7.

———. *People of the Trail: How the Northern Forest Indians Lived*. Vancouver, BC: Douglas & McIntyre, 1992.
This book explores the unique way of life of the Northern Forest Indians. It tells how they built their lodges, trapped and hunted their food, made clothing from skins and furs, and fashioned the canoes, sleds, toboggans, and snowshoes essential for year-round travel. Grades 3-7.

Roessel, Monty. *Kinaaldá: A Navajo Girl Grows Up*. Minneapolis, MN: Lerner, 1993.
Celinda McKelvey, a Navajo girl, participates in the Kinaaldá, the traditional coming-of-age ceremony of her people. Grades 3-7.

Ross, Gayle, reteller. *How Turtle's Back Was Cracked: A Traditional Cherokee Tale*. New York: Dial Books for Young Readers, 1995.
Turtle's shell is cracked when the wolves plot to stop his boastful ways. Grades 2-5.

Sewell, Marcia. *People of the Breaking Day*. New York: Atheneum, 1990.
This story, told from the viewpoint of a Wampanoag child, reveals what it was like to be a child before the coming of the white man. Grades 2-7.

Sheldon, Dyan. *Under the Moon*. New York: Dial Books for Young Readers, 1994.
After finding an arrowhead in her backyard, a young girl has a dream about what the area was once like. Illustrations by Gary Blythe are breathtaking. Grades 2-5.

Siegel, Beatrice. *Indians of the Northeast Woodlands*. New York: Walker, 1992.
In a question-and-answer format, Siegel details life for Native Americans before and after the Pilgrims' arrival in what is now New England. Grades 5-8.

Smith-Baranzini, Marlene, and Howard Egger-Bovet. *USKids History: Book of the American Indians*. Boston: Little, Brown, 1994.
This book provides insights into the day-to-day lives, customs, and beliefs of various North American Indian tribes before the arrival of the Europeans. It includes ideas for related activities. Grades 4 and up.

Smith-Siska, Heather. *People of the Ice: How the Inuit Lived*. Buffalo, NY: Firefly Books, 1995.
This book describes and illustrates how the Inuit built their igloos, kayaks, and sledges; made their

clothing and prepared their food; played games and carved beautiful objects from soapstone; and hunted and fished. Grades 3-7.

Sneve, Virginia Driving Hawk. *The Iroquois: A First Americans Book*. New York: Holiday House, 1995.
The author retells the creation myth of the Iroquois and describes their history, beliefs, and daily way of life, as well as their status today. Grades 2-5.

———. *Jimmy Yellow Hawk*. New York: Holiday House, 1972.
Indian life is well-portrayed along with Little Jim's success in trapping a mink and earning his father's approval. Grades 3-5.

———. *The Navajos: A First Americans Book*. New York: Holiday House, 1993.
Sneve provides an overview of the history, culture, and ways of life of the Navaho (Pueblo) Indians. Grades 2-5.

———. *The Nez Percé: A First Americans Book*. New York: Holiday House, 1994.
Sneve describes the lifestyle and history of the Nez Percé Indians. Grades 2-5.

———. *The Seminoles: A First Americans Book*. New York: Holiday House, 1994.
The author describes the history, lifestyle, customs, and current status of the Seminoles. Grades 2-5.

Stewart, Elisabeth J. *On the Long Trail Home*. New York: Clarion Books, 1994.
A young Cherokee girl and her brother escape their captors on the Trail of Tears and begin a long, hazardous trip back to their home in the mountains. The story is based on the life of the author's great-grandmother. Grades 5-7.

Swentzell, Rina. *Children of Clay: A Family of Pueblo Potters*. Minneapolis, MN: Lerner, 1992.
Members of a Tewa Indian family living in Santa Clara Pueblo in New Mexico follow the age-old tradition of their people as they create various objects of clay. Grades 2-5.

Thomas, Dr. David Hurst, and Lorann Pendleton, consulting eds. *Native Americans*. New York: Time Life Books, 1995.
This book is part of The Nature Company Discoveries Library, a new reference series for children. It is an excellent research reference. Grades 4 and up.

Thompson, Jean. *Brother of the Wolves*. New York: William Morrow, 1978.
A young Indian boy raised by wolves returns to his tribe. Grades 6-8.

Thomson, Peggy. *Katie Henio: Navajo Sheepherder*. New York: Cobblehill Books, 1995.
The text and photographs illustrate the life of Katie Henio. Grades 3-5.

Trimble, Stephen. *The Village of Blue Stone*. New York: Macmillan, 1990.
A year in the life of the Anasazis is re-created in this book, which clearly details their everyday activities. It is filled with rituals, codes of behavior, and customs of that age. Weaving, pottery, and jewelry making are among the many crafts discussed. Grades 3-8.

Whelan, Gloria. *Night of the Full Moon*. New York: Alfred A. Knopf, 1993.
This story is based on true accounts of the Potawatomi Indians' forced migration. Libby's innocent wish to be an Indian girl comes true in a terrifying way when government officials come to move the Indians from their land. Grades 2-4.

Yue, David, and Charlotte Yue. *The Tipi: A Center of Native American Life*. New York: Alfred A. Knopf, 1984.
Details about tipis are abundant, including how they are constructed and why they make the best kind of shelter. Grades 3-6.

Theme Resources

Commercial Resources

Beard, Andrea. *Native Americans: Literature-Based Activities for Thematic Teaching*. Cypress, CA: Creative Teaching Press, 1992.
This resource provides many activities for trade books dealing with Native Americans for grades 4 and up.

Caduto, Michael J., and Joseph Bruchac. *Keepers of the Night: Native American Stories and Nocturnal Activities for Children*. Golden, CO: Fulcrum, 1994.

Hands-on activities for students in grades 4 and up include nighttime observational activities and walks to teach sensory awareness as well as traditional dances to enjoy and learn. Grades 4 and up.

Claydon, Dina. *Novel Ties: Stone Fox*. New Hyde Park, NY: Learning Links, 1990.
This resource contains pre-reading and post-reading activities, vocabulary skills, comprehension questions, and writing activities in a chapter-by-chapter format

for *Stone Fox*. It is appropriate for students in grades 4-7.

Cobblestone: The History Magazine for Young People. Peterborough, NH: Cobblestone.

The subject of the November 1992 issue is "Indians of the Northwest Coast." It is appropriate for students in grades 4 and up.

The subject of the April 1993 issue for students in grades 4 and up is "The Cultures of Pre-Columbian North America." Articles in this issue include "Early Hunters of the Plains" and "Who Were the First Americans?"

The November 1994 issue's title is "Indians of the Northeast Coast." Articles in this issue for students in grades 4 and up include "Native Peoples of the Northeast" and "Historic Moments in a 100,000-Year Heritage."

Copycat Magazine. Racine, WI: Copycat Press.

The November-December 1989 issue contains information and activities for students in grades 3-6 surrounding the study of Native Americans. It also includes several craft activities, a corncob game, and reproducible "Hopi Family" figures.

The November-December 1994 issue includes an article titled "A Wampanoag Child's Day," which has information on life, clothing, and food of the Wampanoag for students in grades 3-6.

Fitcher, George S. *American Indian Music and Musical Instruments.* New York: David McKay, 1978.

Fitcher describes every category of music from war chants to music for curing illnesses for students in grades 4 and up. He includes instructions and diagrams for making Indian musical instruments, as well as the music for several Indian songs.

Hoven, Leigh. *Thematic Unit: Native Americans.* Huntington Beach, CA: Teacher Created Materials, 1990.

This resource includes ideas to use with the books for *Arrow to the Sun*, *Rainbow Crow*, and *The Legend of Bluebonnet* for students in grades 2-5. It also includes poetry, writing, and other content-area related activities.

Kavasch, E. Barrie. *Earthmaker's Lodge: Native American Folklore, Activities, and Foods.* Peterborough, NH: Cobblestone, 1994.

This is a collection of histories, introductions, stories, legends, poems, wordlore, folktales, projects, activities, games, and recipes of Native American peoples for students in grades 4 and up.

Kids Discover: America 1492. New York: Kids Discover.

The August-September 1992 issue for grades 4 and up contains much information and illustrations of life of Native Americans in 1492.

Kuipers, Barbara J. *American Indian Reference Books for Children and Young Adults.* Englewood, CO: Libraries Unlimited, 1991.

This resource will help in locating reference books on the American Indian for use with children in grades 3-12. It includes more than 200 books, describes the strengths and weaknesses of each, and explains how to use them in your curriculum.

National Geographic. Washington, DC: National Geographic Society.

The title of the October 1991 issue is "1491: America Before Columbus." It looks closely at Native people and cultures before the arrival of Columbus. A double-map supplement illustrates the heritage of Native Americans. Suitable for use with students in grades 7 and up.

Norris, Crystal. *Novel Ties: The Light in the Forest.* New Hyde Park, NY: Learning Links, 1991.

This resource contains pre-reading and post-reading activities, vocabulary skills, comprehension questions, and writing activities for students in grades 6-8 in a chapter-by-chapter format for *The Light in the Forest*.

Penner, Lucille Recht. *A Native American Feast.* New York: Macmillan, 1994.

Included in this book are recipes, cooking techniques, and customs of various Native American tribes Europeans encountered when they arrived in North America. Suited for students in grades 3-6.

Slapin, Beverly, and Doris Seale. *Through Indian Eyes: The Native Experience in Books for Children.* Philadelphia: New Society Publishers, 1992.

This book includes reviews of texts and resource books, as well as fiction, and looks at the issues of cultural and historical bias. This book is recommended as a resource for teachers to use when choosing trade books dealing with Native Americans for use with students.

Villanella, Rosemary. *Novel Ties: The Sign of the Beaver.* New Hyde Park, NY: Learning Links, 1991.

This resource contains pre-reading and post-reading activities, vocabulary skills, comprehension questions, and writing activities for students in grades 5-8 in a chapter-by-chapter format for *The Sign of the Beaver*.

Zaun, Kathy. *Whole Language Theme Unit: Native Americans.* Grand Rapids, MI: Instructional Fair, 1994.

This unit contains four 17-by-22-inch full-color posters and a thirty-two-page reproducible resource guide on Native Americans. The resource guide includes integrated student activity pages, ideas for bulletin boards, and field trip suggestions. For use with students in grades 4-6.

Videos

Discovery Channel's How the West Was Lost: Navaho, A Clash of Cultures. New York: Time/Life Video, 1995. (58 minutes)

Native Americans were pushed farther and farther west from their homes. This video shows the Navajo plight through editorials of the time, eyewitness accounts, and history passed down from soldiers and tribe members alike.

Mystery of the Maya. Evanston, IL: Journal Films, 1990. (25 minutes)

The ancient Maya created one of the great civilizations of the world . . . and then disappeared. This program seeks answers to the three great mysteries of the Maya: their unusual choice of inhospitable areas for their cities, how they achieved such incredible knowledge, and why they abandoned their cities at the height of their brilliance.

The Song of Sacajawea. Rowayton, CT: Rabbit Ears Productions, 1992. (30 minutes)

This is an animated version of the story of a young Native American woman who courageously guides the Lewis and Clark expedition across the Rocky Mountains to the Pacific Ocean.

Trumpet Video Visits: Gary Paulsen. Holmes, PA: Trumpet Club, 1993. (24 minutes)

Gary Paulsen tells about the exciting adventures he has had.

End-of-Unit Celebration

The Indian Diet

At the time the first settlers arrived in America, the Indians were enjoying an abundant and varied diet, drawing on more than 2,000 different plant foods, plus nuts, fruit, fish, seafood, and available game. Their diets were limited only when nature intervened.

The Indians were skilled farmers, adapting their methods to the earth and to the needs of the people. They steadily improved the cultivation of the bean and of corn.

It has been estimated that more than 65 percent of our contemporary diet can be traced directly to the contributions of the American Indians. The single most important contribution, however, is corn.

Corn feeds the animals that produce meat, poultry, milk, and cheese.

Corn oil is found in or is used in the making of or packaging of soap, insecticides, mayonnaise, salad dressings, and monosodium glutamate.

Corn syrup is found in or used in the making of candy, catsup, ice cream, processed meats, soft drinks, beer, gin, vodka, and sweetened condensed milk.

Cornstarch is found in or used in the making of or packaging of puddings, baby foods, jams, pickles, vinegar, yeast, instant coffees, powdered sugar, and a variety of other items.

The following recipes can be used to concoct sweet treats for an end-of-unit celebration. Depending on the age of the students, this could be a group activity. Otherwise, make the treats yourself and bring them to school to share.

Recipes

Maple Syrup Candy

INGREDIENTS

Maple syrup

Snow—If snow is not available, freeze water in a shallow pan. Before it is completely solid, use a knife to scrape the semi-frozen ice and place it in a bowl.

PROCEDURE

1. Cook maple syrup over medium heat in a saucepan until it reaches 275 degrees or the hard-ball stage (the syrup forms a hard ball when dropped into a cup of cold water).

2. Fill a large cake pan with a mound of clean snow.

3. Slowly pour cooked syrup over snow, dribbling it in thin strips.

4. Let syrup cool.

Source: Barchers, Suzanne I., and Patricia C. Marden. *Cooking Up U.S. History: Recipes and Research to Share with Children.* Englewood, CO: Teacher Ideas Press, 1991.

Indian Pudding

INGREDIENTS

$\frac{1}{4}$ cup cornmeal	$2\frac{1}{2}$ cups heated milk
$\frac{3}{4}$ cup molasses	$\frac{1}{4}$ teaspoon salt
$1\frac{1}{2}$ cups cold milk	4 tablespoons margarine
$\frac{1}{2}$ teaspoon cinnamon	2 well-beaten eggs

PROCEDURE

1. In the bottom half of a double boiler, heat water until it boils.

2. In the top of the double boiler, stir cornmeal into 1 cup of the cold milk.

3. Stir in the $2\frac{1}{2}$ cups of heated milk.

4. Cook and stir until smooth.

5. Cover the pan.

6. Reduce heat so that the water simmers lightly. Cook for 25 to 30 minutes.

7. Remove from heat.

8. Stir in the remaining ingredients except for the cold milk.

9. Using the 4 tablespoons of margarine, grease a 2-quart baking pan.

10. Pour the mixture into the greased 2-quart baking pan.

11. Pour the remaining cold milk on top.

12. Bake at 350 degrees for about 1 hour or until firm.

Serves 4 to 6.

Source: Barchers, Suzanne I., and Patricia C. Marden. *Cooking Up U.S. History: Recipes and Research to Share with Children.* Englewood, CO: Teacher Ideas Press, 1991.

Native American Research Project

Divide your class into groups of two or three to research the following topics. When the projects are completed, hold a presentation day.

Crazy Horse

Pocahontas

Sacajawea

Sequoyah

Sitting Bull

The Effect of Colonization on Native Americans

The French and Indian War

The League of Five Nations

Native American Reservations Today

Oral/Written Language

Rituals and Ceremonies

Tribal Government

Students could also choose a specific Native American tribe to research. They may wish to choose one from your area of the United States.

Chapter 2

Exploration

Introduction

Explorers search for new things and make discoveries. In Europe there were many daring explorers who set out to discover new lands.

The fiction and nonfiction trade books recommended in this chapter were selected to help give students some insight into the lives of these explorers, including the dangers they faced and the tremendous discoveries they made.

To introduce the topic of exploration to your class, read aloud *The Discovery of the Americas* by Betsy and Gulio Maestro. It begins with the history of early peoples walking to the Americas over a land bridge and ends with Magellan's voyages. The book also relates some of the negative effects of discovery on the way of life of the native peoples.

Whole Group Reading

📖 Conrad, Pam. *Pedro's Journal: A Voyage with Christopher Columbus, August 3, 1492 – February 14, 1493*. Honesdale, PA: Caroline House, 1991.

Pam Conrad created Pedro deSalcedo, who leaves his mother and Spain behind for a job as a cabin boy aboard the *Santa María*. He sails with Christopher Columbus on his first journey to the Americas. Pedro keeps a journal throughout his voyage, which he intends to present to his mother on his return. This book is recommended for use with the whole class because it is very well written and gives the reader an excellent view of what life might have been like for early explorers. Grades 3-7.

Author Information

Pam Conrad was born June 18, 1947 in New York City. She began writing in February of 1957 when she was bedridden with the chicken pox. Her mother gave her paper to draw on, but she began writing poetry instead. For many years—during college, early in her marriage, and in early motherhood—she did not write. She returned to college and to writing when her youngest daughter was three years old. She wrote many books and received many awards for her writing.

Pam Conrad died in 1996.

Activities

1. Throughout the reading of this novel, read aloud sections of *I, Columbus: My Journal, 1492–1493* by Peter and Connie Roop. This is an edited translation of Columbus's ship's log. Compare what Columbus wrote of the journey with Pedro's writings.

2. Have students write a letter from Pedro to his mother telling her of the journey, his shame, and his fear that he will never see her again.

3. On a world map, have students locate the following:

   India   Palos
   Saltes River   Canary Islands

4. Have students decide what five items they would have wanted to take with them on a ship if they were Pedro. They can draw pictures of these items and write captions underneath each, telling their reasons for choosing them.

Discussion

Give the class the following instruction: As we read this book, we will be discussing the following questions. Write down your ideas about these questions and add to them as needed.

1. Why was Pedro hired as a ship's boy?

2. Where is the *Santa María* headed?

3. What did Columbus think happened to the rudder of the *Pinta*?

4. Why were many men afraid to make the voyage?

5. What signs have made the crew think that they are approaching land?

6. What reward has Columbus offered to the first person to spot land?

7. During the journey, who does Pedro think about and worry about?

8. Why did Columbus decide to change the direction in which they were sailing?

9. What makes the crew think that they are lost at sea?

10. One day, the crew wished to turn back; the next day they wanted to keep going. Why?

11. When the crew set foot on the island, what kind of greeting did they receive from the natives?

12. What country did Columbus think that they were close to and why?

13. How does Pedro feel about what they are doing and why?

14. What happened to the *Santa María*?

15. Where had the *Pinta* been?

16. What was it that Pedro thought were mermaids?

17. Describe their journey back to Spain.

18. Why did Columbus instruct Pedro to put his message to the King and Pedro's letters into a barrel to be put out to sea?

Vocabulary

brocade (p2)
   a fabric woven with a raised design, often in gold or silver threads

rudder (p5)
   a broad, flat, movable piece of wood or metal that is hinged to the rear of a boat or whip and is used to steer the vessel

ingenious (p6)
   skillful or clever

boatswain (p8)
   the officer of a ship who supervises the crew in the care and maintenance of the hull, rigging, and other equipment

caulker (p8)
   someone who makes the seams of a boat tight by plugging them with tar, putty, or other material

meteorite (p15)
a part of a meteor that is not burned up and strikes the earth as a lump of stone or metal

tern (p16)
a small, gull-like bird with a slender body, pointed wings, and forked tail

fathom (p16)
a measure of length equal to six feet, used mainly in measuring the depth of water

gunwale (p19)
the upper edge of the side of a ship or boat

petrel (p23)
any of several small, dark, long-winged sea birds

frigate birds (p23)
either of two types of large sea birds noted for great powers of flight

mutiny (p25)
a rebellion against authority, as by a group of soldiers or sailors against their commanders

league (p28)
an old measure of length, usually equal to about three miles

scabbard (p51)
a case or sheath to protect the blade of a weapon, as a sword or bayonet

renegade (p64)
traitor

manatee (p67)
a mammal that lives off Florida and in the Gulf of Mexico; it has flippers and a broad, flat tail, and eats only plants

envoy (p70)
a messenger on a special mission

skirmish (p71)
a minor conflict

goliath (waves) (p77)
giant

pilgrimage (p78)
any long or difficult journey

Small Group Reading

Brenner, Barbara. *If You Were There in 1492*. New York: Bradbury Press, 1991.

This is a lively account of what life was like for people, including children, in 1492. Each section includes comments about Christopher Columbus, and an afterword describes what happened after his discovery of the New World. Grades 4-7.

Author Information

Barbara Brenner was born June 26, 1925 in Brooklyn, New York. She attended Seton Hall College (now Seton Hall University), Rutgers University, New York University, and New School for Social Research.

Brenner's working career has included: copywriter for Prudential Insurance, freelance artist's agent, writer-consultant in the publications division of Bank Street College of Education, senior editor at Bank Street College of Education, college instructor at Parson's School of Design in New York City, and freelance writer from 1957 to present.

Her interest in writing began at age nine. An avid reader, she credits *The Tale of Peter Rabbit*, *When We Were Very Young*, *Pinnochio*, and *Blackie's Children's Annual* as being somewhat responsible for her becoming a children's book writer.

Brenner has written in a wide variety of genres for preschool age through adult. Her books include: *If You Were There in 1776*, *Wagon Wheels*, and *Dinosaurium*.

Activities

1. On a world map, have students locate the following:

Africa	Asia	Canary Islands
Alexandria, Egypt	Atlantic Ocean	China
Antarctica	Australia	Cuba
Antwerp, Belgium	Bristol, England	Delhi, India

Europe	Iceland	Persia
Florence, Italy	Japan	Poland
France	Lisbon, Portugal	Rome, Italy
Genoa, Italy	Majorca, Spain	Scotland
Granada, Spain	Mediterranean Sea	Seville, Spain
Greece	North America	South America
Haiti	Nuremberg, Germany	Turkey
Holland	Palos, Spain	Venice, Italy
Iberian Peninsula		

2. Ask your school's music teacher to teach a lesson to your class on fifteenth-century music and the instruments used during that time.

3. Using *If You Were There in 1492*, have students in the group write short biographies of the following people to present to the class:

Martin Behaim	Henry the Navigator
Copernicus	Marco Polo
Bartholomew Dias	King John of Portugal
King Ferdinand	Amerigo Vespucci
Queen Isabella	

4. Have students create small posters showing life in the fifteenth century. Topics to include are: food, clothing, art, entertainment, crime and punishment, and expulsion. Display these posters in your classroom.

5. Ask your school's art teacher to conduct a lesson about fifteenth-century artists. Include Verrocchio, Botticelli, Bramante, Ghirlandoio, Michelangelo, and Leonardo da Vinci.

Discussion

1. Describe what life was like for people in 1492.

2. How were maps of the world in 1492 different than the maps of today?

3. The average European knew little about Asia in 1492. What would they have been surprised to find out about Asia?

4. What did Spain and Portugal compete for in 1492?

5. Discuss slave trade in 1492.

6. What does the Iberian Peninsula look like?

7. What was the Rock of Gibraltar called in 1492?

8. In 1492, what two kingdoms was Spain divided into? Who were the rulers of these two kingdoms?

9. Why were Spain and Portugal in 1492 called the "hot spots" of history?

10. What ideas did Christopher Columbus present to King John of Portugal?

11. How was Spain different from France and England in 1492?

12. Why did a traveler from France say, "The pigpens of France were better than the inns of Spain"?

13. Why was Spain in 1492 (and America today) called a "melting pot"?

14. When and why did Christopher Columbus travel to Spain?

15. How did the Spanish Catholics feel about the Moors?

16. What deal did the sultan of Granada, Abdallah, make with King Ferdinand and Queen Isabella?

17. What did people in Spain eat in 1492? How was it different from the food you eat today?

18. How did clothing in Spain in 1492 differ from what you wear today?

19. In 1492, how did the people of Europe control sickness?

20. When the ordinary people of Europe got sick, what did they do to try to become well again?

21. In what way were the lives of royal children difficult in the fifteenth century?

22. Why was Queen Isabella considered an unusual queen?

23. Discuss your feeling about Queen Isabella's religious views.

24. What do some historians believe about Queen Isabella's decision to finance Columbus's voyage?

25. If you were a child in 1492, what type of education would you have received?

26. What type of entertainment was popular in 1492?

27. Who were the great artists of the fifteenth century?

28. Why was the book business booming in 1492?

29. How did the availability of books change people's lives in 1492? How is this also true today?

30. What subjects did Christopher Columbus enjoy reading about?

31. How were people who committed crimes punished in 1492?

32. What was the Spanish Inquisition?

33. Discuss your feelings about the treatment of Jews in Spain in the fifteenth century.

34. What did mapmakers draw on maps in the areas they knew nothing about?

35. Who constructed the first globe of the world? Discuss the mistakes made on the globe.

36. Why did people love the ocean in 1492?

37. What type of duties did cabin boys on ships perform?

38. Why did Columbus have difficulty getting sailors to come on his voyage?

39. Discuss the lives of the Lucayan and Taino people before the arrival of Columbus. How did the arrival of Columbus change their lives?

40. What land did Columbus believe he had reached?

Vocabulary

crucial (p2)
likely to have a very important result or effect; critical

merchant (p5)
a person who buys and sells things for a profit

porcelain (p5)
a fine, hard, white earthenware used to make plates, dishes, cups; china

barbarian (p5)
a member of a nation, group, or tribe whose way of life is considered primitive or backward

passport (p6)
an official document that identifies a citizen and gives him or her the right to travel abroad under the government's protection

monarch (p10)
a ruler, such as a king or queen

astronomer (p10)
a person who is an expert in the study of the stars and planets

mania (p11)
a mental disorder marked by excessive excitement, sometimes violence, and often swift changes of mood

notion (p11)
a general idea or impression

terrain (p13)
an area of land

ravine (p13)
a long, narrow, deep depression in the earth that has steep sides, usually eroded by a flow of water; gorge

mesa (p13)
a hill or small plateau with a flat top and steep sides

primitive (p14)
coming from or belonging to the earliest times

nobles (p14)
members of the nobility; a group of people who have hereditary titles and rank, such as kings, queens, duchesses, dukes, countesses, earls

forlorn (p14)
sad from being alone or neglected

province (p15)
a main division of a country, similar to a state in the United States, having its own local government

elegance (p16)
"good taste," such as in household furnishings or decorations

pomegranate (p17)
a tropical fruit about the size of an orange

date (p17)
the sweet fruit of a type of palm tree

hospitality (p17)
friendly, welcoming treatment of guests or strangers

filigree (p17)
delicate ornamental work, such as intertwined gold and silver wire

synagogue (p17)
a place of meeting for Jewish worship and religious instruction

architecture (p17)
the profession of designing and constructing buildings

melting pot (p18)
a place where people of different races or cultures live

monastery (p18)
a place where monks live in seclusion

monk (p18)
a man who is a member of a religious order and usually lives in a monastery

culture (p20)
the way of life of a particular people, including its customs, religions, ideas, inventions, and tools

merciless (p20)
having or showing no mercy

heretic (p21)
a person who believes or teaches heresy, a belief different from or contrary to an accepted belief of a church, profession, or science

infidel (p21)
among Christians, a person who is not a Christian

sultan (p22)
the ruler of a Muslim country

hostage (p22)
a person held by an enemy until certain promises or conditions are fulfilled

exile (p23)
to banish someone from his or her native land

brine (p27)
water with a high concentration of salt, often used for pickling

crude (p29)
lacking refinement or good taste

tunic (p29)
a close-fitting jacket, often worn as part of a uniform

homespun (p29)
cloth made of homespun yarn or a strong, loose fabric

cloak (p32)
a loose outer garment, usually without sleeves

stagnant (p33)
water that is stale and dirty because it is not moving or flowing

plague (p33)
a very contagious, often fatal disease that spreads rapidly through a large area

apothecary (p34)
a drug store or pharmacy

dispensaries (p34)
places where medicine or first-aid treatment is given free or at a low cost

immune (p36)
protected against a disease

feudal landholdings (p38)
land given by lords in return for performance of other duties in an economic and political system of medieval Europe

jousting (p39)
formal fighting between two mounted knights armed with lances

shrewd (p40)
having practicalness or common sense

lute (p40)
an old stringed instrument similar to a guitar

brocade (p40)
a fabric woven with a raised design, often in gold or silver threads

fanaticism (p42)
devotion or enthusiasm that goes beyond the bounds of reason

expulsion (p42)
being driven out

notoriously (p43)
known widely, especially for bad reasons

hornbook (p44)
a leaf or page on which the alphabet and other information was printed, covered, and framed, formerly used in teaching reading to children

parchment (p44)
the skin of sheep, goats, and other animals prepared to be written or painted on

flogging (p44)
a hard beating, such as with a whip or stick

muleteer (p49)
a mule driver

mandolin (p49)
a musical instrument with a pear-shaped body and eight to twelve metal strings

mausoleum (p51)
a large tomb

renaissance (p51)
rebirth

cosmopolitan (p51)
common to all the world; not local or limited

apprentice (p51)
a person who works for another to learn a trade or business

linen (p55)
thread or cloth made of flax fibers

gallows (p58)
a wooden framework with a suspended noose, used for hanging criminals

persecution (p61)
mistreatment or oppression because of religion, race, or beliefs

prejudice (p61)
hatred of or dislike for a particular group, race, or religion

heresy (p63)
a belief different from or contrary to an accepted belief of a church, profession, or science

blasphemy (p63)
words or actions showing a lack or respect for God or sacred things

exempt (p63)
to free or excuse, as from a duty or obligation

refugee (p69)
a person who flees from persecution or danger

effigy (p70)
a painting or statue of a person

prosperous (p76)
successful; flourishing; thriving

crimson (p76)
deep red

caravel (p77)
a small fast-sailing ship of the fifteenth and sixteenth centuries

quadrant (p80)
an instrument having a ninety-degree scale, used to measure angles

mutiny (p85)
a rebellion against authority, such as by a group of soldiers or sailors against their commanders

exploitation (p95)
improper or selfish use

feasible (p98)
capable of being done or put into effect

Small Group Reading

Fritz, Jean. *Around the World in a Hundred Years: From Henry the Navigator to Magellan*. New York: G. P. Putnam's Sons, 1994.

Fritz examines the great wave of European exploration during the fifteenth century, resulting in more accurate maps. Grades 5 and up.

Author Information

The daughter of missionary parents, Jean Fritz spent her first twelve years in China. As a child, she often wondered about America and what it meant to be an American.

After she had married and had two children, Fritz began writing for magazines such as *The New Yorker* and *Redbook*.

Each of Fritz's historical novels grew from her personal interest in the subject. Her enthusiasm for her subjects brings the past to life in an entertaining, informative, and detailed fashion.

Fritz was the 1986 recipient of the Laura Ingalls Wilder Award of the American Library Association, which is given once every three years to an author whose work has made a "substantial and lasting contribution to literature for children."

Activities

1. On a world map, have students locate the following places mentioned in the book:

Africa	Iceland	North Carolina
Antarctica	India	Pacific Ocean
Australia	Indian Ocean	Persian Gulf
Brazil	Ireland	Peru
Canary Islands	Jamestown, VA	Portugal
Cape Verde Islands	Japan	Puerto Rico
Cuba	Jerusalem	Red Sea
Dominican Republic	Kenya	Rio de Janeiro
Florida	Lisbon	San Salvador
Genoa, Italy	Mediterranean Sea	Singapore
Gibraltar	Mexico	Sudan
Greenland	Mississippi River	Texas
Haiti	Morocco	Venice, Italy
Hawaii	Nile River	Zanzibar

2. To show students how difficult it was for mapmakers to map the world, have them draw and label maps of your town, or a section of the town if it is large.

3. Have students write short essays telling what explorer that they might like to have traveled with on their journey and why.

4. Have this group create small posters of five explorers. The posters should illustrate their contributions to the world and the area explored. Students can then share their finished products with the rest of the class.

Discussion

Give the small group the following instruction: As your group reads this book, discuss the following questions.

1. What made it difficult for the first mapmakers to map the world?

2. Discuss the main reasons for the need for further exploration in the fifteenth century.

3. What happened when Prince Henry sent Goncalves and Vaz with some settlers to Porto Santo?

4. What did Europeans believe about people who were different from them?

5. Why was Prince Henry known as Prince Henry the Navigator?

6. Where did Bartholomew Diaz place the stone marker he was so proud of?

7. What was the shortcut that Columbus wanted to take to the Indies?

8. Why did Columbus think that the new world he had discovered was China?

9. What did Vasco da Gama accomplish by going to Calicut?

10. What was Pedro Alvares Cabral able to prove to King Manual?

11. What did John Cabot explore?

12. What has the controversy about Amerigo Vespucci been?

13. When was the first accurate measurement of longitude made possible?

14. What did editors do to news of Vespucci's exploration?

15. How did America get its name?

16. Why did Ponce de Leon name Florida, La Florida?

17. What was Ponce de Leon searching for in his travels?

18. Why were English settlers in Jamestown, Virginia accused of trespassing on Spanish territory?

19. Why did Balboa decide to become a settler?

20. What new sea did Balboa discover?

21. What did people in the sixteenth and early seventeenth centuries believe about America?

22. What was Magellan's expedition? Why did he look for so long? Why was it so important?

23. Why was the Panama Canal built?

24. What continent is still being explored today?

Vocabulary

astronomy (p10)
the study of the stars, planets, and other heavenly bodies, including information on their makeup, positions, and motions

latitude (p10)
an imaginary line parallel to the equator

longitude (p10)
distance east or west of the prime meridian, running through Greenwich, England, measured as an angle at the earth's axis and expressed in degrees or units of time

equator (p10)
a imaginary line that encircles the earth exactly halfway between the North Pole and the South Pole

sacrilegious (p11)
characterized by sacrilege; an act of disrespect for anything sacred

flotilla (p13)
a small fleet of ships

missionary (p15)
a person sent out to convert people to a certain religion

pilgrimage (p15)
a journey to a place that is held in reverence or honor

cartographer (p25)
someone who makes maps and charts

caravel (p25)
a small, fast-sailing ship of the fifteenth and sixteenth centuries

navigable (p27)
water deep and wide enough for ships to sail through

arrogance (p29)
too much pride and too little regard for others

mutiny (p35)
a rebellion against authority, as by a group of soldiers or sailors against their commanders

exile (p35)
to banish someone from his or her native land

destiny (p41)
the outcome or fate that is bound to come

heathen (p48)
a person who is regarded as irreligious, uncivilized, or unenlightened

heretic (p48)
a person who believes or teaches heresy, a belief different from or contrary to an accepted belief of a church, profession, or science

scurvy (p55)
a disease caused by a lack of vitamin C in the diet, marked by swollen and bleeding gums and great physical weakness

diplomacy (p56)
the handling of relations, friendly or unfriendly, short of war, between nations

viceroy (p57)
a person who rules a country, colony, or province as the deputy of a sovereign

caravan (p63)
a group of traders, pilgrims, or nomads traveling together, especially through a desert

prominent (p70)
well known

immortalize (p71)
to give eternal life or fame

chronometer (p73)
a very precise clock, used in science, navigation, and other fields

strait (p73)
    a narrow body of water connecting two larger bodies of water

forgery (p74)
    an imitation meant to deceive

covetous (p92)
    strongly desiring something belonging to someone else

elusive (p96)
    escaping or avoiding capture

entreat (p98)
    to ask earnestly; implore; beg

etiquette (p98)
    the rules established for behavior in polite society or in official or professional life

monarch (p98)
    a ruler, as a king or queen

archives (p98)
    a place for keeping public records and historical papers

barter (p101)
    to trade or exchange

insubordination (p102)
    refusal to obey or submit; disobedience

desolate (p104)
    dreary; barren

treachery (p104)
    disloyal action; betrayal

Small Group Reading

Jacobs, Francine. *The Tainos: The People Who Welcomed Columbus*. New York: G. P. Putnam's Sons, 1992.

This book describes the history, culture, and mysterious fate of the first Native Americans to welcome Columbus in 1492. Jean Fritz says, "Why am I going to spread the good news about this book? Quite simply because I do not see how young people can truly understand Columbus and his successors without reading Francine Jacobs's book about the Tainos, the people who welcomed Columbus." Grades 5 and up.

Author Information

Francine Jacobs was born May 11, 1935 in New York City. She grew up in a small, oceanside community on Long Island, New York.

Jacobs worked as an elementary school teacher in Rye, New York from 1956 to 1958 and again from 1967 to 1968 in Chappaqua, New York.

She studied elementary education and child psychology at Queens College in New York City. When her children started school, she began writing for young readers. Ideas for her books sometimes come from her experience while traveling.

Books that Jacobs has written include: *The Wisher's Handbook*, *The King's Ditch*, and *Breakthrough: The True Story of Penicillin*.

Activities

1. On a world map, have students locate:

Amazon River, South America	Jamaica
Angulla, West Indies	Japan
Asia	Newfoundland
Bahama Islands	Puerto Rico
Caribbean Sea	South America
Cuba	Trinidad
Haiti	Venezuela
Hispaniola	Virgin Islands

2. Have students do further research on Leif Ericson, Marco Polo, Queen Isabella, and King Ferdinand for extra credit.

3. Have students write personal essays regarding their feelings about the plight of the Tainos and share them with the rest of the class.

4. As a group, have students create a poster showing the life of the Tainos before and after the arrival of Christopher Columbus. The poster could include illustrations of Taino homes, food, jobs, leisure activities, Columbus's arrival, the search for gold, and the ultimate extinction of the Tainos. Students should write captions below the illustrations. Display the poster in your classroom.

Discussion

1. Describe the life of the Arawalk people.

2. How did archaeologists discover the origins of the Tainos? Where did they come from?

3. How could these archaeologists tell that the Arawalk migrations came in stages?

4. Why do social scientists call new generations of the Arawalks, Tainos?

5. Why did the Tainos fear the Island Caribs?

6. How were Taino villages able to thrive in Haiti?

7. Describe the government of the Tainos in Haiti.

8. What did the homes of the Tainos look like?

9. What did the shaman (the village priest who was also the doctor) use to heal people who were sick?

10. What crops did the Tainos plant?

11. What did the Tainos eat?

12. Discuss the jobs the men and women performed. Compare their jobs to those of men and women today.

13. What leisure activities did the Tainos enjoy?

14. How do you think the Lucayans, the Tainos of the Bahamas, felt when they first saw the three great wooden ships?

15. What did Columbus give to the Lucayans? What did the Lucayans give to Columbus?

16. Where were Columbus and his men headed for on their voyage, and why?

17. Why did Columbus encourage the Lucayans to participate in Christian services?

18. Where did Columbus believe he had landed?

19. Why did Columbus have Lucayan guides take him to so many different islands?

20. What happened to the *Santa María*?

21. What plan did Columbus propose to the Tainos?

22. How was Columbus treated when he returned to Spain? What promises did Columbus make to King Ferdinand and Queen Isabella?

23. When Columbus returned to Hispaniola, what did he find?

24. What did Columbus and his men do after returning to Hispaniola?

25. By the end of their first three months at Hispaniola, how did Columbus's men feel about him?

26. What consequence did Columbus's greed have for the Tainos?

27. What plan did Columbus have to settle his debt with Queen Isabella?

28. Discuss how the Spaniards treated the Tainos. How did the treatment change?

29. What did the Spaniards find at San Cristobal?

30. What was the tribute, or blood tax? What result did this tax have on the Tainos?

31. What did Queen Isabella order in June of 1500? What happened to Columbus at this time?

32. What occurred at Hispaniola after Columbus left?

33. What happened to the shipment of gold when it was being taken to Spain?

34. How did the Tainos feel about being paid?

35. Discuss Ovando's meeting with the caciques of the southwestern districts.

36. Why did the war of Higüey take place?

37. Discuss the ecomienda policy that Ovando started.

38. How did families of the Taino mine workers survive?

39. After Queen Isabella died, how did King Ferdinand's ruling about the Tainos change?

40. When Diego Columbus became the new governor of Hispaniola, were the Tainos treated any differently?

41. What message did the Dominican friars bring to the colonists? How did the colonists react?

42. Discuss the Laws of Burgos.

43. What was Bartolomé de Las Casa's plan for reform? How did this change the lives of the Tainos?

44. Discuss your feeling about the plight of the Tainos following the arrival of Christopher Columbus.

Vocabulary

ancestry (p11)
line of descent; birth

forebears (p11)
ancestors

arid (p11)
without enough rainfall to grow things; dry, parched

cultivation (p11)
the work of preparing the land for growing plants, such as by loosening soil

perish (p12)
to be completely destroyed

petroglyph (p12)
a carving or line drawing on rock, especially one made by prehistoric people

archeologist (p12)
an expert in the study of past times and cultures mainly carried out by digging up and examining remains, such as of the cities or tombs of ancient cultures

anthropologist (p12)
an expert in the science of the physical, social, and cultural development of human beings

missionaries (p13)
people sent out to convert other people to a certain religion

diverse (p15)
distinctly different

coveted (p16)
desired strongly

emigrate (p16)
to move from one country or section of a country to settle in another

intrepid (p16)
very brave; courageous; fearless

chieftain (p19)
the head of a clan or tribe

immigrant (p19)
a person who comes into a country or region where he or she was not born, to live there

ferocity (p20)
extreme fierceness, savagery, cruelty

inferior (p20)
not as good, such as in quality, work, or usefulness

vulnerable (p20)
open to attack; without sufficient defenses

manioc (p20)
another name for cassava, a tropical plant with starchy roots used to make tapioca

nobility (p22)
a group of people who have hereditary titles and rank, such as kings, queens, duchesses, dukes, countesses, and earls

sacred (p22)
deserving reverence, honor, or respect

ritual (p22)
a system of rites and ceremonies

serf (p23)
in feudal times, a person who could not leave the land he or she worked on, and who could be sold along with the land

erosion (p24)
the wearing away or gradual destruction of something, such as by the action of wind, water, or acid

delicacy (p26)
a choice food

ingenuity (p26)
skill or cleverness, as shown in inventing or solving things

revelry (p30)
noisy or boisterous merrymaking

sovereign (p36)
  a monarch; king or queen

imperial (p36)
  of or having to do with an empire, an emperor, or an empress

litter (p39)
  a vehicle consisting of a couch on two poles carried by people or animals

emissaries (p41)
  people sent as special representatives or to carry out special orders

hull (p41)
  the body or frame of a ship

provisions (p41)
  food, or a supply of food

garrison (p43)
  the troops stationed in a fort or town

dominion (p44)
  supreme power or authority

skeptical (p45)
  not believing easily; inclined to question or doubt

feigned (p46)
  purely imaginary; made up

arrogant (p47)
  too proud and disdainful of others

stamina (p47)
  vitality; vigor; strength; endurance

malaria (p48)
  a disease spread by an infected anopheles mosquito and marked by recurrent attacks of chills, fever, and sweating

prophecy (p49)
  a prediction made under divine influence

mutiny (p49)
  a rebellion against authority, such as by a group of soldiers or sailors against their commanders

famine (p52)
  a widespread lack of food that causes many to starve

smallpox (p53)
  a highly contagious viral disease causing a high fever and skin eruptions that usually leave permanent scars

yellow fever (p53)
  an infectious disease of warm countries caused by a virus transmitted to humans by the bite of certain mosquitoes, marked by fever, vomiting, and yellowing of the skin

plague (p53)
  a highly contagious, often fatal disease that spreads rapidly through a large area

immunity (p53)
  the condition of being able to resist a disease

caravel (p54)
  a small, fast-sailing ship of the fifteenth and sixteenth centuries

renegade (p54)
  a person who gives up faith, principles, or party to join the opposite side; traitor

tyranny (p58)
  absolute power unfairly or cruelly used

liberty (p68)
  freedom from control by others

tenets (p70)
  opinions, doctrines, or principles held to be true by a person or group

imminent (p71)
  likely to happen soon

exile (p71)
  to banish someone from his or her native land

avenge (p72)
  to get revenge

catastrophe (p72)
  a sudden and widespread disaster

omen (p72)
  something that is looked upon as a sign of what is going to happen

subjugate (p75)
  to bring under control; to conquer

insurrection (p77)
  a rebellion or uprising

pacify (p80)
  to quiet or calm

atrocity (p81)
  the resulting action of being wicked, criminal, or cruel

friar (p82)
  a member of certain Roman Catholic religious orders

eloquence (p82)
  skillful use of language, especially in speaking

sacrament (p83)
  any of certain very holy rites in Christian churches, such as baptism and communion

dilemma (p89)
  a position where either of two choices is as bad or as unpleasant as the other

extinction (p91)
  no longer existing

Small Group Reading

Schlein, Miriam. *I Sailed with Columbus*. New York: HarperCollins, 1991.
Schlein describes Columbus's first voyage as seen through the eyes of a twelve-year-old ship's boy. Grades 4-7.

Author Information

Miriam Schlein has written dozens of books for children, both fiction and nonfiction. She has had several books chosen as Junior Literary Guild selections; some have been named "Outstanding Science Trade Books for Children."

Activities

1. Have the students draw illustrations of the *Santa María* using the description on page 10.

2. Have the students compare Julio's diary entries in *I Sailed with Columbus* with those of Pedro in *Pedro's Journal*.

3. Have students make a chart of the distance the *Santa María* traveled each day as recorded by Julio in his diary. At the bottom of the chart, they should list some of the reasons for the differences in distances shown.

4. Cristobal Colon (whom we know as Christopher Columbus) told Julio, "A man can do so much more when he can read." Have students discuss this statement and brainstorm a list of the things a reader can do that a nonreader cannot do.

5. On a world map, have students locate the following:

   Africa   Haiti
   Asia   Indies
   Bahamas   Japan (Cipangu)
   Canary Islands   Mediterranean Sea
   Cuba   Portugal
   Dominican Republic   San Salvador
   Genoa

6. Have students write a letter from Julio to the Franciscan Brothers, telling them about the voyage. Students can share their letters with the rest of the class.

Discussion

Give the small group the following instruction: As your group reads this book, discuss the following questions.

1. Why did Julio live with the Franciscan Brothers?

2. What did Julio do to help the Brothers?

3. Why did Captain Vincente Pinzon want Julio to come on the voyage to the Indies?

4. If you were Julio, would you have gone on the voyage?

5. How did Julio feel as the *Santa María* left the harbor?

6. What did Maestro Gabriel tell Julio his job would be?

7. What do some of the men fear?

8. Imagine you are out at sea and cannot see land. How would you feel?

9. What surprised Julio about why many of the men were on the voyage?

10. Why did the *Niña*, the *Pinta*, and the *Santa María* stay fairly close together?

11. How did the Canary Islands get their name?

12. Why do you think the Captain General (Cristobal Colon) lied to the men about how far they had traveled?

13. By October 9th, how did the men feel about the voyage?

14. Discuss the reaction of the men when land was sighted.

15. Why were the men shocked when they saw the native people of what the Captain General named San Salvador?

16. Why did the Captain General call the native people of San Salvador "Indians"?

17. How were the men finally able to communicate with the Indians?

18. Why did the Indian guides want to escape?

19. What do the men search for as they explore?

20. What happened to the *Santa María* on Christmas Day?

21. What was the Admiral's plan for Villa de la Navidad?

22. Why did Julio believe that the Admiral thought they may not survive the journey home?

23. Why did King John of Portugal tell the Admiral that he wondered why he had let such a wonderful chance slip by?

24. What does Julio plan for his future?

25. In the author's note at the end of the book, Schlein says that the "false" figures Columbus gave to the crew each day turned out to be more accurate than what he had thought were the true figures. Why is that?

26. What happened to the settlers Columbus left at Villa de la Navidad?

27. Columbus was certain he had reached the Indies. Why then did some others begin to think he had found a new world?

Vocabulary

friary (p4)
a monastery occupied by friars

mimic (p4)
to imitate the speech or actions of

harbor (p4)
a place or port where ships can anchor or be protected in a storm

flagship (p8)
the ship carrying the commander of a fleet and displaying the commander's flag

friar (p10)
a member of certain Roman Catholic religious orders

bulwark (p10)
the side of a ship above the deck

insignia (p10)
badges or emblems used as special marks of membership, office, or honor

starboard (p11)
the right-hand side of a ship or boat

stern (p17)
the rear part, as of a ship or boat

binnacle (p17)
a stand or case for a ship's compass, located near the steering wheel

helmsman (p17)
the person who steers a ship

tiller (p17)
a bar or handle for turning the rudder in steering a boat

port (p21)
the left-hand side of a ship or boat, facing the bow

bilge (p21)
a ship's bottom

wallow (p21)
to roll or tumble about; to flounder, as in mud or water

prow (p24)
the usually pointed forward end or bow of a ship or boat

crow's nest (p24)
a high, partly sheltered platform on a ship's mast used for a lookout

cobbler (p27)
a shoemaker

amnesty (p27)
an official pardon for offenses committed against a government

navigator (p32)
a person trained in charting the position and course of a ship or aircraft

caravel (p34)
a small, fast-sailing ship of the fifteenth and sixteenth centuries

rudder (p35)
a broad, flat, movable piece of wood or metal that is hinged to the rear of a boat or ship and is used to steer the vessel

meteorite (p39)
a part of a meteor that is not burned up and strikes the earth as a lump of stone or metal

fathom (p45)
a measure of length equal to six feet, used mainly in measuring the depth of water

surly (p58)
rude and ill-humored

mutiny (p59)
a rebellion against authority, as by a group of soldiers or sailors against their commanders

courtesy (p70)
politeness and consideration for others; good manners

tunic (p74)
a close-fitting jacket, often worn as part of a uniform

vespers (p90)
in certain churches, a service of worship held in the late afternoon or evening

reef (p91)
a ridge of sand, rocks, or coral at or near the surface of the water

console (p97)
to comfort in sorrow or disappointment; to cheer

parchment (p114)
the skin of sheep, goats, and other animals, prepared to be written or painted on

viceroy (p117)
a person who rules a country, colony, or province as the deputy of a sovereign

monastery (p120)
a place where monks live in seclusion

Small Group Reading

West, Tracey. *Voyage of the Half Moon*. New York: Silver Moon Press, 1993.

Young John Hudson joins his father, the great explorer Henry Hudson, on a journey to the New World. They and the crew of the *Half Moon* are the first Europeans to explore the Hudson River. Grades 4-7.

Author Information

Tracey West was born October 1, 1965 in New Jersey. She lives in Piermont, New York. West attended Douglass College at Rutgers University in New Jersey. Since college, she has worked as a freelance writer and as an editor of children's books and educational books.

She says that she always wanted to write. As a child she loved to read and did so constantly. West says, "All I thought about was being a writer. I remember how important books were to me, and it's nice to think you could do that for someone else."

West has written two other historical fiction books for children, *Fire in the Valley* and *Mr. Peale's Bones*. She also coauthored *Countdown to Two Thousand* and *Great-Uncle Dracula* (under a pseudonym) with Bonnie Bader.

Activities

1. On a map of the United States, have students locate the Hudson River in New York.

2. Have students do further research on Henry Hudson and present their findings to the class.

3. Have students write journal entries from Henry's and John's points of view.

Discussion

Give the small group the following instruction: As your group reads this book, discuss the following questions.

1. What happened to John Colman upon reaching the New World?

2. How did James Robinson feel about the attack?

3. What was Henry Hudson's goal for this voyage?

4. How do you think John felt when he and his father went ashore to meet the native people?

5. How did John's new friend Etow save John's life?

6. Why was the *Half Moon* forced to turn around and head for home?

7. What happened to the *Half Moon* before reaching the ocean?

8. On Henry Hudson's fourth voyage on the *Discovery*, what did he discover?

9. What finally became of Henry and John Hudson?

10. Henry Hudson wrote in his diary of seeing a mermaid. What do experts today believe it was?

11. Why was finding a shortcut to Asia so important?

Vocabulary

anguish (p1)
great suffering of mind or body; agony

bow (p1)
the forward part, as of a ship or boat

harbor (p6)
a place or port where ships can anchor or be protected in a storm

hostage (p8)
a person given up to or held by an enemy until certain promises or conditions are fulfilled

taunt (p9)
a scornful, mocking, or sarcastic remark

skeptical (p13)
showing doubt

embroidery (p14)
stitches or decoration made by needlework

musket (p28)
an old type of firearm, replaced by the rifle

fathom (p31)
a measure of length equal to six feet, used mainly in measuring the depth of water

foremast (p31)
the mast that is closest to the bow of a ship

scoundrel (p40)
a mean or dishonest person; a villain

mutiny (p45)
a rebellion against authority, as by a group of soldiers or sailors against their commanders

stern (p45)
the rear part, as of a ship or boat

eerie (p46)
causing or arousing fear; weird; strange

Bibliography

Individual Titles

Adler, David A. *A Picture Book of Christopher Columbus.* New York: Holiday House, 1991.
This is a brief account of the life and accomplishments of Christopher Columbus. Grades 2-5.

Alper, Ann Fitzpatrick. *Forgotten Voyager: The Story of Amerigo Vespucci.* Minneapolis, MN: Carolrhoda Books, 1991.
The author describes the Florentine world of Amerigo Vespucci. She tells of how Amerigo used the new navigational instruments to determine longitude and latitude and his realization that he was in a new land, not the lands described by Marco Polo. Grades 2-5.

Blumberg, Rhoda. *The Incredible Journey of Lewis and Clark.* New York: Lothrop, Lee & Shepard, 1987.
This is a wonderfully illustrated account of the expedition sponsored by Thomas Jefferson in 1804. It

is packed with details of medicine and animal and plant life, and anecdotes of the explorers not usually made available to children. Grades 5-6.

———. *The Remarkable Voyages of Captain Cook.* New York: Bradbury Press, 1991.

This book gives accounts of the three major voyages of Captain Cook as he explored the South Pacific on behalf of King George III of England. Grades 5 and up.

Brown, Warren. *The Search for the Northwest Passage.* New York: Chelsea House, 1991.

This is an account of the search for and discovery of the Northwest Passage. Grades 6 and up.

Burton, Rosemary, Richard Cavendish, and Bernard Stonehouse. *Journeys of the Great Explorers.* New York: Facts on File, 1992.

A seven-page spread in the center of the book details the journey of Marco Polo. It includes a map, a biographical chronology, and several reproductions. It also includes sections on Columbus, Lewis and Clark, Hillary and Tenzing, and the explorers of space, as well as an extensive time line. Grades 4 and up.

Clare, John D., ed. *The Voyages of Christopher Columbus.* San Diego, CA: Gulliver Books, 1992.

This book describes the four voyages of Columbus to the New World and his activities there. Grades 4 and up.

Dorris, Michael. *Morning Girl.* New York: Hyperion Books for Children, 1992.

The author describes the lives of a Taino brother and sister before the coming of Columbus. At the end, the book foreshadows the changes to come. Grades 3 and up.

Everett, Felicity, and Struan Reid. *The Usborne Book of Explorers.* New York: Scholastic, 1991.

This is an excellent resource for your class to use in researching explorers. Grades 4 and up.

Fisher, Leonard Everett. *Prince Henry the Navigator.* New York: Macmillan, 1990.

In 1416, Prince Henry established the first school of navigation, which enabled explorers who came later to make their important discoveries. Grades 2-5.

Fradin, Dennis Brindell. *The Niña, the Pinta, and the Santa María.* New York: Franklin Watts, 1991.

This is a biography of Christopher Columbus, focusing on his voyage to America aboard the three famous ships. Grades 4 and up.

Fritz, Jean. *Where Do You Think You're Going, Christopher Columbus?* New York: G. P. Putnam's Sons, 1980.

Fritz's account of Columbus's journey is filled with facts about Queen Isabella, the islands Columbus discovered, and the many setbacks he encountered. Grades 3-6.

Grant, Neil. *The Great Atlas of Discovery.* New York: Alfred A. Knopf, 1992.

Maps and text show major areas and routes of exploration from about 6000 B.C. to the present. Grades 5 and up.

Haney, David. *Captain James Cook and the Explorers of the Pacific.* New York: Chelsea House, 1992.

This book examines the life and journeys of Captain Cook. Grades 6 and up.

Humble, Richard. *Exploration Through the Ages: The Voyage of Magellan.* New York: Franklin Watts, 1988.

This book tells the story of Magellan's important voyage of discovery. Grades 4 and up.

Kent, Zachary. *The World's Great Explorers: Marco Polo.* Chicago: Childrens Press, 1992.

Kent describes the travels of the medieval Italian explorer and his adventures and discoveries in the Far East. Grades 6 and up.

Kroll, Steven. *Lewis and Clark: Explorers of the American West.* New York: Holiday House, 1994.

This book introduces Lewis and Clark and their expedition of 1804–1806 through the Louisiana Territory, opening the Mississippi River to the Pacific Ocean. Grades 2-4.

Leon, George DeLucenay. *Explorers of the Americas Before Columbus.* New York: Franklin Watts, 1989.

This book examines the voyages of explorers who reached the shores of North America before Columbus. Leon discusses Eric the Red, Leif Ericson, the Norse Settlements, and ancient visitors to South and Latin America. Grades 6 and up.

Levinson, Nancy Smiler. *Christopher Columbus: Voyager to the Unknown.* New York: Lodestar Books, 1990.

This is a biography of the fifteenth-century Italian seaman and navigator who unknowingly discovered a new continent while looking for a western route to India. Grades 4 and up.

Litowinsky, Olga. *The High Voyage: The Final Crossing of Christopher Columbus.* New York: Dell, 1992.

Fernando is overwhelmed when his father, Christopher Columbus, invites him to come along on his next voyage. In this historic adventure, taken from Fernando's diaries, and told from his point of view, readers see the New World as it may have appeared to its first explorers. Grades 5-9.

Lomask, Milton. *Exploration: Great Lives.* New York: Charles Scribner's Sons, 1988.

The author focuses on twenty-five significant geographical explorers, covering a time span from the fourth century to 1957. Grades 4-6.

Macaulay, David. *Ship*. Boston: Houghton Mifflin, 1993.

Macaulay combines excellent technical drawing skills with expert narrative to explain how small wooden ships opened the seas to the Age of Exploration in the fifteenth and sixteenth centuries. Grades 4 and up.

Maestro, Betsy, and Giulio Maestro. *The Discovery of the Americas*. New York: Lothrop, Lee & Shepard, 1991.

This is an excellent resource for introducing the discovery of the Americas. It begins with the first history of early peoples walking to the Americas over a land bridge and ends with Magellan's voyages. The book relates some of the negative effects of discovery on the way of life of the native peoples. Grades 1-5.

———. *Exploration and Conquest: The America's After Columbus: 1500-1620*. New York: Lothrop, Lee & Shepard, 1994.

The authors discuss further exploration of the New World by Europeans after Columbus. Grades 3-7.

Margeson, Susan M. *Eyewitness Books: Viking*. New York: Alfred A. Knopf, 1994.

The author discusses who the Vikings were, describes their discovery of new lands, and presents a multitude of information about them. The illustrations, and particularly the photographs of Viking artifacts, provide a tremendous resource. Grades 4 and up.

Martell, Hazel Mary. *Worlds of the Past: The Vikings*. New York: New Discovery Books, 1992.

Martell describes aspects of life in the European and North American Viking settlements as revealed through archaeological excavations. Grades 4 and up.

Mason, Antony. *The Children's Atlas of Exploration*. Brookfield, CT: Millbrook Press, 1993.

This atlas depicts exploration through the ages, from the wanderings of prehistoric peoples to modern space missions. Grades 4 and up.

Meltzer, Milton. *Columbus and the World Around Him*. New York: Franklin Watts, 1990.

Black-and-white maps and reproductions extend a text that not only gives a psychological portrait of Columbus but also sets him squarely in his historical context. Grades 6-12.

O'Dell, Scott. *Steams to the River, River to the Sea: A Novel of Sacagawea*. Boston: Houghton Mifflin, 1986.

A young Indian woman, accompanied by her infant and cruel husband, experiences joy and heartbreak when she joins the Lewis and Clark Expedition seeking a way to the Pacific. Grades 5 and up.

Roop, Peter, and Connie Roop. *I, Columbus: My Journal, 1492–1493*. New York: Walker, 1990.

The authors have edited a translation of Columbus's ship's log from the years 1492 and 1493 to offer a glimpse of the voyage through his own eyes. Grades 2-7.

Roth, Susan L. *Marco Polo: His Notebook*. New York: Doubleday, 1990.

This book contains many reproductions of drawings and maps collected from museums. Readers will find it easy to pretend and follow the adventurous Marco Polo from the time he leaves Venice as a teenager in 1271, to his arrival at the Great Kublai Khan's Summer Palace in 1274, to his return to Venice twenty-four years later, in 1295. Grades 3-9.

Ryan, Peter. *Explorers & Mapmakers*. New York: Lodestar Books, 1989.

This book chronicles the efforts of early explorers to map the globe. Illustrations and photographs enhance this well-written book. Grades 4 and up.

Schaff, Louise E. *Skald of the Vikings*. New York: Lothrop, Lee & Shepard, 1966.

Schaff tells the story of young Thrain, who was chosen to accompany the Viking expedition to Vinland as its skald. A skald is a balladeer who would sing of the adventurers' exploits in the years to come. In Vinland, Thrain is taken hostage by Indians and must plan his escape. Grades 5 and up.

Sis, Peter. *Follow the Dream*. New York: Alfred A. Knopf, 1991.

With maps, a pictorial log, and a unique style of painting, Sis combines documented fact and legend to portray Columbus and his dream of finding a new route to the Orient. Grades K-4.

Smith, Carter, ed. *The Explorers and Settlers: A Sourcebook on Colonial America*. Brookfield, CT: Millbrook Press, 1991.

This book describes and illustrates the first discoveries and settlements in North America. Grades 3 and up.

Stefoff, Rebecca. *Accidental Explorers: Surprises and Side Trips in the History of Discovery*. New York: Oxford University Press, 1992.

Stefoff discusses the role of chance in the discoveries of explorers such as Columbus and Ponce de Leon. Grades 6 and up.

———. *Ferdinand Magellan and the Discovery of the World Ocean*. New York: Chelsea House, 1990.

This is a biography of the Portuguese sea captain who commanded the first expedition that sailed around the world, providing the first proof that the earth is round. Grades 6 and up.

———. *Marco Polo and the Medieval Explorers*. New York: Chelsea House, 1992.

Stefoff provides a straightforward account of Marco Polo's life and journey, with maps and reproductions from his time. Grades 6 and up.

———. *Women of the World: Women Travelers and Explorers*. New York: Oxford University Press, 1992.

Stefoff describes some of the explorations and discoveries made by women throughout history. Grades 6 and up.

Townson, W. D. *Illustrated Atlas of the World in the Age of Discovery, 1453–1763.* New York: Warwick Press, 1981.

In this atlas, exploration is portrayed at succeeding stages by a combination of clear and simple maps, colorful photographs and drawings, and an informative text. Grades 5 and up.

Twist, Clint. *Christopher Columbus: Discovery of the Americas.* Austin, TX: Raintree/Steck-Vaughn, 1994.

Twist introduces the background, voyages, discoveries, and historical significance of Christopher Columbus. This book is packed with full-color photographs and maps. Grades 5-8.

———. *Magellan and Da Gama: To the Far East and Beyond.* Austin, TX: Raintree/Steck-Vaughn, 1994.

This book describes the explorations of Ferdinand Magellan and Vasco da Gama in the sixteenth century, which led to the establishment of Spanish and Portuguese empires around the world. This book is filled with maps and full-color photographs. Grades 5-8.

Ventura, Piero. *1492: The Year of the New World.* New York: G. P. Putnam's Sons, 1991.

Ventura gives an account of Columbus's voyage and links descriptions of life in various countries in fifteenth-century Europe with those of life among various Indians in the New World. Grades 5 and up.

Theme Resources

Commercial Resources

Artman, John. *Explorers: An Activity Book.* Carthage, IL: Good Apple, 1986.

This activity book for students in grades 4-8 has information on activities regarding ten of the most noted explorers of all time.

Aten, Jerry. *Hooray for Columbus!* Carthage, IL: Good Apple, 1991.

The interdisciplinary ideas and activities in this resource book enhance student research and creative problem-solving skills. Included is an interactive map in which students chart the important events of each of Columbus's four voyages to the New World. Use with students in grades 3-6.

Cobblestone: The History Magazine for Young People. Peterborough, NH: Cobblestone.

The subject of the October 1984 issue for students in grades 4 and up is "Who Came to America Before Columbus?" Articles include "Did the Phoenicians Come to America?" and "The Voyage of Leif the Lucky."

Devorsey, Louis, Jr. *Jackdaw: First American Encounters: Columbus & The Age of Explorers.* Amawalk, NY: Jackdaw Publications, 1992.

This is a portfolio of primary source material featuring fourteen reproductions of historic documents. The documents for use with students in grades 5 and up include a map of America engraved by Cornelius de Jode in 1593; the first engraving of Martin Behaim's world map, 1730; and a portrait of Christopher Columbus done by Laurens Lotto in 1512. The portfolio also includes notes on the documents, a reading list, and critical-thinking questions.

Kids Discover: Columbus. New York: Kids Discover.

The October 1992 issue contains many photos and much information about Christopher Columbus and his voyage to the new world. It includes a detailed illustration of the *Santa María.* Suitable for use with students in grades 4 and up.

Kids Discover: Explorers. New York: Kids Discover.

The February 1994 issue would be an excellent resource to have in your classroom or school library for research purposes. Suitable for use with students in grades 4 and up.

Kids Discover: Vikings. New York: Kids Discover.

The November 1995 issue for students in grades 4 and up contains much information about the Viking explorers.

Klimowski, Kevin. *Inquiring into the Theme of Exploration: Based on Charles Bohner's Journey: West with Lewis and Clark.* Logan, IA: Perfection Learning, 1995.

This resource provides activities, background information for the theme, and much more. Grades 6-8.

Pofahl, Jane. *United States History: Early Explorers.* Grand Rapids, MI: T. S. Dennison, 1994.

This resource, suitable for use in grades 3-6, includes cross-curricular activities and reproducible activity pages on explorers.

Starkey, Dinah. *Scholastic Atlas of Exploration.* New York: Scholastic, 1993.

This resource book features more than thirty full-color maps, which students can use to follow explorers from the time of Ancient Greece all the way to present-day space and underwater expeditions. Use with students in grades 4 and up.

Sterling, Mary Ellen. *Thematic Unit: Explorers*. Huntington Beach, CA: Teacher Created Materials, 1992.
This theme-based resource includes many activities for all curriculum areas regarding explorers for grades 4 and up.

Computer Resources

Explorers of the New World. [CD-ROM]. Great Neck, NY: Future Vision Multimedia, 1995.
Students can follow the footsteps of Columbus, Magellan, and Cortes on their journeys to the New World. A database includes information about sixty additional explorers.

Columbus and the Age of Discovery. [CD-ROM]. Chicago: Clearview, 1995.
Students will travel through time to learn about many of the great explorers and navigators before, during, and after Columbus.

Videos

Where Do You Think You're Going, Christopher Columbus? Weston, CT: Weston Woods, 1991. (35 minutes)
This video is based on the book *Where Do You Think You're Going, Christopher Columbus?* by Jean Fritz.

End-of-Unit Celebration

Exploration Research Project

Divide your class into groups of two to research the following topics. When the projects are completed, hold a presentation day.

Prince Henry the Navigator	Jacques Cartier
Robert de La Salle	Juan Ponce de Leon
Bartholomew Diaz	Giovanni Verrazano
Christopher Columbus	Vasco Nunez de Balboa
Vasco da Gama	Francisco Coronado
Sir Francis Drake	Ferdinand Magellan
Pedro Alvares Cabral	Francisco Pizarro
Leif Ericson	Henry Hudson
John Cabot	Hernando de Soto
Samuel de Champlain	Hernando Cortes
Amerigo Vespucci	

Chapter 3

The American Revolution and the Constitution

Introduction

The American Revolutionary War began in Lexington, Massachusetts in 1775 and ended at Yorktown, Virginia in 1781. The war was fought because colonists longed for independence from Great Britain. Many believed that they were not really free even though they had left British soil. Although the majority wanted to be free of the British, there were many colonists who still supported Great Britain and King George III. They were called Loyalists and fought against some of their own neighbors.

The Declaration of Independence was signed on July 4, 1776, and bolstered the colonists' belief that they had a right to set up their own government. The U.S. Constitution took effect in 1789.

Many excellent trade books about this time period in United States history have been published. *The Fighting Ground*, as well as the small group titles recommended, represent some of the very best.

Whole Group Reading

Avi. *The Fighting Ground*. New York: J. B. Lippincott, 1984.

Thirteen-year-old Jonathan joins a small group of townspeople who are marching toward the Hessians. During the next twenty-four hours, he fights in battle, runs away, is captured by three Hessians, saves a little boy, and eventually returns to his group. In *School Library Journal*'s review of *The Fighting Ground*, it says, "Avi has accomplished his intent: to have readers experience minute by minute what it's like to be involved in war." Grades 5 and up.

Author Information

Avi Wortis was born December 23, 1937 in New York City. He received a master's degree in Library Science from Columbia University in 1964. He has worked as a librarian, as well as teaching college courses in children's literature.

In high school, Avi could not write or spell. What little grammar he learned was not learned in school but from books he had read. He would read anything and everything. His third year in high school marked a turning point in his life. His English teacher insisted that he be tutored during the summer to improve his writing skills. During that summer, his motivation to write began.

Avi began writing for young people when his own children were born. Of this writing he says, "I do believe that young people are special, as fascinating, as complex and compelling as any other person, no matter what age. To make contact with them is a sort of grace. Young people don't easily take adults into their private world or trust. To be welcomed there is a gift."

When Avi's first children's book, *Things That Sometimes Happen*, was about to be published, his agent called him to ask what name he wanted on the book. Avi thought about it and said, "Oh well, just put Avi down." Since then, all of Avi's books have been without a last name.

Activities

1. Have students compare twenty-four hours in their own lives to the twenty-four-hour period in Jonathan's life in *The Fighting Ground*.

2. As students read *The Fighting Ground*, have them keep a journal of their reactions to the novel.

3. On a map of the United States, have students locate the following places:

Alexandria, NJ	Rocktown, NJ
Fleming, NJ	Snydertown, NJ
Linvale, NJ	Trenton, NJ
Pennington, NJ	Well's Ferry, NJ
Philadelphia, PA	

4. Have students write an essay about their feelings about war.

5. Have students write an epilogue for *The Fighting Ground*. It should take place twenty years after the war and could include what has happened to Jonathan, his parents, the Corporal, and the young boy whom Jonathan found alone in the shed.

Discussion

Give the class the following instruction: As we read this book, we will be discussing the following questions. Write down your ideas about these questions and add to them as needed.

1. What did the ringing of the bell mean?

2. What did Jonathan realize about his father?

3. Why do you think Jonathan made the decision to fight in the war?

4. What do you think Jonathan's feelings were when they finally reached the fighting ground?

5. Why did Jonathan call the German soldiers the "real enemies"?

6. Describe Jonathan's feelings about war when he was caught by the Hessians.

7. Why did Jonathan hesitate to escape?

8. What was Jonathan's reaction upon finding the young boy in the shed?

9. Why did the Hessians seem to trust Jonathan?

10. How did you feel when Jonathan found the boy's parents?

11. Predict what Jonathan will do once the Hessians are all asleep.

12. Why couldn't Jonathan shoot the Hessian?

13. Where might Jonathan go with the boy?

14. How do you think the Corporal knew where the Hessians were?

15. Who had really killed the boy's parents?

16. How have Jonathan's feelings about the fighting changed since the beginning of the novel?

17. What did the Corporal mean when he said the Hessians were "ducks in a pond"?

18. Why did soldiers want Jonathan to go into the house first? What was Jonathan's reaction?

19. What decision did Jonathan make in the house? What do you think you would have done, and why?

20. What did Jonathan come to understand about his father's fear at the end of the novel?

Vocabulary

regiment (p3)
an army unit, larger than a battalion and smaller than a division, usually commanded by a colonel

tyrannical (p4)
of or like a tyrant; harsh; cruel

mercenary (p4)
a soldier who serves for pay in the army of a foreign government

ally (p4)
a person or country joined with another for a particular purpose

Hessians (p4)
German soldiers hired to fight for the British in the American Revolution

Tories (p4)
Americans who sided with the British

flintlock (p4)
a gunlock in which a piece of flint is struck against steel to light the gunpowder

musket (p4)
an old type of firearm, replaced by the rifle

turncoat (p9)
a person who goes over to the opposing side or party; a traitor

militia (p11)
a body of citizens given military training outside the regular armed forces and called up in emergencies

inadvertently (p19)
unintentionally

ambush (p22)
to attack from a concealed place

quarry (p29)
an excavation from which stone is taken for use in building

monotonous (p35)
boring because of lack of variety or change

fife (p35)
a small flute having a shrill tone, used with drums in military music

daft (p37)
crazy or foolish

bayonet (p41)
a daggerlike weapon that may be attached to the muzzle of a rifle

Grenadier (p43)
a member of a special regiment in the British army

wary (p69)
watchful or suspicious; very careful; cautious

perplex (p71)
to cause to hesitate or doubt; to confuse

plaintive (p73)
expressing sadness; mournful

camaraderie (p79)
the spirit of loyalty and friendship among comrades

flanks (p82)
the side of an animal or person between the ribs and the hip

docile (p85)
easy to teach, manage, or handle; obedient

scrutinize (p89)
to look at closely; to examine very carefully

encroaching (p90)
intruding upon the rights of another's property; trespassing

retched (p98)
vomited

peepers (p102)
an animal that chirps or peeps, such as a chick or a kind of tree frog

mote (p105)
a tiny particle

silhouette (p109)
the outline of a person or object seen against a light or a light background

elusive (p110)
escaping or avoiding capture

johnnycake (p114)
a flat cornmeal cake baked on a griddle

garrison (p122)
the troops stationed in a fort or town

disheveled (p142)
untidy, in reference to hair or clothing

stupefaction (p142)
amazement; astonishment

spasmodically (p144)
like a spasm; sudden, often intense, and irregular

shrouded (p146)
covered; concealed

mirage (p151)
an optical illusion, as of a lake and palm trees in a desert or an upside-down ship at sea, that appears quite close but is actually an image of a distant object reflected by the atmosphere

Small Group Reading

📖 Collier, Christopher, and James Collier. *My Brother Sam Is Dead*. New York: Scholastic, 1974.
The story, which is based partially on fact, is of a Connecticut family divided by loyalties during the Revolutionary War. Grades 6-9.

Author Information

Christopher Collier was born January 29, 1930 in New York City. He teaches American history at the University of Connecticut and is also the historian for the state of Connecticut.

His motivation to write captivating books of history is due to his dislike for the dry textbooks often used to educate young people. His and his brother James's stories, which blend historical facts and fictional characters, portray ordinary people who undertake heroic struggles. Christopher Collier writes, "There is no better way to teach history than to embrace potential learners and fling them into a living past."

James Lincoln Collier was born June 27, 1928 in New York City. Along with spending some time in military service, he has worked as a magazine editor, performed many odd jobs, and played the trombone in a jazz band in New York City. He has written numerous books for children and adults. Several historical fiction novels for children were written with his brother, Christopher Collier.

James Collier was born into a family of writers. He says, "I thus became a writer the way other young people go into the family business. It never occurred to me that I couldn't write; it was what people did, and it has been what I have done since I've been an adult." He credits his upbringing for providing him with the self-discipline required of writing.

Activities

1. On a map of the United States, have students locate the following:

Albany, NY	Lexington, MA	Redding, CT
Boston, MA	Litchfield, CT	Wethersfield, CT
Concord, MA	Long Island, NY	Wilkes Barre, PA
Danbury, CT	New Haven, CT	Windham, CT
Hartford, CT	Norwalk, CT	Yale University, CT
Hudson River, NY	Peekskill, NY	

2. Have students in the group each choose a scene to illustrate and write a description of what took place in the scene. Students can then present them to the rest of the class.

3. Have students write a book talk for *My Brother Sam Is Dead* and present it to the class.

4. Have students write a speech that Tim may have given to General Putnam in an attempt to save Sam's life. Students should attempt to make the speeches as persuasive as possible.

5. Have students write a eulogy for Sam, telling what kind of person he was and what he did for the Patriots.

Discussion Guide

Give the small group the following instruction: As your group reads this book, discuss the following questions.

1. How does Tim feel about his brother Sam?

2. Why did Sam call the British soldiers "Lobsterbacks"?

3. How does Sam and Tim's father feel about the possibility of war?

4. What secret did Sam tell Tim?

5. Why was Tim and Sam's father crying in the taproom?

6. Discuss the Patriots' or Rebels' point of view in the Revolutionary War.

7. Discuss the Loyalists' or Tories' point of view in the Revolutionary War.

8. What position has Tim been put in between Sam and their father?

9. Why did the Rebels come to Redding?

10. What happened that made Tim understand that the war was real?

11. What did having their guns taken mean to the people of Redding?

12. Why did Tim envy Sam?

13. What does Tim's father want him to become, and why?

14. What does Mr. Heron want Tim to do for him? Why do you think Tim's father said no?

15. Why does Tim want to work for Mr. Heron badly enough that he would go behind his father's back?

16. Why wouldn't Betsy tell Tim where Sam was?

17. What made Betsy so insistent that Tim could not deliver the letter for Mr. Heron?

18. Tim said he'd never been on a trip as long as forty miles in his life. Compare this with your own travels.

19. Why were Tim and his father stopped on their way to Verplancks Point?

20. Why do you think Tim is confused about whether he should be a Loyalist or a Rebel?

21. What happened to Tim's father?

22. How did Tim trick the cowboys into letting him go?

23. Why did it concern Tim to take commissary notes as payment at the tavern?

24. Discuss what losing his father meant to Tim. How did his life change?

25. After seeing Sam again, how did Tim's opinion of him change?

26. Why did Sam want Tim to butcher the cattle?

27. How did Sam come to be arrested?

28. Why do you think General Putnam made the decision that he did regarding clemency for Sam?

29. Discuss Tim's feelings upon watching his brother be executed. How did you feel?

Vocabulary

minutemen (p2)
groups of men and young boys who were trained to be soldiers and had to be ready to fight at a moment's notice

Patriot (p2)
a person who loves his or her country and loyally defends and supports it

massacre (p2)
to kill or slaughter in large numbers

garrison (p4)
the troops stationed in a fort or town

peppered (p5)
showered with bullets

prevail (p6)
to gain control; to be victorious

treason (p6)
an act of betrayal or breach of allegiance to one's country

Tories (p6)
Americans who sided with the British

virtue (p6)
moral excellence; right living; morality; goodness

Parliament (p8)
the legislature of Great Britain

sloth (p9)
laziness

swill (p13)
partly liquid garbage

subversion (p21)
an attempt to overthrow completely, as a government

gaudy (p22)
showy or bright in a way that lacks taste

militia (p33)
a body of citizens given military training outside the regular armed forces and called up in emergencies

skirmish (p65)
a brief fight between groups such as troops

surveyor (p65)
a person who measures and maps land

apprentice (p66)
a person who works for another to learn a trade or business

speculating (p66)
investing money where there is a considerable risk of loss but also the possibility of large profits

shilling (p68)
a now-defunct British coin

Loyalists (p71)
people who remained loyal to the British government during the American Revolution

cholera (p72)
an infectious bacterial disease that attacks the intestines, often causing death

consumption (p72)
an old-fashioned word for tuberculosis of the lungs

commissary (p80)
a store that sells food and daily supplies, as at a camp or military post

ambush (p83)
to attack from a concealed place

hardtack (p87)
a hard, unsalted, crackerlike biscuit

recalcitrance (p87)
a stubborn refusal to obey

sledge (p90)
a vehicle on runners, used for carrying people or loads over snow or ice

musket (p93)
an old type of firearm, replaced by the rifle

forage (p95)
food suitable for horses, cattle, and other livestock

sedition (p102)
speech or conduct that stirs up revolt against government

wharves (p104)
structures, usually platforms, built along or out from a shore, alongside which ships or boats may dock to load or unload

skiff (p104)
a light rowboat, sometimes having a small sail and a centerboard

johnnycake (p112)
a flat, cornmeal cake baked on a griddle

depreciation (p129)
a reduction in value

treason (p131)
an act of betrayal, treachery, or breach of allegiance to one's country

porridge (p132)
a soft food made by boiling oatmeal or some other grain in water, milk, or other liquid

vanguard (p136)
the advance troops of an army

fusillade (p141)
a burst of fire, such as from guns or cannons

adjutant (p172)
an officer who helps a commanding officer by assuming such duties as preparing orders, writing letters, and keeping records

unscrupulous (p174)
having no scruples, principles, or conscience; dishonest

mortar (p176)
a mixture of lime or cement with sand and water, used in building to keep bricks together or to plaster walls

mutiny (p180)
a rebellion against authority, as by a group of soldiers or sailors against their commanders

foreboding (p184)
a feeling that something bad is going to happen; premonition

defection (p185)
a deserting of one's country or side, especially to go over to an opposing group

compulsory (p192)
required; enforced

clemency (p194)
mildness in judging; mercy

Small Group Reading

📖 Collier, Christopher, and James Collier. *War Comes to Willy Freeman*. New York: Dell, 1983.
This is the first of the Arabus family saga novels. Thirteen-year-old Willy Freeman witnesses her father's death at the hands of the British and discovers that her mother had been captured and taken to New York. Disguised as a boy, Willy begins her long search in New York and becomes aware that to be black, free, and female exposes her to dangers and decisions she'd never dreamed possible. This book was named a National Council of Social Studies—Children's Book Council Notable Children's Trade Book in the field of Social Studies. Grades 4-7.

Author Information

See page 49.

Activities

1. As we are told by James and Christopher Collier, much of the story of Jack Arabus is true. Try to acquire a copy of *Arabus v. Ivers*, A.D. 1784, from the *Connecticut Reports of Trials* to have students read the official account. A copy of this document can be obtained by calling (806-566-4601) or writing the Law Unit of the Connecticut State Library at 231 Capitol Ave., Hartford, CT 06106.

2. To find out if Jack Arabus was ever able to buy the freedom of Aunt Betsy and Dan, have students read *Jump Ship to Freedom*, by James and Christopher Collier. Another Arabus family story is *Who Is Carrie?*

3. On a map of the United States, have students locate the following:

Baker's Cove, CT	Housatonic River, CT	Norwalk, CT
Brooklyn, NY	Hudson River, NY	Pequonnock River, CT
Danbury, CT	Long Island Sound, NY	Stony Point, NY
Fairfield, CT	Long Point, CT	Stratford, CT
Greenwich, CT	New Haven, CT	Trenton, NJ
Groton, CT	New London, CT	Yorktown, VA

4. Have students learn more about Sam Fraunces by reading *Phoebe the Spy* by Judith Berry Griffin.

5. To share *War Comes to Willy Freeman* with the rest of the class, have each group member tell a part of Willy's story, including summaries of the following:

   • Willy witnessing her father's death

   • Willy's discovery that her mother was captured, and the beginning of her search

   • The time Willy spent at Sam Fraunces's tavern in New York City

   • Willy's trip to see her mother after the war ended

   • Willy's struggle at the end of the novel to see that she and her Uncle Jack would be freed

Discussion

Give the small group the following instruction: As your group reads this book, discuss the following questions.

1. How did Willy's father earn freedom from slavery for himself and his family?

2. Why do you think Willy and her family didn't have a last name before being set free?

3. What is Willy frightened of?

4. When the two soldiers killed their cow, why was Willy surprised that they were black? How did the soldiers react to finding out that Willy and her mother were black?

5. Why do you think the cow meant so much to Willy's mother?

6. Why did some black people believe there was no point in fighting for the Americans?

7. Discuss how you would have felt if you were Willy, having to go with her father to the fort to warn the soldiers that the British were coming.

8. How did Willy end up inside the fort with her father?

9. Why do you think Willy felt she would be treated differently if those in the fort knew that she was a girl?

10. Discuss what Willy saw in the fort when she took the cartridges up to the soldiers. What would you have done in her place?

11. Why did the British soldier let Willy go?

12. Why did British soldiers capture Willy's mother and some other blacks?

13. What made Willy decide to go to her Aunt Betsy in Stratford?

14. Why was Aunt Betsy afraid of Willy staying with them?

15. What do you think Captain Ivers has in mind for Willy?

16. Discuss what Willy meant when she said, "When you was a woman you was half a slave, anyway." How have times changed since the American Revolution?

17. How was the fighting "like children growing up" to Willy?

18. How did Willy manage to escape from the soldiers in the woods?

19. How did Willy end up at Sam Fraunces's Queen's Head Tavern?

20. How did Canvas Town get its name?

21. Why didn't Willy want Horace to know she was a girl?

22. What did the people of New York City do when the war was over and the British soldiers left?

23. Why was going to see her mother such a hard decision for Willy after she had searched for her for so long?

24. Where had Willy's mother been during the war?

25. Imagine that you are Uncle Jack. What would you have done after Willy's mother died?

26. Do you think Mr. Goodrich will help Willy and Uncle Jack?

27. Discuss your feelings when the Judge made his decision about Uncle Jack and Willy.

28. What did Willy mean when she said, "I'd got it figured out that being argumentative was the same as being free"?

Vocabulary

bayonet (p1)
  a daggerlike weapon that may be attached to the muzzle of a rifle

militia (p2)
  a body of citizens given military training outside the regular armed forces and called up in emergencies

pallet (p5)
  a poor bed or mattress, usually made of or filled with straw

lieutenant (p14)
  a military rank in the U.S. Army

musket (p15)
  an old type of firearm, replaced by the rifle

palisade (p24)
  a fence of strong stakes set in the ground as a barrier against attack

massacre (p25)
  to kill or slaughter in large numbers

powder magazine (p25)
  a storage place for holding gunpowder

pike (p29)
  a long pole with a metal spearhead

writhing (p34)
  twisting or distorting the body or part of the body, as with pain

frigate (p39)
a fast, square-rigged sailing warship of medium size, in use in the eighteenth and early nineteenth centuries

wharves (p39)
structures built along or out from a shore, alongside which ships or boats may dock to load or unload

moored (p41)
secured or fastened with cables, ropes, or anchors, such as a ship

mast (p42)
a long pole set upright in a sailing ship to hold up the sails or yards

gunnel (p42)
another spelling for gunwale, the upper edge of the side of a ship or boat

brig (p42)
a square-rigged sailing vessel having two masts

sloop (p43)
a sailing vessel with one mast, a mainsail, and at least one jib (a triangular sail set forward of the foremast)

furlough (p47)
an official leave or absence granted to a member of the armed forces

skirmish (p52)
a brief fight between small groups of troops

tiller (p57)
a bar or handle for turning the rudder in steering a boat

starboard (p58)
the right-hand side of a ship as one faces the front or bow

dory (p58)
a flat-bottomed rowboat having high sides and well adapted to rough weather, used by fishermen

keel (p62)
the main structural timber or steel bar running along the center of a ship's bottom

inlet (p62)
a narrow strip of water leading from a larger body of water into the land

tuppence (p78)
another spelling for twopence, a sum equal to two pennies

Loyalist (p80)
a person who was loyal to the British during the American Revolution

refugees (p81)
people who flee from persecution or danger

populace (p86)
the common people of a community or an area

sconce (p88)
an ornamental wall bracket for holding a candle or other light

cipher (p92)
to work out an arithmetic problem

drover (p94)
a person who drives cattle, sheep, or other animals to market in droves

apothecary shop (p95)
a drugstore or pharmacy

rebel (p108)
a person who refuses to submit to authority and fights against it instead

constable (p152)
a police officer

flogging (p156)
a beating, as with a whip or stick

ague (p159)
a fever, such as malaria, marked by alternating periods of chills, fever, and sweating

habeas corpus (p164)
a legal order demanding that a prisoner be produced in court to determine if it is lawful to hold him or her

manacles (p166)
handcuffs

victualler (p176)
a provider of food

Small Group Reading

📖 Griffin, Judith Berry. *Phoebe the Spy*. New York: Scholastic, 1977.

This book appeared originally as *Phoebe and the General*. Thirteen-year-old Phoebe Fraunces is assigned by her father, the owner of New York City's Queen's Head Tavern, to act as a spy and help uncover a plot to assassinate General Washington. In this story based on a historical incident, she saved him from eating poisoned peas put on his plate by one of his own bodyguards. Grades 2-5.

Author Information

Judith Berry Griffin attended the University of Chicago and Columbia University. Along with her writing career, she has worked as an elementary school teacher in White Plains, New York.

Activities

1. Have students brainstorm how the war may have turned out differently if it were not for Phoebe Fraunces.

2. Have students find out more information about George Washington's life and share it with the class. The following books would be helpful:

    Egger-Bovet, Howard, and Marlene Smith-Baranzini. *Brown Paper School USKids History: Book of the American Revolution.* Boston: Little, Brown, 1994.

    Giblin, James Cross. *George Washington: A Picture Book Biography.* New York: Scholastic, 1992.

    Gross, Ruth Belove. *If You Grew Up with George Washington.* New York: Scholastic, 1993.

3. Have students write a letter from Phoebe to a friend, telling him or her about her adventures as George Washington's housekeeper. They should share these with the rest of the class.

Discussion

Give the small group the following instruction: As your group reads this book, discuss the following questions.

1. Why did Mr. Fraunces feel that General Washington was in great danger?

2. Why did Mr. Fraunces fear for his own safety as well?

3. Why did some people want to see the colonies separated?

4. How would Phoebe working as a housekeeper for General Washington help the cause?

5. What did Phoebe's father mean when he said, " 'Tis a strange freedom we're fighting for, alongside General Washington." Do you agree or disagree? Explain your answer.

6. What was Phoebe's main duty while she worked as General Washington's housekeeper?

7. Why did Phoebe's father say that she should not trust anyone with their plan?

8. Do you have any ideas about who is plotting to kill General Washington and how they might do it?

9. How did Phoebe find out who was out to kill the General?

10. When the war was over, what job did General Washington give to Mr. Fraunces?

11. Imagine that you are asked to do something for your country as dangerous as what Phoebe did. Would you do it? Why or why not?

Vocabulary

scoundrel (p11)
a mean or dishonest person

patriot (p15)
a person who loves his or her country and loyally defends and supports it

spire (p21)
the pointed top, as of a tower or steeple

harbor (p27)
a port where ships can anchor or be protected in a storm

solemn (p34)
    serious

uproar (p44)
    a condition of disturbance or noisy confusion

salt cellar (p39)
    a small container for salt, commonly either an
    open dish or a shaker, for use at the table

Small Group Reading

McGovern, Ann. *The Secret Soldier: The Story of Deborah Sampson*. New York: Four Winds Press, 1975.

This is the absorbing story of Deborah Sampson who, disguised as a man, fought in the Continental Army. Grades 1-5.

Author Information

Ann McGovern was born May 25, 1930 in New York, New York. Her career has included being an associate editor of Arrow Book Club, as well as editor and founder of See Saw Book Club. She has worked as a full-time writer since 1967 and has had numerous books published throughout her career.

McGovern writes, "Looking backward (and forward) at my books, I realize that they reflect my life in three ways: 1. ideas I strongly believe in; 2. desire for knowledge (I never finished college); and 3. exciting personal experiences." She began writing when she was eight years old because she couldn't speak. A severe stutter kept her from expressing herself verbally, so she turned her feelings and thoughts to reading and writing. Many years later, as a divorced mother, she turned to writing as a way to earn additional income, and found fulfillment as well.

Activities

1. On a map of the United States, have students locate the following:

Boston, MA	Philadelphia, PA
Concord, MA	Plympton, MA
Lexington, MA	Providence, RI
Middleborough, MA	Sharon, MS
New York, NY	Yorktown, VA

2. Have students research the following topics and present their findings to the class.

The Boston Tea Party	The Declaration of Independence
Causes of the Revolutionary War	George Washington

3. Have students write a diary entry of Deborah's first day as Robert Shurtliff.

4. Have students share a summary of the book with the class, along with a poster they have created and the research they did.

Discussion

Give the small group the following instruction: As your group reads this book, discuss the following questions.

1. What happened to Deborah's father?

2. Why did Deborah's mother have to give her children away?

3. What did Deborah enjoy doing most of all with her cousin Miss Fuller?

4. How do you think Deborah felt when she had to go and live with Mrs. Thatcher?

5. What did Deborah do for the Thomases when she went to live with them? How was it better than living with Mrs. Thatcher?

6. Because Deborah was not allowed to go to school, how did she continue learning at the Thomases?

7. Compare the America of today with the America of the late 1700s.

8. What did many people in the colonies think was unfair?

9. Discuss the issue of the colonies being ruled by the King of England. Do you think you would have sided with the King or with the colonists who felt that their treatment was unfair? Explain your answer.

10. What was the Boston Tea Party?

11. What caused the first battle of the Revolutionary War? Where did it take place?

12. Who was chosen to be the leader of the American Army?

13. In your own words, describe the Declaration of Independence.

14. What were people of the colonies who still wanted to belong to England called?

15. What did turning eighteen mean to Deborah?

16. How did Deborah end up becoming a school-teacher?

17. What was the difference between a husband's rights and a wife's rights at this time in history?

18. Why did Deborah want to be a soldier?

19. When Deborah dressed as a man for the first time, with whom did she check to make sure no one would know she was really a woman?

20. What name did Deborah use when she became a Continental soldier?

21. What made Deborah realize there was more to war than adventure?

22. Why did Deborah refuse help when she was shot?

23. Why do you think Dr. Binney kept her secret when she was so sick in Philadelphia?

24. How did General Paterson feel when he found out Deborah's secret?

25. What did Deborah do after she was discharged from the army?

26. Why do you think people were so interested in hearing Deborah speak about her life as Robert Shurtliff?

27. Discuss your feelings about what Deborah did to help America free itself from England.

Vocabulary

feeble (p6)
lacking strength; weak

minutemen (p19)
groups of men and young boys who were trained to be soldiers and had to be ready to fight at a moment's notice

Tories (p22)
colonists who were on the British side of the American Revolution

Continental soldiers (p31)
soldiers who would sign up for the army for three years at a time

enlist (p33)
to join a branch of the armed forces voluntarily

discharge (p56)
a certificate of release

Small Group Reading

Reit, Seymour. *Guns for General Washington: A Story of the American Revolution*. San Diego, CA: Harcourt Brace Jovanovich, 1990.
This is a fictionalized account of Henry Knox's true story of how Knox and his men transported guns from Fort Ticonderoga to Washington's camp in the middle of winter. Grades 3-7.

Author Information

Seymour Reit was born and raised in New York City. He attended New York University and began his writing career as an undergraduate student.

Besides being an author, Reit has worked as an animation cartoonist and as an editor. He created the character "Casper the Friendly Ghost" for television.

Activities

1. On a map of the United States, have students locate the following:

    Adirondack Mountains, NY   Kinderhook, NY
    Albany, NY   Lake Champlain, NY
    Berkshire Mountains, MA   Lake George, NY
    Boston, MA   Lansing's Ferry, NY
    Cambridge, MA   Lexington, MA
    Charlestown, MA   Mohawk River, NY
    Chelsea, MA   Mystick River, MA
    Claverack, MA   Philadelphia, PA
    Concord, MA   Prospect Hill, MA
    Connecticut River, VT   Roxbury, MA
    Dowe's Wharf, MA   Sabbath Day Point, MA
    Fort Ticonderoga, NY   Saratoga, NY
    Framingham, MA   Springfield, MA
    Glens Falls, NY   Westfield, MA
    Great Barrington, MA   Worcester, MA
    Hudson Valley, NY

2. Have students do further research on the following:

    John Adams   John Hancock
    Samuel Adams   HMS Somerset
    Ethan Allen   Major General William Howe
    Benedict Arnold   William Knox
    General Burgoyne   General Philip Schuyer

    Students can use the information they find in creating small posters, which they can hang in the classroom after sharing them aloud with the rest of the class.

3. Have students illustrate the liberation of Boston from the Royal Navy. They should include General Howe's warships in the harbor and General Washington's rebel cannons at Dorchester Heights.

4. Have students write a letter to Lucy from Henry Knox describing the victory at Boston.

Discussion

Give the small group the following instruction: As your group reads this book, discuss the following questions.

1. What was William Knox hoping for?

2. What were General William Howe's feelings about the patriots?

3. When General Washington was asked to lead the Continental Army, in what shape did he find it?

4. Why had men joined the Continental Army's cause?

5. What did General Washington do to organize his troops?

6. How did General Washington's troops' weapons compare with those of the troops of General Howe?

7. Why did Paul Revere's father leave Isaac Clemens in charge of his silversmith shop?

8. Do you agree or disagree with Paul Revere Junior's feeling that "being lonely was the worst of all feelings"? Explain your answer.

9. Discuss the change in Boston since it had been taken over by the British.

10. Why had Paul Revere Junior stayed behind in Boston alone?

11. Describe Henry Knox's plan for getting artillery for the rebels.

12. What dangers might Henry and William Knox meet on their journey to and from Fort Ticonderoga?

13. Why was Fort Ticonderoga built where it was by the French?

14. What did the Knox brothers find when they reached Fort Ticonderoga?

15. What news and rumors did Paul Revere Junior hear in Boston?

16. Why were Will and Henry Knox hoping for snow on their journey overland?

17. Discuss how the snow that they had wished for turned into their enemy.

18. How did privateers help the Continental Army?

19. What was the good news that Major General William Howe received from London?

20. How did Henry Knox and his men strengthen the ice on the Mohawk River?

21. Why did only a fraction of men re-enlist in the Continental Army when their tour of duty was over?

22. How did Bloody Pond get its name?

23. What new problem did Henry Knox face after crossing the Hudson River?

24. Why did Will Knox feel that the mountains were going to be a worse enemy than the British? What problems did they encounter?

25. What plans did General Washington make once he had the artillery that he so desperately needed?

26. Do you think General Washington's plan will work? Explain your answer.

27. What was General Washington's goal for the cannon firing at Dorchester Heights?

28. Although there is no written record, what do historians believe about a bargain between General Howe and General Washington?

29. Describe the celebration following the freeing of Boston.

30. What did the triumph in Boston mean to the colonists?

Vocabulary

palisade (p1)
a fence or strong stakes set in the ground as a barrier against attack

rebel (p1)
a person who refuses to submit to authority and fights against it instead

sentinel (p1)
a watcher or guard; a sentry

redcoat (p1)
a British soldier during the American Revolution

blockade (p2)
the shutting off of a place, such as a coast city, by enemy ships or troops

regiment (p2)
an army unit, larger than a battalion and smaller than a division, usually commanded by a colonel

frontiersmen (p2)
people who live on the frontier, next to the wilderness

militia (p2)
a body of citizens given military training outside the regular armed forces and called up in emergencies

rampart (p2)
a bank of earth, often with a parapet on top, surrounding a fort as a defense

frigate (p2)
a fast, square-rigged sailing warship of medium size, in use in the eighteenth and early nineteenth centuries

patriot (p3)
a person who loves his or her country and loyally defends and supports it

port side (p4)
the left-hand side of a ship or boat, as one faces the front or bow

sloop (p4)
a sailing vessel with one mast, a mainsail, and at least one jib (a triangular sail set forward of the foremast)

brig (p4)
a square-rigged sailing vessel having two masts

starboard (p5)
the right-hand side of a ship, as one faces the front or bow

schooner (p5)
a ship having two or more masts rigged with fore-and-aft sails

batteries (p5)
a group of big guns used together in battle

musket (p5)
an old type of firearm, replaced by the rifle

skirmish (p5)
a brief fight between small groups of troops

scurvy (p6)
a disease caused by lack of vitamin C in the diet, marked by swollen and bleeding gums and great physical weakness

cask (p6)
a barrel-shaped wooden container

hasty pudding (p8)
porridge made of cornmeal

staunch (p9)
firm and dependable; loyal

tyranny (p10)
a government in which a single ruler has absolute power

arsenal (p10)
a building for making or keeping such supplies as guns and ammunition

liberate (p11)
to set free; to release

smallpox (p12)
a highly contagious viral disease causing a high fever and skin eruptions that usually leave permanent scars

traitor (p14)
a person who betrays friends, a cause, or an obligation, especially a person who betrays a country

Tory (p14)
a colonist who sided with the British

besiege (p16)
to seek to capture by surrounding and wearing down resistance

Whigs (p21)
a political party that wanted independence for the colonies

infantry (p22)
soldiers, or a branch of the army, trained and equipped to fight on foot

garrison (p26)
the troops stationed in a fort or town

mortar (p28)
a short cannon, loaded through the muzzle and fired at a high angle

scow (p28)
a flat-bottomed barge

bateaux (p28)
a wide-beamed shallow vessel

piragua (p28)
a small, fast sailboat

howitzer (p28)
a short cannon that fires off shells at a high angle

flotilla (p31)
a fleet of boats or small ships

platoon (p35)
a subdivision of a company, troop, or other military unit, commanded by a lieutenant

berths (p39)
spaces for sleeping on a ship, train, or airplane

privateer (p40)
an armed ship that is privately owned but is given permission by a government to attack enemy ships in a war

flagon (p41)
a container with a handle and spout and often a lid on hinges, used for serving liquids

juggernaut (p75)
a slow and irresistible force or object that destroys everything in its path

chasm (p77)
a deep crack or gorge in the surface of the earth

foray (p86)
a raid or expedition, as in a war

adjutant (p87)
    an officer who helps a commanding officer by assuming such duties as preparing orders, writing letters, and keeping records

fascines (p88)
    huge bundles of branches tied tightly together

salvo (p91)
    the firing of a number of guns at the same time to hit a target or give a salute

audacious (p92)
    showing no fear; daring; bold

Small Group Reading

📖 Woodruff, Elvira. *George Washington's Socks*. New York: Scholastic, 1991.

Matt, his sister Katie, and Matt's friends camp out in Tony's backyard. They have formed an Adventure Club. At each meeting they read an adventure from *Great Adventures in History*, a book title created by Woodruff for this story. The night of their campout finds them in colonial America with General George Washington through the help of a time-traveling boat. Their adventure has become real! Grades 4-8.

Author Information

Elvira Woodruff was born June 19, 1951 in Somerville, New Jersey.

Along with being a writer, Woodruff has worked as a janitor, gardener, baker, window decorator, ice-cream truck driver, storyteller, and library aide.

Of her career as a writer she says, "Becoming a writer has been one of the most pleasant surprises I've had in my life. I have always enjoyed reading and especially writing, though I never seriously considered it as a profession until I was well into my thirties."

Activities

1. Have students illustrate George Washington and his troops crossing the Delaware River.

2. Have students write an essay telling what time period in history they would want to travel to if they had the opportunity and why.

3. Start an Adventure Club in you classroom or school building. The club could meet once a month or more often to read more American history adventures.

4. On a map of the United States, have students locate the following:
    Delaware River   Marblehead, MA
    Fort Ticonderoga, NY   Trenton, NJ
    Haverston, MA

5. Have students research the following subjects:
    Boy's Roles in the War   Corporal Adam Hibbs
    Colonel John Glover   Fort Ticonderoga
    Colonel Henry Knox   George Washington

6. Have students who enjoyed reading this novel read *Travelers Through Time #2: Back to Paul Revere* by Beatrice Gormley, or *The Riddle of Penncroft Farm* by Dorothea Jensen.

7. Have students choose their favorite scene from the book and write a short script for it that they can perform for the rest of the class.

Discussion

Give the small group the following instruction: As your group reads this book, discuss the following questions.

1. What does Matthew's club do?

2. Why did Matt invite his sister Katie along on the club's campout?

3. Describe the legend of Lake Levart.

4. What do you think happened to Matt, Katie, and Matt's friends?

5. How would you feel if you were part of the Adventure Club and suddenly found yourself face to face with General George Washington?

6. Why was the American Army called "Washington's ragtag band of rebels"?

7. How did Matt end up a rebel soldier with a bayonet in his hands?

8. What did Matt mean when he said his life in the twentieth century was luxurious?

9. Why did Israel Gates think that Matt had called him an old goat?

10. How did Israel Gates end up being a soldier?

11. Why was Matt thankful that he had done his homework?

12. What does a drummer do for his regiment?

13. How do you think Matt felt when he found out about Israel?

14. Why was Temperance Hornbee so afraid of having Matt in the Hornbee home?

15. What did Mr. and Mrs. Hornbee think of Matt when he told them the truth about where he was from?

16. What did Matt mean when he realized that the people he had met weren't much different from the people of his own time?

17. What did Hooter and Tony find out about Adam Hibbs?

18. How do you think the boys will rescue Katie and Q from the Hessians?

19. What did the Indian boy think of Tony's pocket video game?

20. Why were the Hessians in America fighting for King George?

21. What did the boys and Katie learn about Gustav that helped them to better understand soldiers on both sides of the war?

22. Why did the rebels think the children were Tory spies?

23. How were the children saved by General Washington?

24. Why did Matt think that Israel and Gustav might have been friends if it weren't for the war?

25. How did Katie help them to return home?

26. What did they discover that Emit Levart meant?

27. Do you think that the Adventure Club will take the old rowboat out again?

28. If you had the old rowboat, where would you want to go and why?

29. Why do you think the author chose *George Washington's Socks* for the title of the book?

Vocabulary

allegiance (p7)
    loyalty to a government or ruler

bayonet (p7)
    a daggerlike weapon that may be attached to the muzzle of a rifle

rebel (p13)
    a person who refuses to submit to authority and fights against it instead

comrade (p23)
    a close companion or friend

iridescent (p27)
    showing the colors of the rainbow in changing patterns

Tory (p38)
    a colonist who sided with the British

seafaring (p39)
    traveling on the sea

enlisted men (p39)
    men who joined a branch of the armed forces voluntarily

Hessians (p41)
German soldiers hired to fight for the British during the American Revolution

mercenary (p41)
a soldier who serves for pay in the army of a foreign government

musket (p41)
an old type of firearm, replaced by the rifle

tarry (p47)
to stay for a while; to linger

regiment (p48)
an army unit, larger than a battalion and smaller than a division, usually commanded by a colonel

haggard (p53)
looking ill, starved, exhausted, or in pain

tinker (p61)
a person who travels about and repairs pots, pans, and other utensils

vexed (p61)
irritated or annoyed

scow (p64)
a large boat having a flat bottom and square ends, usually towed, used to carry such things as coal, oil, gravel, or garbage

Patriot (p65)
a person who loves his or her country and loyally defends and supports it

howitzer (p65)
a short cannon that fires off shells at a high angle

mortar (p65)
a short cannon, loaded through the muzzle and fired at a high angle

expedite (p66)
to facilitate a process; to speed up

tyrannical (p68)
of or like a tyrant; harsh; cruel

beseeches (p71)
asks in a very serious way; begs

militia (p86)
a body of citizens given military training outside the regular armed forces and called up in emergencies

forsooth (p89)
in truth or in fact

daft (p93)
crazy or foolish

terrain (p118)
an area of land

gait (p118)
any of the ways by which a horse moves, such as a trot or gallop

grenadier (p119)
a member of a special regiment in the British Army

turncoat (p138)
a person who goes over to the opposing side or party; a traitor

Bibliography

Individual Titles

Adler, David. *A Picture Book of Paul Revere.* New York: Holiday House, 1995.
This is an easy-to-read biography of Paul Revere. Grades 3 and up.

———. *Remember Betsy Floss: And Other Colonial American Riddles.* New York: Holiday House, 1987.
There are sixty riddles included in this book, with illustrations. Grades 2-6.

Avi. *Night Journeys.* New York: Pantheon Books, 1979.
Two young indentured servants in the late 1700s escape and receive help from an unexpected source. Grades 5-8.

Bangs, Edward. *Steven Kellogg's Yankee Doodle.* New York: Parents Magazine Press, 1976.
A young Yankee Doodle accompanied by his small dog pushes his way through the revolutionary scene, encountering British and American forces. Grades PreK-3.

Banim, Lisa. *Drums at Saratoga.* New York: Silver Moon Press, 1993.
Nathaniel, who has run away from his home in Canada to follow the British army down the Hudson Valley, comes to learn what the war is truly about. Grades 4-8.

Benchley, Nathaniel. *George the Drummer Boy.* New York: HarperCollins, 1977.
Through the eyes of George, a British drummer boy, readers see the incidents at Lexington and Concord, Massachusetts that started the American Revolution. Grades 3-6.

———. *Sam the Minute Man.* New York: HarperCollins, 1969.

This is the story of the first battle of the American Revolution as seen through the eyes of a very young minuteman. Grades 3-6.

Berleth, Richard. *Samuel's Choice.* New York: Scholastic, 1990.

Samuel is a fourteen-year-old black slave in Brooklyn who plays a heroic role in the Battle of Long Island during the American Revolution. Grades 4-6.

Brady, Esther Wood. *Toliver's Secret.* New York: Crown, 1976.

During the Revolutionary War, a ten-year-old girl disguised as a boy crosses enemy lines to deliver a loaf of bread containing a message for the Patriots. Grades 3-7.

Brenner, Barbara. *If You Were There in 1776.* New York: Bradbury Press, 1994.

Brenner demonstrates how the concepts and principles expressed in the Declaration of Independence were drawn from the experiences of living in America in the late eighteenth century. Grades 4-8.

Brown, Drollene P. *Sybil Rides for Independence.* Niles, IL: Whitman, 1985.

A Revolutionary War story of sixteen-year-old Sybil Ludinton's ride to alert her father's soldiers of a British attack. Grades 2-5.

Chew, Ruth. *Trapped in Time.* New York: Scholastic, 1986.

When Audrey and Nathan find a strange old watch, they are suddenly transported back to New York in the time of the Revolutionary War. Grades 5 and up.

Collier, Christopher, and James Collier. *The Bloody Country.* New York: Four Winds Press, 1985.

This is a Revolutionary War–era novel about two close friends, one a landowner's son and the other a slave, whose sympathies differ on the issues of war and slavery. Grades 7-9.

———. *Jump Ship to Freedom.* New York: Dell, 1981.

Daniel's late father, having served under Washington, left continental notes to buy his family's freedom. Instead the slaves' owner confiscates the notes and takes Daniel aboard his ship to sell him in the West Indies. Grades 6-9.

———. *Who Is Carrie?* New York: Delacorte Press, 1984.

This is the third book in the Arabus Family Saga. While the newly formed United States struggles to form a new government that gives peace and freedom to all, young Carrie, the spunky black slave from Fraunces Tavern, seeks to learn her true identity. Grades 4-8.

———. *The Winter Hero.* New York: Scholastic, 1978.

This is a fictionalized account of Shay's Rebellion, set in Massachusetts in 1787. Grades 6-9.

Davis, Burke. *Black Heroes of the American Revolution.* New York: Harcourt Brace Jovanovich, 1976.

This book contains selections profiling some African-American Revolutionary heroes. Includes several photographs. Grades 3 and up.

DeFord, Deborah, and Harry S. Stout. *An Enemy Among Them.* Boston: Houghton Mifflin, 1987.

This is a story of friendship between two young people on opposite sides of the Revolutionary War. Margaret is a farm girl from Pennsylvania, and Christian is a soldier hired by the British. They must examine their long-standing values, beliefs, and loyalties as the war escalates, testing their resolve. Grades 6 and up.

Edwards, Sally. *George Midgett's War.* New York: Charles Scribner's Sons, 1985.

The Ocracoke islanders, who live off the coast of North Carolina, remain aloof from the Revolution until British raiders steal their pigs and murder a deaf woman. This book shows that personal, as well as political, choices must sometimes be made in wartime. Grades 5-7.

Egger-Bovet, Howard, and Marlene Smith-Baranzini. *Brown Paper School USKids History: Book of the American Revolution.* Boston: Little, Brown, 1994.

This book highlights the events leading up to the Revolutionary War, life in the colonies during the war, and important figures of the time. It includes ideas for related activities. Grades 4 and up.

Fast, Howard. *April Morning.* New York: Bantam Books, 1961.

April Morning explores the nature of courage, grief, and fear of death as experienced by a fifteen-year-old boy who faced the British at Lexington, saw his father shot, fled in panic, and then sniped at the Redcoats as they marched back to Boston. Grades 6-9.

Forbes, Esther. *Johnny Tremain.* New York: Dell, 1943.

This is the story of a young silversmith's apprentice, who plays an important part in the American Revolution. Grades 6-9.

Fritz, Jean. *And Then What Happened, Paul Revere?* New York: Scholastic, 1988.

This book describes Paul's active participation in the Sons of Liberty, as well as the nonpolitical activities that occupied his time. The ride to Lexington is described thoroughly with hilarious and harrowing details. Grades 3-6.

——. *Can't You Make Them Behave, King George?* New York: Coward, McCann & Geoghegan, 1977.

This story describes George's life, from his bashful childhood until the signing of the peace proclamation with the colonies. Grades 3-6.

——. *Early Thunder.* New York: Coward-McCann, 1967.

In this story, set in Salem, Massachusetts in 1774, fourteen-year-old Daniel West reexamines his loyalties and changes from Tory to Whig. Grades 6-9.

——. *George Washington's Breakfast.* New York: Trumpet Club, 1989. Reprint.

George W. Allen knows all there is to know about our first president—except what he had for breakfast. Grades 3-5.

——. *Shh! We're Writing the Constitution.* New York: G. P. Putnam's Sons, 1987.

This story about the writing of the Constitution provides young readers with interesting and relevant facts about this critical period in American history. Grades 4-7.

——. *Where Was Patrick Henry on the 29th of May?* New York: Coward, McCann & Geoghegan, 1975.

Patrick's life, from birth on May 29 to his death, is covered in this book. Grades 3-5.

——. *Why Don't You Get a Horse, Sam Adams?* New York: Coward, McCann & Geoghegan, 1974.

Sam would not ride a horse because he wanted to be able to talk to people easily about the wrongs done by the British government. Grades 2-6.

——. *Will You Sign Here, John Hancock?* New York: Coward, McCann & Geoghegan, 1976.

John was one of the richest men in New England but would not pay his taxes to England. This story describes his extravagant lifestyle and the role, as a first signer of the Declaration of Independence, that he played in the founding of our nation. Grades 2-6.

Gauch, Patricia Lee. *This Time Tempe Wick?* New York: Coward, McCann & Geoghegan, 1974.

This is a fictionalized account of a true story of the Jockey Hollow, New Jersey, heroine who hid her horse in her bedroom to save it from mutinous Pennsylvania soldiers in the winter of 1781. Grades 2-3.

Giblin, James Cross. *George Washington: A Picture Book Biography.* New York: Scholastic, 1992.

Giblin examines the family life and career of the first American president. He also discusses myths and legends, monuments to Washington, and Mount Vernon. This book is beautifully illustrated by Michael Dooling. Grades 2-5.

——. *Thomas Jefferson: A Picture Book Biography.* New York: Scholastic, 1994.

Giblin discusses the family life and contributions to American democracy of Thomas Jefferson. Michael Dooling's illustrations are wonderful. Grades 2-5.

Gormley, Beatrice. *Travelers Through Time #2: Back to Paul Revere.* New York: Scholastic, 1994.

Matt and Emily's grandfather has invented a way to travel back in time. Matt, Emily, and Matt's best friend, Jonathan, decide to take a trip to the night that the American Revolution began. They arrive just in time to see Paul Revere ride by. Grades 3-6.

Gross, Ruth Belove. *If You Grew Up with George Washington.* New York: Scholastic, 1993.

In a question-and-answer format, Washington's daily life and his times are briefly told. Grades 4-7.

Jensen, Dorothea. *The Riddle of Penncroft Farm.* San Diego, CA: Harcourt Brace Jovanovich, 1989.

A young ghost from George Washington's day comes forward in time to help Lars solve a current-day mystery and gives him a better understanding of the American Revolution. Grades 5-7.

Johnson, Neil. *The Battle of Lexington and Concord.* New York: Four Winds Press, 1992.

The author re-creates "the shot heard 'round the world" and the rest of the Revolutionary War's opening engagement. This book includes color photos of modern reenactments. Grades 4 and up.

Keller, Charles, and Richard Baker, compilers. *The Star-Spangled Banana and Other Revolutionary Riddles.* Englewood Cliffs, NJ: Prentice-Hall, 1974.

This hilarious book of riddles will truly help to lighten up your discussions about the Revolutionary War. Grades 2-6.

Lawson, Robert. *Ben and Me.* Boston: Little, Brown, 1939.

Amos, a mouse, immodestly reveals that he, Ben Franklin's closest friend and adviser, was largely responsible for the great man's inventions, discoveries, and successes. Grades 3-7.

Levine, Ellen. *Secret Missions.* New York: Scholastic, 1988.

This is a true story of a Quaker housewife, Lydia Darragh, who spies on the British during the Revolutionary War and hides messages in the buttons of her son's coat. Fourteen-year-old John takes the messages to Washington's camp, where his older brother Charles reads them. Grades 3-7.

Levy, Elizabeth. *If You Were There When They Signed the Constitution.* New York: Scholastic, 1987.

Questions are posed and answered in simple terms about the Constitution. Important figures, arguments among the colonies, and delegation of power are some of the topics addressed. Grades 3-5.

Loeper, John, J. *Going to School in 1776*. New York: Atheneum, 1973.

This book tells what it was like to be a child in the early days of our country. The events are based on actual historical records. Grades 4 and up.

Longfellow, Henry Wadsworth. *Paul Revere's Ride*. New York: Greenwillow Books, 1985.

This is a well-known account of Paul Revere's famous ride in picture-book format. Grades 4-6.

Marko, Katherine McGlade. *Away to Fundy Bay*. New York: Walker, 1985.

Set in Nova Scotia, this story deals with spies, counterspies, and press gangs as experienced by a young boy during the time of the American Revolution. Grades 5-8.

Marrin, Albert. *The War for Independence*. New York: Atheneum, 1988.

This presentation of the Revolution dramatizes monumental events as well as the struggles of individuals. Grades 5 and up.

Meltzer, Milton. *The American Revolutionaries: A History in Their Own Words, 1750-1800*. New York: Thomas Y. Crowell, 1987.

Letters, diaries, memoirs, interviews, ballads, newspaper articles, and speeches depict life and events in the American colonies in the second half of the eighteenth century, with an emphasis on the years of the Revolutionary War. Grades 5 and up.

Monjo, F. N. *King George's Head Was Made of Lead*. New York: Coward, McCann & Geoghegan, 1974.

A statue of King George III tells the story of the events leading up to the Revolutionary War. Grades 3 and up.

O'Dell, Scott. *Sarah Bishop*. Boston: Houghton Mifflin, 1980.

Sarah, orphaned by the war, becomes a fugitive from the British army and turns a cave into her home. She lives in constant fear of starvation, wild animals, and other people until she is befriended by a young Quaker. Grades 7 and up.

Rappaport, Doreen. *The Boston Coffee Party*. New York: HarperCollins, 1988.

A small segment of the Revolutionary War is used as the basis for a simply written piece of fiction for beginning readers. Grades 1-3.

Rinaldi, Ann. *The Fifth of March: A Story of the Boston Massacre*. San Diego, CA: Harcourt Brace, 1993.

Fourteen-year-old Rachel Marsh, an indentured servant in the Boston household of John and Abigail Adams, is caught up in the colonists' unrest that eventually escalates into the massacre of March 5, 1770. Grades 6-9.

Roop, Peter, and Connie Roop. *Buttons for General Washington*. Minneapolis, MN: Carolrhoda Books, 1986.

This is a fictional account of the mission of a fourteen-year-old spy who during the Revolutionary War sends messages to George Washington's camp in the buttons of his coat. Grades K-4.

Smith-Baranzini, Marlene, and Howard Egger-Bovet. *Brown Paper School USKids History: Book of the New American Nation*. Boston: Little, Brown, 1995.

This book explores how the people in the thirteen colonies came together to form a new country called the United States of America. Grades 4-8.

Spier, Peter. *We the People: The Story of the U.S. Constitution*. New York: Doubleday, 1987.

This is an excellent introduction to a study of the Constitution. Spier divides the Preamble into nine important parts and offers an abundance of illustrations to describe its meaning. Grades K-3.

Stein, Conrad R. *Cornerstones of Freedom: The Story of Valley Forge*. Chicago: Childrens Press, 1985.

This is a factual account of Washington and his troops at Valley Forge. The severity of winter is well depicted. Grades 3-6.

Theme Resources

Commercial Resources

Brand, Oscar. *Songs of '76: A Folksinger's History of the Revolution*. New York: Evans, 1972.

This book contains songs and music from 1775 to 1783. Grades 4-8.

Brophy, Susan. *Novel Ties: The Fighting Ground*. New Hyde Park, NY: Learning Links, 1991.

This resource contains pre-reading and post-reading comprehension questions, and writing activities to use with students in grades 5 and up in a chapter-by-chapter format for *The Fighting Ground*.

Cobblestone: The History Magazine for Young People. Peterborough, NH: Cobblestone.

The September 1983 issue contains patriotic tales of the American Revolution for grades 4 and up.

The September 1989 issue for grades 4 and up focuses on Thomas Jefferson.

The September 1991 issue's focus for grades 4 and up is "Our Bill of Rights." Articles include "The Road to Rights" and "Mr. Madison Keeps His Promise."

Dobrow, Vicki. *Novel Ties: Johnny Tremain.* New Hyde Park, NY: Learning Links, 1995.

This resource contains pre-reading and post-reading comprehension questions, and writing activities to use with students in grades 6-9 in a chapter-by-chapter format for *Johnny Tremain.*

Friedland, Joyce, and Rikki Kessler. *Historical Ties: Colonial America and the Revolution.* New Hyde Park, NY: Learning Links, 1993.

Study guides, maps, questions, and resources to use with students in grades 6 and up provide instructional aids for *My Brother Sam Is Dead, April Morning, Johnny Tremain,* and *The Witch of Blackbird Pond.*

Haack, John Lockett. *Literature Unit: Johnny Tremain.* Huntington Beach, CA: Teacher Created Materials, 1994.

This book includes sample plans, author information, vocabulary ideas, and cross-curricular activities to use with students in grades 6-9.

Johnson, David, compiler. *Jackdaw: The American Revolution.* Amawalk, NY: Jackdaw Publications, 1995.

This is a portfolio of primary source material including eighteen reproductions of historical documents. Among them are a letter from a colonist to the East India Company in London about the Boston Tea Party, a copy of the original Declaration of Independence with notes and amendments, and a map of the battlefields of the American Revolution. Comprehensive notes on the documents and a reading list and critical-thinking questions are also included. This resource can be used with students in grades 5 and up.

Kamerman, Sylvia E., ed. *Patriotic & Historical Plays for Young People.* Boston: Plays, 1987.

This resource contains one-act plays and programs about heroic figures of Revolutionary times for use with students in grades 6 and up.

Kids Discover: Colonial America. New York: Kids Discover.

The November 1994 issue focuses on the thirteen English colonies along the Atlantic coast of North America. It spans 168 years, beginning in 1607. Colonists eventually began to resent the control of a government that was thousands of miles away and interested mainly in economic benefit. Conflict finally erupted into the Revolutionary War in 1775. Grades 4 and up.

Laughlin, Mildred Knight, Peggy Tubbs Black, and Margery Kirby Loberg. *Social Studies Readers Theatre for Children.* Englewood, CO: Teacher Ideas Press, 1991.

This book provides teachers of grades 3-8 with many scripting suggestions for this time period.

Murphy, Michael. *Novel Ties: My Brother Sam Is Dead.* New Hyde Park, NY: Learning Links, 1991.

This resource contains pre-reading and post-reading comprehension questions, and writing activities to use with students in grades 6 and up in a chapter-by-chapter format for *My Brother Sam Is Dead.*

Pofahl, Jane. *United States History: The American Revolution.* Grand Rapids, MI: T. S. Dennison, 1994.

This resource includes cross-curricular activities and reproducible activity pages on the American Revolution that can be used with students in grades 3-6.

Rabson, Carolyn. *Songbook of the American Revolution.* Peaks Island, ME: Neo Press, 1974.

This book contains words and music of ballads, national songs, and hymns from the Revolutionary War, which can be used with students in grades 5 and up.

Reeves, Barbara. *Novel Ties: April Morning.* New Hyde Park, NY: Learning Links, 1992.

This resource contains pre-reading and post-reading comprehension questions, and writing activities to use with students in grades 6 and up in a chapter-by-chapter format for *April Morning.*

Thematic Unit: The Revolutionary War. Huntington Beach, CA: Teacher Created Materials, 1991.

This resource includes many Revolutionary War–related activities to use with students in grades 5 and up in all curricular areas.

Sterling, Mary Ellen. *Thematic Unit: U.S. Constitution.* Huntington Beach, CA: Teacher Created Materials, 1993.

This book includes a variety of theme-based activities about the U. S. Constitution to use with students in grades 5 and up.

Videos

American Independence. Bala Cynwyd, PA: Schlessinger Video, 1996. (25 minutes)

Students will learn about history through graphics and animation, live-action portrayals of historic figures, and stories told from a child's point of view. Topics covered are the Boston Tea Party, the Declaration of Independence, the life of Thomas Jefferson, the Liberty Bell, and Independence Hall.

Great Events and People in New York State History: New York State in the Revolution. Burlington, VT: Young People's Historical Society, 1987. (10 minutes)

This video was originally a filmstrip produced in 1984. It was transferred to video in 1987. *Great Events* illustrates the pre-Revolutionary war years, major events of the American Revolutionary War, and post-Revolutionary war years regarding New York state. People highlighted include Alexander Hamilton, George Washington, John Jay, Israel Bessel, Sir William Howe, General Barry St. Leger, Major General John Burgoyne, General Horatio Gates, Tadesuz Kosciuszka, and General Cornwallis.

Johnny Tremain and the Sons of Liberty. Burbank, CA: Walt Disney Home Video, 1957. (80 minutes)
This video is based on the book *Johnny Tremain* by Esther Forbes.

People of the American Revolution. National Geographic Society, 1986. (51 minutes) Three filmstrips/three cassettes.
Features "Signers of the Declaration," "Soldiers of the Revolution," and "Women of the Revolutionary War Era." This set discusses the major events that led to the American Revolution, the major battles and happenings of the war, and the men and women who fought to attain independence from England.

1776. Burbank, CA: Columbia Pictures, 1991. (148 minutes)
This is a musical celebration of the founding of the United States based on the award-winning Broadway production.

United States History Video Collection: The American Revolution. Bala Cynwyd, PA: Schlessinger Video Productions, 1996. (35 minutes)
Causes of the American Revolution, England's imperial policies, Patriots and Loyalists, the Declaration of Independence, the War for Independence, and the Treaty of Paris are presented.

End-of-Unit Celebration

Recipes

Create the following edible treats to celebrate the completion of this unit.

Cornmeal Spoon Bread

INGREDIENTS

1¾ cups milk	3 tablespoons butter
¼ teaspoon salt	2 eggs
⅔ cup cornmeal	

PROCEDURE

1. Boil milk in a medium-sized saucepan.
2. Add salt.
3. Stir in cornmeal and continue to stir until mixture thickens.
4. Add butter and stir.
5. Remove mixture from heat.
6. Beat eggs well and then stir into cornmeal mixture.
7. Butter a 9-inch square baking pan.
8. Pour mixture into the pan.
9. Bake at 375 degrees for 1 hour.

Makes 9 1-inch square pieces.

Source: Barchers, Suzanne I., and Patricia C. Marden. *Cooking Up U.S. History: Recipes and Research to Share with Children.* Englewood, CO: Teacher Ideas Press, 1991.

Virginia Pound Cake

INGREDIENTS

2 cups butter

2 cups sugar

9 eggs

1½ teaspoons vanilla

½ teaspoon nutmeg

2 tablespoons orange juice

4 cups flour

PROCEDURE

1. Cream butter.

2. Using an electric mixer, beat in sugar until smooth and creamy (or beat by hand for 5 minutes).

3. Beat eggs in a separate bowl until thick and light yellow.

4. Add eggs to butter mixture and mix well (or beat by hand for 5 minutes).

5. Beat in vanilla, nutmeg, and orange juice.

6. While mixer is running, beat in flour, a small amount at a time (or beat well by hand).

7. Grease 2 9-inch loaf pans.

8. Pour half of the mixture into each pan.

9. Bake at 325 degrees for about 1 hour or until a toothpick inserted into the center comes out clean.

Serves 15 to 20.

Source: Barchers, Suzanne I., and Patricia C. Marden. *Cooking Up U.S. History: Recipes and Research to Share with Children.* Englewood, CO: Teacher Ideas Press, 1991.

Other Activities

1. Following the completion of *The Fighting Ground* and further discussion about Loyalists and Patriots and their roles in the Revolutionary War, hold a classroom debate. Divide the students into two groups: One group would be Loyalists defending their position of loyalty to the King of England. The other group would be Patriots defending their desire to be free from England.

2. Have students research the causes of the American Revolutionary War and list them on a poster to be hung in the classroom.

3. Have your school's music teacher teach "Yankee Doodle" and other songs of the time period to your class. These could then be performed for another class or the whole school.

American Revolution Research Project

Assign a topic to each student or small groups of two or three in the class. Their responsibility is to research that topic and write a summary of important information. These summaries could then be shared orally and hung around the classroom or compiled into a booklet.

"No taxation without representation"	The Minutemen
Boston Massacre of 1770	George Washington
Committees of Correspondence	The Battles of Lexington and Concord
Boston Tea Party	The Declaration of Independence

The Battle of Saratoga

Francis Marion—"Swamp Fox"

General Nathanael Greene

Lord Cornwallis

British Surrender at Yorktown

Peace Treaty of Paris of 1783

The Constitution of the United States

Mary Hays
   (otherwise known as Molly Pitcher)

Deborah Sampson

Battle of Bunker Hill

Benedict Arnold

Battle of Fort Ticonderoga

Chapter 4

Slavery and the Civil War

Introduction

Included in this chapter on the Civil War are a multitude of trade book recommendations and teacher resources. This is caused by the volume of fiction and nonfiction trade books available on this period in U.S. history. These trade books are of a variety of genre: fiction, nonfiction, biography, fantasy, and poetry. Although it is unlikely you will have the funds needed to purchase all of the materials listed here, they are included so that you can choose those that are the most appropriate for use with your students.

Every attempt has been made to include trade books that focus on all aspects of the war, including the roles of women, black soldiers, and children.

Begin this unit by introducing the topics of slavery and the Civil War. Read aloud the poem "A Visitor" by Sarah Smith Caldwell (see p. 72). Sarah was my great-great-great-aunt and an abolitionist in New York State. She wrote this poem in 1841. As slavery was a major cause of the Civil War, have your students think about and discuss the poem's meaning in this context. Find out what your students already know about slavery, the Underground Railroad, and the Civil War, and put this information on a wall chart.

Read *Nettie's Trip South* by Ann Turner (New York: Macmillan, 1987) to your class to spur further discussion about slavery. It is the story of a young white girl who writes to her friend about her horror at seeing how slaves were treated in the South. This story is based on a diary of the author's great-grandmother. The book was named an International Reading Association/Children's Book Council Children's Choice book in 1988.

Read *Pink and Say* by Patricia Polacco (New York: Scholastic, 1994) to your class to provide a springboard for further discussion about the Civil War. This is a wonderful story of the friendship between a black soldier and a white Ohio recruit during the Civil War. It is based on a tale that was passed down through the author's family.

Shades of Gray was chosen as the novel to be read with the entire class because it emphasizes differing views of the war. Carolyn Reeder's portrayal of the war's effect on families is excellent. Reading this novel with your class will help them to understand the war's devastating effects on our country, which went beyond the casualties of the soldiers. In turn, the students will have a means for comparison and insight when reading in small groups and independently.

A Visitor

One cold winter evening when loud was
   the storm
The wind raged without, but within all was
   calm.
The fire sparkled brightly illuming our
   room
Bespeaking that comfort encircled our
   room.
Our friends were all seated and cheerful
   the look
As I affectionately gazed on this family
   group.
Conversing and thinking how kind was
   their lot
Enjoying the comforts that many had not.
When a faint gentle rap was heard at our
   door,
Announcing a friend or a wanderer near,
I aroused me and hastened to welcome a
   guest
Who then from the storm would find
   shelter and rest.
When a woe begone being presented to
   sight
Whose brow all beclouded by sorrows dark
   night
His clothes were all tattered, his shoes
   were all torn
His head was uncovered, exposed to the
   storm.
As I welcomed him in he looked in my face
And convulsively said, "Are you a friend
   of my race?"
I told him as asylum to all I could give,
In the name of my Master from whom all I
   receive.

I asked why thus in distress he appeared
His clothes why thus tattered, his limbs
   why thus seared.
I knew in an instant, I knew by his sigh,
I knew by the teardrops that fell from his
   eye.
That a fugitive slave my compassion had
   sought
And with him the spirit of Freedom had
   brought.
I warmed him, I fed him, I clothed and
   hastened him on
Where the slave breathes in freedom,
   where libertys gone
To the land of Victoria, where slaves
   cannot live
But are free as the Monarch whose gifts
   they receive.
Has liberty then, I despairingly thought,
Left the land which our ancestors
   purchased and bought?
By their blood and their tears and their
   sacrificed homes
To gain an asylum from oppressions strong
   arm.
Has the proud bird of Liberty folded his
   wings?
Are his notes all expended that no longer
   he sings?
Or is Justice unwilling her part to perform?
That a brother thus braved and encountered
   the storm.

Sarah Smith Caldwell—
Marion, New York, 1841

Whole Group Reading

📖 Reeder, Carolyn. *Shades of Gray*. New York: Macmillan, 1989.
   Twelve-year-old Will Page lost his entire family during the Civil War. Now he has gone to live with his uncle, who had refused to fight. Will wonders how he can he live in the house of a coward. But slowly Will comes to understand that some actions take a different kind of courage. Winner of the Scott O'Dell Award for Historical Fiction in 1989. Grades 4 and up.

Author Information

Carolyn Reeder was born November 16, 1937 in Washington, D.C. She is an elementary school teacher and history buff. Her interest in the Civil War grew when vacationing at the battlefields of Antietam, Gettysburg, and New Market. Firsthand accounts of the Civil War's effect on local residents were her inspiration for *Shades of Gray*, her first novel.

Of her writing, Carolyn Reeder says, "At first I wrote only during school vacations, but before long I began to write during the school year, too. Now I feel I am restless if I'm away from the computer for more than a few days. I enjoy the excitement of creating my characters and their story, and I enjoy the detective work of finding out all the things I need to know to make the background accurate."

Activities

1. After completing the novel, have the students write an epilogue. This epilogue should take place twenty years after the main story takes place and should tell about what life is now like for all of the main characters: Will, Aunt Ella, Uncle Jed, and Meg.

2. Have students write a different ending for *Shades of Gray*—with Will making the decision to leave Winchester to go live with Doc Martin.

3. Have students create character sketches of Will, Meg, Uncle Jed, and Aunt Ella.

4. Have students illustrate Uncle Jed and Aunt Ella's farm using the descriptions in the novel.

5. At various points during the reading of *Shades of Gray*, have students write diary entries from Will Page's point of view.

6. Have students imagine that they are Jim Woodley, the Union soldier, and write a letter to his family telling them of his stay with the Joneses.

7. When your class has finished reading chapter 10, brainstorm advantages of Will staying to live with the Joneses and the advantages of going to live with Doc Martin. Put this information on a wall chart.

Discussion

Give the class the following instruction: As we read this book, we will be discussing the following questions. Write down your ideas about the questions and add to them as needed.

1. Why was Will so upset about having to go and live with his mother's sister and her family?

2. What happened during the war that Will could not forget?

3. How were slaves treated in different parts of the South?

4. Describe Will's Uncle Jed's feeling about the war.

5. What did states' rights have to do with the Civil War?

6. Why did Will refuse to call his uncle "Uncle Jed"?

7. Why did Will's mother and his Aunt Ella lose touch during the war?

8. What was Meg's feeling for Will at the end of chapter 3 and why?

9. How do you think Will felt working side by side with his Uncle Jed? Explain your answer.

10. Think about what Uncle Jed said to Mr. Jenkins: "Jonas Jenkins, who do you think is the coward, a man who walks away from a fight or a man who makes a challenge he knows won't be accepted?" Explain this statement in your own words. Do you agree or disagree with it?

11. When Will took the rabbit to the Jenkinses, he ended up defending his Uncle Jed. Do you think his feelings toward him are changing? Why or why not?

12. What happened to Will's brother Charlie during the war?

13. Why was pride so important to Will?

14. Even though Uncle Jed did not face enemy soldiers, what enemies has he faced?

15. What were some of the reasons soldiers joined the army?

16. How did Will feel when he read Doc Martin's letter?

17. Uncle Jed had some very strong feelings about the war and what he had lost. What were they?

18. How was it an "accident of geography" that a soldier was a part of one army or the other?

19. Why did Will keep putting off answering Doc Martin's letter?

20. What did the Union soldier, Jim Woodley, tell Will that confused him?

21. What led to Will's understanding about his Uncle Jed's feelings about the war?

22. Uncle Jed told Will that life is easier if you can believe that things will turn out all right. Do you agree or disagree? Explain your answer.

23. What did Will tell Jim Woodley in the letter he wrote to him? Why was it so hard for him to write this letter?

24. Describe your feelings about Will's decision at the end of the novel. Would you have made the same decision? Why or why not?

25. In what ways has the author, Carolyn Reeder, helped you to see that the war had effects other than casualties?

Vocabulary

florid (p1)
having a ruddy, flushed color

traitor (p2)
a person who betrays his or her country or the trust of another person or group

forded (p3)
crossed (such as a river) at a shallow place

meager (p13)
very little

cavalry (p11)
soldiers trained to fight on horseback

courteous (p14)
having good manners; polite

gruel (p16)
a thin, liquid food made by boiling cereal in water or milk

apprehensive (p31)
fearful of what may happen; nervous

menacing (p32)
threatening

auger (p39)
a tool for boring holes in the earth or wood

ominous (p41)
threatening or foreboding; signaling a bad omen

resolute (p44)
determined or bold

exasperation (p55)
the feeling of being annoyed or irritated

dubious (p59)
not sure or certain; doubtful

obliged (p67)
placed under obligation, such as for a service or favor

artillery (p69)
large, heavy firearms, such as cannons

regiment (p67)
a military unit made up of several battalions

vanquish (p70)
to defeat or overcome

indignation (p79)
anger that is aroused by something that is not right, just, or fair

fraternize (p82)
to associate in a friendly way

succulent (p86)
full of juice; juicy

monotonous (p99)
boring because of lack of variety or change

sultry (p99)
uncomfortably hot, humid, and still

oppressive (p101)
burdensome; harsh; cruel

defiant (p110)
> full of defiance; resisting

confrontation (p120)
> standing face to face with; facing boldly

disdain (p131)
> scorn or haughty contempt, especially toward
> someone or something considered inferior

dismay (p133)
> a feeling of alarm, uneasiness, and confusion

conviction (p165)
> a firm belief

Small Group Reading

Beatty, Patricia. *Charley Skedaddle*. New York: William Morrow, 1987.

A Bowery Boy from New York City joins the Union Army as a drummer boy and runs away only to encounter a bitter mountain woman. Winner of the 1987 Scott O'Dell Award for Historical Fiction. Grades 5-9.

Author Information

Patricia Beatty was born August 26, 1922 in Portland, Oregon. She worked as a high school teacher of English and history, a technical library worker, a business and science librarian, and a teacher of fiction writing for children.

Beatty was a prolific and award-winning writer of historical fiction for children. She re-created the eras of her fictional characters with the accuracy and attention to detail of a first-rate historian. Her heroes and heroines take part in exciting yet believable conflicts, often drawn with humor and touching on themes of heroism and mortality, that make her books popular with children of many ages and interests. Through her writing career, Beatty gained a reputation as a leading writer of historical novels for children. She died July 9, 1991 in Riverside, California.

Activities

1. On a map of the United States, have students locate the following:

Alexandria, VA	Fredericksburg, VA
Atlanta, GA	Gettysburg, PA
Blue Ridge Mountains, PA	New York City
Chancellorsville, VA	Petersburg, VA
Culpeper, VA	Rapidan River, VA
Elmira, NY	Richmond, VA

2. Have students research the following topics:

Battle of Gettysburg	General Meade
Fredericksburg	140th New York Veterans Volunteers
Ulysses S. Grant	The Underground Railroad
Robert E. Lee	

3. Have students write a letter to Granny Bent from Charley once he has settled in the West, telling her of his journey there.

4. Have students write a group epilogue for *Charley Skedaddle*. The epilogue should take place ten years after the Civil War and should tell what has become of Charley Quinn, Granny Bent, and Sarie. Students could share their epilogue, as well as a summary of the book, with the rest of the class.

Discussion

Give the small group the following instruction: As your group reads this book, discuss the following questions.

1. What are Bowery Boys and Dead Rabbits?

2. Why do you think Charley Quinn seems to be looking for a fight?

3. How has the death of Charley's brother Johnny affected him?

4. Describe Charley's feelings when he saw the 140th Volunteers marching by.

5. What does Charley think of Abe Lincoln?

6. Why was Charley so eager to join the Union Army?

7. What are bounty jumpers?

8. How did Charley feel about his friend Con by the time their ship reached its destination?

9. What do bugler boys and drummer boys do in the army?

10. Describe the difference between what Charley has seen in the Bowery and what he now sees in Virginia.

11. What are Charley's feelings about slavery?

12. How did Charley feel when Silas Gorman said he was proud of him?

13. What do soldiers say war is like?

14. How did Charley react to his first encounter with fighting?

15. Why did Charley tell the Confederate soldier that his name was Charley Skedaddle?

16. What made the Confederate officer decide to let Charley go?

17. Discuss what you think will happen to Charley now that he has been released by the Confederate officer.

18. Why did the old woman want to keep Charley with her in the mountains?

19. What made Charley's fight with Cois MacRae different from the many others he has been in?

20. Describe your feelings when you found out what Granny Bent and her husband did concerning runaway slaves.

21. What was Granny Bent's Christmas present to Charley, and why did it mean so much to him?

22. Discuss the many things that made Charley begin to think of Granny Bent as family.

23. When Charley is a grown man, do you think he will return to the mountains of Virginia? Explain your answer.

Vocabulary

menace (p1)
to threaten with evil or harm

taunt (p2)
a scornful, mocking, or sarcastic remark

Metropolitan (p4)
a person who lives in a large city or who has the characteristics associated with city people

state militia (p4)
a body of citizens from a state that are given military training outside the regular armed forces and are called up in emergencies

cloak (p6)
a loose outer garment, usually without sleeves

consumption (p7)
an old-fashioned word for tuberculosis of the lungs

betrothed (p8)
engaged to be married

wheedle (p11)
to coax or persuade by flattering

incorrigible (p11)
incapable of being corrected, improved, or reformed

jaunty (p12)
having a lively or self-confident air or manner

haversack (p15)
a bag, slung over the shoulder, for carrying provisions on a march or hike

regiment (p22)
an army unit, larger than a battalion and smaller than a division, usually commanded by a colonel

infantry (p34)
foot soldiers

veranda (p42)
a long, open, outdoor porch, usually roofed, along the perimeter of a building

emancipate (p46)
to set free, as from slavery or oppression

oblique (p59)
not direct or straightforward

skirmish (p63)
a brief fight between small groups of troops

bayonet (p69)
a daggerlike weapon that may be attached to the muzzle of a rifle

courier (p72)
a messenger required to deliver a message quickly

hardtack (p73)
a hard, unsalted, crackerlike biscuit

gaunt (p85)
very thin and bony, as from illness or hunger; worn

benefactor (p97)
a person who has given help or money

circuit rider (p144)
a minister who travels and preaches at places along a route

Small Group Reading

Chang, Ina. *A Separate Battle: Women and the Civil War.* New York: Lodestar Books, 1991.
A Separate Battle uses diaries, letters, and photographs to show how women influenced the course of the Civil War and transformed their own lives in the process. Grades 5-9.

Author Information

Ina Chang lives with her husband in Seattle, Washington. She has worked as a freelance writer, reporter, and editor. *A Separate Battle: Women and the Civil War* is her first book.

Activities

1. Have the students create posters depicting women's roles in the Civil War. They could also choose specific women to highlight on their posters. When finished, they should present them to the class, then hang them in the classroom. Women that students could highlight on the posters include Sojourner Truth, Harriet Beecher Stowe, Harriet Tubman, Clara Barton, Louisa May Alcott, Dorothea Dix, Sarah Edmonds, Elizabeth VanLew, and Belle Boyd.

2. Have students use one or more of the following books to research a specific woman of the time:

   Dubowski, Cathy East. *Clara Barton: Healing the Wounds.* Morristown, NJ: Silver Burdett Press, 1990.

   Ferris, Jeri. *Walking the Road to Freedom: A Story About Sojourner Truth.* Minneapolis, MN: Carolrhoda Books, 1988.

   Gaines, Ernest J. *The Autobiography of Miss Jane Pittman.* New York: Dial Press, 1971.

   McGovern, Ann. *"Wanted Dead or Alive": The True Story of Harriet Tubman.* New York: Scholastic, 1965.

   McKissack, Patricia, and Frederick McKissack. *Sojourner Truth: Ain't I a Woman?* New York: Scholastic, 1992.

   McMullan, Kate. *The Story of Harriet Tubman, Conductor of the Underground Railroad.* New York: Dell, 1991.

   Reit, Seymour. *Behind Rebel Lines: The Incredible Story of Emma Edmonds, Civil War Spy.* San Diego, CA: Harcourt Brace Jovanovich, 1988.

Shura, Mary Francis. *Gentle Annie: The True Story of a Civil War Nurse.* New York: Scholastic, 1991.

Sterling, Dorothy. *Freedom Train: The Story of Harriet Tubman.* New York: Scholastic, 1954.

Stevens, Bryna. *Frank Thompson: Her Civil War Story.* New York: Macmillan, 1992.

3. For extra credit, have a student recite to the class Sojourner Truth's speech on page 5 of *A Separate Battle.*

4. On a map of the United States, have students locate the following:

Akron, OH	Chicago, IL	Manassas, VA
Alexandria, VA	Chickamauga, TN	New Orleans, LA
Annapolis, MD	Columbia, SC	Philadelphia, PA
Antietam, MD	Combahee River, SC	Richmond, VA
Appomattox, VA	Concord, MA	Syracuse, NY
Auburn, NY	Flint, MI	Vicksburg, MS
Baton Rouge, LA	Gettysburg, PA	Washington, DC
Beaufort, SC	Macon, GA	Winchester, VA
Charleston, SC		

5. Included at the end of this chapter is a crossword puzzle of famous women of the Civil War for students to complete following their reading of *A Separate Battle.*

Discussion

Give the small group the following instruction: As your group reads this book, discuss the following questions.

1. Many of the women discussed in this book were abolitionists. What does this mean? What did they do for their fellow women?

2. What made Angela Grimke decide to leave the South?

3. What specific things did women do for the abolitionist cause?

4. How did Harriet Beecher Stowe make an impact on the antislavery movement?

5. Discuss your own feelings about slavery.

6. How did Harriet Tubman help runaway slaves?

7. Why were the Confederate States of America formed?

8. What did women do to help supply the Union and Confederate armies?

9. How did the invention of the foot-treadle sewing machine help the war effort?

10. Clara Barton founded a branch of the Red Cross in 1881. How does this organization continue to bring help to people all over the world today?

11. Before the Civil War, almost all nurses in army hospitals were men. Why? Why did this change during the war?

12. During the Civil War, field hospitals were used to take care of the wounded. Describe these field hospitals.

13. Dozens of women were discovered to be posing as male soldiers during the Civil War. There may have been many more women who were never discovered. What were their reasons for doing this?

14. What were some of the things women did to spy for the Union or Confederate armies?

15. Describe how the war affected women, children, and others who were left at home while their husbands, fathers, sons, and brothers went off to war.

Vocabulary

countenance (p2)
the expression of the face

flogged (p2)
beat hard, as with a whip or stick

abolitionist (p2)
someone who wanted to end slavery in the United States

patriotism (p14)
love for one's country and loyal devotion to it

havelock (p20)
a cotton cap with a piece of cloth that hung down in the back and shaded the neck

somber (p36)
gloomy and melancholy; sad

initiative (p37)
the first step in starting or doing something

undulated (p38)
moved or caused to move like a wave or in waves

typhoid fever (p38)
an infectious disease caused by a bacterium found in infected food or water and marked by fever, diarrhea, a red rash, and an intestinal inflammation

tyrant (p40)
a ruler having absolute power

cumbersome (p41)
hard to move or manage

battalion (p50)
two or more companies of soldiers led by a lieutenant colonel or major

swagger (p50)
to walk with a proud or insolent air; to strut

reminiscence (p51)
the act or practice of thinking or speaking about the past

masquerading (p51)
disguising oneself

cunning (p60)
clever or tricky

exploits (p61)
brave or daring acts

smallpox (p64)
a highly contagious viral disease causing a high fever and skin eruptions that usually leave permanent scars

scarlet fever (p64)
a contagious disease chiefly affecting young people, marked by a sore throat, fever, and a red rash

contraband (p72)
seized property (in this case, former slaves seized by the Union Army)

refugee (p72)
a person who flees from persecution or danger

despondent (p85)
discouraged or depressed

forlorn (p86)
sad or pitiful because of being alone or neglected

liberated (p86)
set free; released

eloquent (p88)
effective or skillful in expressing feelings or ideas

Small Group Reading

Clark, Margaret Goff. *Freedom Crossing*. New York: Scholastic, 1980.
A young Southern girl finds her loyalties challenged when she returns to her home in the North and discovers that her father and brother have been helping runaway slaves. Grades 4-7.

Author Information

Margaret Clark was born March 7, 1913 in Oklahoma City, Oklahoma. She worked as an elementary school teacher, a teacher of creative writing in adult education programs, and a deputy town clerk. She was adopted by the Seneca Indians in 1962.

She began writing when her two children were young. The age level of her stories grew as her children grew. The inspiration for most of her books came from her own experiences.

Activities

1. Have students write to the Niagara County, New York, historian for more information and photos (if available) of Tryon's Folly.

2. Have students illustrate Tryon's Folly. They could do an outside view and an inside view—with the four cellars. The finished products can be displayed in the classroom.

3. Have students research Frederick Douglass, the Fugitive Slave Act of 1850, and Harriet Beecher Stowe, the author of *Uncle Tom's Cabin*.

4. On a chart, have students compare and contrast Laura's feelings about slavery from the beginning of the novel to the end of the novel. The group can share their chart with the rest of the class.

5. On a map of the United States, have students locate the following:

Buffalo, NY	Niagara Falls
Lake Ontario	Niagara River
Lewiston, NY	North Carolina
Lockport, NY	Rochester, NY

6. Have students write a group letter to Laura's Aunt Ruth and Uncle Jim from Laura. In this letter, they should try to persuade her aunt and uncle that slavery is wrong.

Discussion

Give the small group the following instruction: As your group reads this book, discuss the following questions.

1. Why had Laura been living with her aunt and uncle in Virginia for four years?

2. How did Laura's Aunt Ruth and Uncle Jim feel about the Underground Railroad?

3. Why was Bert concerned about Laura's reaction to Bert and Joel helping Martin?

4. Describe the difference between Laura's life in Virginia and what it is like now, at home in New York.

5. Joel tells Laura that she is hard-hearted. What does that mean? Do you agree or not?

6. Laura believes that "slaves don't feel the way we do. They—they're like children and they want to be safe and cared for." Explain how she has come to believe that.

7. What did Laura's father mean when he once said that she and Bert were "thick as thieves"?

8. Why did people in the South have more time for music, books, and parties?

9. Why was it against the law to teach a slave to read?

10. Why did Laura decide to let Martin hide in the secret room under her bedroom?

11. Who is Moses? What is this person well known for?

12. Recall Joel's note to Laura:

    > Though some may fail,
    > Those who try on and on will succeed.
    > Sometimes folly leads to freedom,
    > And the rabbit escapes from the trap.

    What do you think it means?

13. Why do you think the sheriff was so sure he could get Laura and Bert's carriage back for them?

14. Why was Bert arrested?

15. Why would death be better than slavery to Martin? If you were in his place, would you feel the same?

16. Describe your feelings at the end of the novel. If you had been alive during that time period, what would you have done if Martin or another escaped slave had come knocking at your door?

Vocabulary

indignant (p19)
    angry because of something that is not right, just, or fair

rebellious (p24)
    full of the disobedient spirit of a rebel

conviction (p26)
    a strong belief

reverence (p29)
    a feeling of great respect

perishable (p42)
    likely to decay or wither quickly

turmoil (p50)
    great confusion or disorder

earnestly (p64)
    seriously; sincerely

solemnly (p68)
    seriously

abolitionist (p69)
    an individual who wanted to end slavery in the United States

saunter (p76)
    to walk along in a slow, casual way; to stroll

eureka (p80)
    a cry of joy upon making a discovery

console (p89)
    to comfort or cheer

sympathize (p93)
    to express sympathy or compassion

plaintively (p103)
    sadly; mournfully

anguish (p111)
    very great suffering of the body or mind

sentry (p115)
    a person stationed to keep watch and warn others of danger; a guard

emphatic (p128)
    spoken or done with emphasis

Small Group Reading

Coville, Bruce. *The Ghost Wore Gray*. New York: Bantam Books, 1988.

Sixth-graders Nina and Chris unravel a 125-year-old mystery when they accompany Nina's father to an old country inn. A handsome Confederate ghost appears, trying to tell them something. Grades 3-7.

Author Information

Bruce Coville was born May 16, 1950 in Syracuse, New York. He has worked as a teacher, a camp counselor, a toy maker, and even as a grave digger. He is well known as a writer of juvenile fiction. His novels rely on mythical creatures, such as unicorns and dragons, and science fiction traditions, such as aliens and space stations.

Of his decision to become a writer, Coville says, "I think it was sixth grade when I first realized that writing was something that I could do, and wanted to do very much. As it happened, I had spent most of that year making life miserable for my teacher by steadfastly failing to respond to the many creative devices she had to stimulate us to write. Then one day she simply (finally!) just let us write—told us that we had a certain amount of time to produce a short story of substance. Freed from writing topics imposed from without, I cut loose, and over several days found that I loved what I was doing."

Activities

1. On a map of the United States, have students locate Syracuse, New York; the Catskill Mountains in New York; and Charleston, South Carolina.

2. Have students find out more information about the Fugitive Slave Act and present it to the class.

3. Have students write conversation that may have taken place between Samson Carter and Captain Gray when Carter comes to get Gray at the end of the novel.

4. Have students write a letter to Captain Gray's family from him, telling them about how his feelings have changed about slavery and why.

5. Have students research further Harriet Tubman and the Underground Railroad.

Discussion

Give the small group the following instruction: As your group reads this book, discuss the following questions.

1. What is a preservation architect?

2. Do you think Nine really fooled her father when she wanted her friend Chris to come to the Inn with them? Why or why not?

3. Why did Mr. Tanleven think Nine would enjoy the Quackadoodle Inn?

4. Why does everyone call Nina Nine?

5. Discuss the reasons Nine and Chris could see the ghost when no one else could.

6. Who do you think stole the original floor plans for the Inn from Mr. Tanleven's room, and why?

7. Why would Mona want Nine to write a book for her?

8. What was the Fugitive Slave Act? How might the Inn have been involved?

9. What is a quadroon?

10. How did Captain Gray's thoughts about black people and the Underground Railroad change while being treated by Samson Carter when he was injured?

11. Why didn't Samson Carter turn Captain Gray over to Union soldiers?

12. After reading Captain Gray's diary entry, do you have any predictions as to why he is haunting the Inn, or why he has appeared to Nine and Chris?

13. What might Nine and Chris find at the museum at Samson Carter's home?

14. How did Porter Markson know about Captain Gray's treasure?

15. What was Isabella's connection to the treasure and the Samson Carter Institute?

16. Whom do you think the jewels should belong to now?

17. Describe your feelings at the end of the novel. Were any of your predictions correct?

Vocabulary

stalked (p10)
followed someone secretly

meander (p13)
to wander aimlessly without purpose

appalled (p14)
filled with dismay or horror

turret (p14)
a small tower, often at the corner of a large building or castle

dormer (p14)
a small, roofed structure extending out from a sloping roof and containing an upright window

cupola (p14)
a small tower built on a roof and having a dome-shaped top

emphatic (p58)
spoken or done with emphasis

apprehensive (p59)
fearful; worried

unscrupulous (p92)
having no principles or conscience; dishonest

astonishment (p94)
amazement

chauvinist (p100)
someone who has a biased belief that his or her own group is superior

primly (p102)
precisely; formally

resolution (p124)
something determined, or decided on, as a course of action

vengeful (p137)
seeking or showing vengeance; vindictive

Small Group Reading

📖 Murphy, Jim. *The Boys' War: Confederate and Union Soldiers Talk About the Civil War*. New York: Clarion Books, 1990.

Murphy based this book on first-person accounts of boys who fought in the Civil War. Grades 4-9.

Author Information

Jim Murphy was born September 25, 1947 in Newark, New Jersey. Murphy has worked as an editorial secretary and managing editor for Clarion Books. He continues to work as a freelance author and an editor.

Although many reviewers found *The Boys' War: Confederate and Union Soldiers Talk About the Civil War* to be grim, others have praised the book for its sepia-toned photographs and its use of the boys' own words (through letters and diaries) to make the Civil War come alive for the reader. A *Horn Book* commentator said, "This well-researched and readable account provides fresh insight into the human cost of a pivotal event in United States History."

Of his writing, Murphy says, "I thoroughly enjoy my work. The nonfiction projects let me research subjects that I'm really interested in, they provide an opportunity to tell kids some unusual bits of information. The fiction lets me get out some of the thoughts and opinions in my head."

Activities

1. Have students write a diary entry as if they were a drummer boy in the Civil War. They should tell about the importance of their job, their feelings, and the hardships they experience.

2. Have students write letters home to their families from the viewpoint of a boy fighting in the Civil War. They should tell what they have seen, and their feelings of fear and loneliness.

3. Have students debate whether or not boys should have fought in the Civil War. One side would defend the boys by stating the reasons why they joined the army. The other side would justify the reasons boys should not have been involved in the war. This debate should take place in front of the entire class, as a way of sharing what the group has learned from reading the book.

4. Have students create a group poster depicting the boys' role in the war. After explaining their poster to the class, they can hang it on a wall in the classroom.

Discussion

Give the small group the following instruction: As your group reads this book, discuss the following questions.

1. Discuss your feelings about children fighting in the Civil War.

2. How did most Northerners view slavery? Explain your answer.

3. How did the majority of Southerners view slavery? Explain your answer.

4. Why did boys from the North join the army?

5. Why did boys from the South join the army?

6. Union and Confederate armies both had rules that banned boys from enlisting and fighting. How were boys able to enlist regardless of the rules?

7. At the beginning of the war, both sides had a variety of uniforms. Why was this a problem?

8. What valuable service did the drummer boys provide to both sides?

9. Besides drumming, what other jobs did the boys perform?

10. Why was meal time so important to boys during the war—other than in feeding their hunger?

11. What did soldiers do during their free time?

12. Why did soldiers fear doctors?

13. How might modern medical advancements have changed the fate of injured and sick soldiers?

14. How did the boys change as a result of their experience?

15. Fear was a big part of a soldier's life. How did this affect boys?

16. After the war was over, what was the difference between the Union Army's homecoming and that of the Confederacy?

Vocabulary

proclamation (p2)
an official public announcement

eloquent (p3)
effective or skillful in expressing feelings or ideas

insurrection (p5)
a rebellion or uprising

recruit (p8)
a newly enlisted member of the armed forces

telegraph (p9)
a device for sending and receiving messages by means of a series of electrical or electromagnetic pulses

armory (p11)
a place where arms (weapons) are kept

compromise (p15)
an adjustment or settlement in which each side gives up part of its demands

blockade (p16)
the shutting off of a place by enemy ships or troops

hodgepodge (p16)
a confused mixture

demoralize (p28)
to weaken or destroy the spirit or discipline

poignant (p29)
affecting the feelings; touching; moving

allay (p30)
to quiet, soothe, or reduce

musket (p39)
an old type of firearm, replaced by the rifle

chastise (p43)
to punish, especially by beating

quagmire (p48)
an area of deep, soft mud

haversack (p51)
a bag for carrying provisions on a march or hike that was slung over the shoulder

malaria (p56)
a disease spread by the bite of an infected mosquito and marked by recurrent attacks of chills, fever, and sweating

commissary (p57)
a store that sells food and daily supplies, such as at a camp or military post

animosity (p64)
strong dislike or hatred

annihilate (p70)
to destroy completely

carnage (p71)
a bloody killing of great numbers of people, as in war

gangrene (p86)
the decay of tissue in part of the body, caused by a failure in circulation of the blood, as from injury or disease

scurvy (p89)
a disease caused by lack of vitamin C in the diet, marked by swollen and bleeding gums and great physical weakness

Small Group Reading

Smucker, Barbara. *Runaway to Freedom: A Story of the Underground Railway*. New York: Harper & Row, 1978.

Two twelve-year-old slaves run away and try to reach Canada on the Underground Railroad. This book was published originally under the title *Underground to Canada*, in 1977. It was named one of the fifty best books of all time in Canada by the Children's Book Center in 1978. Grades 6-8.

A word of caution: A derogatory word regarding the slaves is used several times. Be sure to read the book yourself first to decide if it will be appropriate for your students to read. It might be better used with older students, as long as you discuss this term (and the reason for its use in the book) with them first. My feeling is that the story is excellent and worthwhile to use with older middle-school students.

Author Information

Barbara Smucker was born September 1, 1915 in Newton, Kansas. She has worked as a high school teacher of English and journalism, a reporter, a bookseller, a children's librarian, and a head librarian.

Smucker is best known for her well-researched historical fiction for young adults. Many of her books have some kind of personal significance. When she was young, her family hired Ella Underwood, a widowed African-American woman to take care of her and her three siblings. Underwood told them many entrancing stories about the days of slavery. Smucker says, "Years later, when I wrote my book *Underground to Canada*, I could hear Ella's voice and the way she pronounced words."

Smucker's initial interest in writing began in sixth grade. A teacher had given the class an assignment to write an original fairy tale. Smucker's tale was one of the best, and she says, "From then on, I was hooked on writing."

Activities

1. Chapter 5 contains a description of the Riley's plantation and of the shacks where the field slaves lived. Have students illustrate both on one large sheet of construction paper or poster board to show the difference in living conditions.

2. Divide the group into smaller groups of two or three. One group should research the Fugitive Slave Act and the other should research Levi Coffin, the "president" of the Underground Railroad. The groups can incorporate the information gathered into small posters to be hung in the classroom.

3. Have students write letters from Julilly and Liza to the Mennonites who helped them.

4. On a laminated map of the United States, have the group locate and label (with a wipe-off marker) the wagon trip from the Hensen plantation in Virginia to the Riley plantation in Mississippi. The students should also trace Julilly and Liza's journey to Canada from Mississippi. Other places to label include Felsheim, Tennessee; Lexington, Kentucky; the Ohio River; Cincinnati, Ohio—the home of Levi Coffin; the Mississippi River; and Lake Erie.

5. When Julilly hears about the Underground Railroad, she wonders if there is a road under the ground that goes to Canada. Have students research the Underground Railroad. What is it really? Find out more from an encyclopedia or the book *If You Traveled on the Underground Railroad* by Ellen Levine.

Discussion

Give the small group the following instruction: As your group reads this book, discuss the following questions.

1. Why did Mammy Sally fear leaving Massa Hensen's plantation? What could leaving mean for the slaves?

2. Mammy Sally came to Julilly at night and told her about Canada. Why was this important? How could slaves get to Canada?

3. Why did the slave traders examine the slaves like they were animals?

4. Describe your feelings about the slaves being separated from their families and sold.

5. How had Julilly's life changed on the wagon trip? Explain her new responsibilities.

6. When Julilly sang, she and the children were comforted. What did it remind them of?

7. Compare and contrast how Massa Hensen and Massa Riley treated their slaves.

8. In chapter 6, Liza tells Julilly what her father once told her: "Liza the soul is all black or white, 'pending on the man's life and not on his skin." Discuss this statement in your group and explain in your own words what he meant.

9. At the end of chapter 8, Julilly thinks about what freedom means. What does freedom mean to you?

10. What dangers may await Julilly, Liza, Lester, and Adam during their journey to freedom?

11. In chapter 11, Lester tells the others that he can read. What was their reaction? Discuss what your life would be like if you could not read.

12. What made slave owners want to keep slaves from being able to read?

13. What was the Fugitive Slave Act? Discuss the Act and your feelings about it in your group.

14. At the end of chapter 12, we are led to believe that Lester and Adam have been caught by slave catchers. What do you think will happen to them? Will Liza and Julilly make it to Canada without them?

15. When Julilly and Liza were able to bathe in a tub with real soap, what was their reaction?

16. Before leaving Levi Coffin's home, Liza seemed like a changed person. How did she change, and why?

17. Liza says, "Freedom ain't easy, Massa Ross." What does she mean?

18. What did reaching Canada and freedom mean to Liza and Julilly?

19. Think about Julilly's joy at the end of the novel. Compare this to an event in your own life or one in another book you have read.

Vocabulary

plantation (p3)
a farm or estate of many acres having a crop of cotton, tobacco, rice, or other products planted and tended by laborers who live there

oppress (p3)
to burden or keep down by unjust use of force or authority

hoecake (p10)
a flat bread made of coarse cornmeal, originally baked on a hoe in the fire

loiter (p11)
to linger or dawdle

mulatto (p15)
a person with one white and one black parent

Quaker (p20)
a member of the Society of Friends, a religious group

abolitionist (p20)
someone who wanted to end slavery in the United States

brambles (p27)
prickly shrubs

quarters (p30)
a place to live in or sometimes just to sleep in

overseer (p30)
a person who supervises laborers at their work

trough (p35)
a long, narrow, open container for holding food or water for animals

solemn (p53)
serious, grave, and earnest

conviction (p56)
a firm belief

bondage (p56)
slavery

cicada (p60)
a large insect with four transparent wings

stately (p60)
dignified

astonished (p63)
surprised; filled with wonder; amazed

serenely (p69)
peacefully, tranquilly, calmly

fugitive (p76)
fleeing, as from danger or arrest

fervour (p80)
very strong emotion or enthusiasm

accusation (p90)
a charge of having done something wrong or illegal or of being something bad

Mennonite (p98)
a member of a Christian sect that is opposed to taking oaths, holding public office, and military service

sustenance (p116)
something that maintains life or strength; nourishment; food

gaunt (p121)
very thin and bony, such as from illness or hunger; worn

notorious (p123)
widely known, especially for bad reasons

schooner (p144)
a ship having two or more masts rigged with sails

Bibliography

Individual Titles

Adoff, Arnold. *I Am the Darker Brother: An Anthology of Modern Poems by Negro Americans.* New York: Macmillan, 1968.
Included in this book are poems about slavery, Frederick Douglass, the Underground Railroad, and the black soldiers who fought in the Civil War. Grades 3-8.

Alphin, Elaine Marie. *The Ghost Cadet.* New York: Henry Holt, 1991.
A young boy travels back in time, witnesses the Battle of New Market in Virginia, and helps a tormented ghost return a family heirloom so that he can be at rest. Grades 4-7.

Archer, Jules. *A House Divided: The Lives of Ulysses S. Grant and Robert E. Lee.* New York: Scholastic, 1995.
From Bull Run to the fall of Richmond, from Shilo to Sherman's march through Georgia, this joint biography describes the military careers and private lives of Lee and Grant. It portrays vividly the bloodiest and most wrenching episode in American history. Grades 3-7.

Barrett, Tracy. *Harper's Ferry: The Story of John Brown's Raid*. Brookfield, CT: Millbrook Press, 1993.

This book includes information on the personal background of abolitionist John Brown and the events surrounding the raid he led on the United States Arsenal at Harper's Ferry, West Virginia, in 1859. Grades 4 and up.

Beatty, Patricia. *Be Ever Hopeful, Hannalee*. New York: William Morrow, 1988.

Following the Civil War, fourteen-year-old Hannalee and her recently reunited family decide to start a new life in Atlanta. This is a sequel to *Turn Homeward, Hannalee*. Grades 5-8.

———. *Jayhawker*. New York: William Morrow, 1991.

A thirteen-year-old boy joins a band of Kansans who cross into Missouri to help slaves escape to freedom. Grades 5-8.

———. *Turn Homeward, Hannalee*. New York: William Morrow, 1984.

Hannalee Reed is forced to move to Indiana with other mill workers from Georgia—leaving her mother with a promise to return home as soon as the war ends. Grades 5-8.

———. *Wait for Me, Watch for Me Eula Bee*. New York: William Morrow, 1978.

Two children are taken captive by Comanche Indians in Texas in 1861. Grades 6-8.

———. *Who Comes with Cannons?* New York: Scholastic, 1992.

After Truth Hopkins's father died in 1861, she went to live with her uncle's family in North Carolina. She and her family are Quakers, who believe that slavery is wrong. When Truth goes with her uncle to deliver a wagonload of hay to a neighbor, she begins her involvement in the Underground Railroad. Grades 3-7.

Bial, Raymond. *The Underground Railroad*. Boston: Houghton Mifflin, 1995.

Raymond Bial uses photographs to show actual places and artifacts of the Underground Railroad. This is an excellent resource for researching the Underground Railroad. Grades 4 and up.

Bolotin, Norman, and Angela Herb. *For Home and Country: A Civil War Scrapbook*. New York: Lodestar Books, 1995.

This scrapbook is filled with photographs, diaries, letters, stories, news clippings, and other artifacts of the Civil War. Grades 5 and up.

Brewton, Sara, and John E. Brewton. *America Forever: A Book of Poems*. New York: Thomas Y. Crowell, 1968.

This anthology includes poems about the South, slavery, the Civil War, and leading figures. Grades 5-8.

Brill, Marlene Targ. *Allen Jay and the Underground Railroad*. Minneapolis, MN: Carolrhoda Books, 1993.

This is the true story of how Allen Jay, a young Quaker boy living in Ohio in 1842, helped an escaped slave flee from his master through the Underground Railroad. Grades 2-4.

Clapp, Patricia. *The Tamarack Tree: A Novel of the Siege of Vicksburg*. New York: Lothrop, Lee & Shepard, 1986.

Seventeen-year-old Rosemary Leigh tells the story of the turbulence of the Civil War and the personal choice many Northerners faced between loyalty to Southern friends and neighbors and the moral conviction that slavery was wrong. Grades 5-9.

Climo, Shirley. *A Month of Seven Days*. New York: Thomas Y. Crowell, 1987.

When twelve-year-old Zoe's Georgia home is taken over by Union soldiers, she uses all of her ingenuity to drive them away. Grades 5 and up.

Collier, James Lincoln, and Christopher Collier. *With Every Drop of Blood*. New York: Delacorte, 1994.

While trying to transport food to Richmond, Virginia, during the Civil War, fourteen-year-old Johnny is captured by a black Union soldier. Grades 4 and up.

Cooper, Michael L. *From Slave to Civil War Hero: The Life and Times of Robert Smalls*. New York: Lodestar, 1994.

Michael Cooper tells of the life of Robert Smalls, the first slave to become a widely known Civil War hero. Grades 4-8.

Cox, Clinton. *Undying Glory: The Story of the Massachusetts 54th Regiment*. New York: Scholastic, 1991.

Cox describes the formation of the all-black 54th Massachusetts Regiment and its battle history from 1863 to 1865. Grades 5 and up.

Crane, Stephen. *Red Badge of Courage*. New York: Dodd, Mead, 1957.

Henry Fleming, a young farm boy, enlists to fight in the Union Army. The horror of war is well depicted. Grades 5 and up.

Davidson, Margaret. *Frederick Douglass Fights for Freedom*. New York: Scholastic, 1968.

This is a biography of the slave who escaped to the North and became an abolitionist, orator, journalist, and one of the most famous freedom fighters of all time. Grades 2-5.

Donahue, John. *An Island Far from Home*. Minneapolis, MN: Carolrhoda Books, 1995.

A twelve-year-old boy, whose Union army doctor father was killed during the fighting in Fredericksburg, comes to understand the meaning of war and the fine line between friends and enemies when he begins corresponding with a young Confederate prisoner of war. Grades 4-8.

Dubowski, Cathy East. *Clara Barton: Healing the Wounds*. Englewood Cliffs, NJ: Silver Burdett Press, 1990.
This is a biography of the nurse who served on the battlefields of the Civil War and later founded the American Red Cross. Grades 5 and up.

Ferris, Jerri. *Walking the Road to Freedom: A Story About Sojourner Truth*. Minneapolis, MN: Carolrhoda Books, 1988.
This book traces the life of the black woman orator who spoke out against slavery throughout New England and the Midwest. Grades 3-6.

Fleischman, Paul. *Bull Run*. New York: HarperCollins, 1993.
In the book, the author has created sixteen characters from all walks of life. He traces their thoughts, emotions, and experiences, from their first hopes for a brave new world through the brutal reality of the first battle of the Civil War. Grades 4-8.

Forman, James D. *Becca's Story*. New York: Charles Scribner's Sons, 1992.
Based on letters and a diary kept by one of the author's ancestors from 1859 to 1866, this is the story of a girl whose two suitors volunteer for Michigan's Seventh Regiment to fight during the Civil War. Their letters to her are included in the book. Grades 7 and up.

Freedman, Florence B. *Two Tickets to Freedom: The True Story of William and Ellen Craft, Fugitive Slaves*. New York: Scholastic, 1971.
This book was originally published by Simon and Schuster in 1971. This is the story of a light-skinned black woman from Georgia who in 1848 dressed as a Southern gentlemen to purchase two tickets—one for her and one for her husband—whom she said was her slave. They eventually left for England, where they stayed and raised their children until after the Civil War had ended and the slaves were freed. Grades 4-8.

Freedman, Russell. *Lincoln: A Photobiography*. New York: Clarion Books, 1987.
This is an excellent resource for use in studying the Civil War. Included are historical photographs of Lincoln, along with letters, posters, and drawings. Grades 5-6.

Fritz, Jean. *Brady*. New York: Coward-McCann, 1960.
This novel about the Underground Railroad is told from the point of view of a white boy who helps some slaves to move from one station to the next. Grades 5-7.

———. *Harriet Beecher Stowe and the Beecher Preachers*. New York: G. P. Putnam's Sons, 1994.
Jean Fritz brings to life Harriet Beecher Stowe, the woman who opposed slavery with a passion. Grades 4-8.

———. *Stonewall*. New York: G. P. Putnam's Son, 1979.
This is a biography of the Southern general who gained the nickname Stonewall because of his stand at Bull Run during the Civil War. Grades 3-7.

Gaines, Ernest J. *The Autobiography of Miss Jane Pittman*. New York: Dial Books, 1971.
This is a fictionalized account of how Pittman, a black woman born into slavery, organizes and participates in a freedom demonstration a century later. Grades 6 and up.

Gauch, Patricia. *Thunder at Gettysburg*. New York: Coward, 1975.
The feeling of Tillie Pierce is described as she is drawn unknowingly into the Battle of Gettysburg. Grades 3-6.

Gehret, Jeanne. *Susan B. Anthony: And Justice for All*. Fairport, NY: Verbal Images Press, 1994.
This is the story of Susan B. Anthony, a dynamic woman whose life story is told from her early work with the abolitionists through her fight for women's right to vote. Grades 4-8.

Hamilton, Virginia. *Anthony Burns: The Defeat and Triumph of a Fugitive Slave*. New York: Alfred A. Knopf, 1988.
After escaping to Boston a slave is recaptured by his Southern master and returned to Virginia by the power of the Fugitive Slave Act. An afterword makes careful distinctions between documented facts and educated guesswork. The book also includes selections from the Fugitive Slave Act of 1850 and a bibliography of primary and secondary sources. Grades 7-12.

———. *The House of Dies Drear*. New York: Macmillan, 1968.
This is a mystery about a black boy's house which was once part of the Underground Railroad. Grades 6-9.

———. *Many Thousand Gone: African Americans from Slavery to Freedom*. New York: Alfred A. Knopf, 1992.
This book traces the history of slavery in America—from the earliest slave trading through the growth of the Underground Railroad and the Emancipation Proclamation. Grades 4-9.

———. *The Mystery of Drear House*. New York: Greenwillow Books, 1987.
This is a sequel to *The House of Dies Drear*, that picks up the story of the Small family and the dilemmas that must be resolved upon the discovery of a long-dead abolitionist's hidden treasure. Grades 5 and up.

Hansen, Joyce. *Between Two Fires: Black Soldiers in the Civil War*. New York: Franklin Watts, 1993.
Hansen documents the recruitment, training, and struggles of black soldiers during the Civil War and examines the campaigns in which they participated. Grades 5 and up.

———. *Which Way Freedom.* New York: Walker, 1986.

Two youngsters run away from slavery on a North Carolina farm. One of them witnesses the Civil War first as a Confederate captive and then as a Union soldier. Grades 5-8.

———. *Out from This Place.* New York: Walker, 1988.

In a sequel to *Which Way Freedom*, the author focuses on Easter, the fourteen-year-old black girl that Obi left behind. Like Obi, Easter is determined, after her escape from bondage, to find and keep freedom. Grades 4 and up.

Haskins, Jim. *The Day Fort Sumter Was Fired On: A Photo History of the Civil War.* New York: Scholastic, 1995.

This book covers military and political history as well as the war's effect on women, blacks, and children. Grades 4-6.

———. *Get on Board: The Story of the Underground Railroad.* New York: Scholastic, 1993.

This is an excellent nonfiction book about the Underground Railroad. It includes many photos, information about stationmasters and conductors, railroad songs, and much more. Grades 4-8.

Hermes, Patricia. *On Winter's Wind.* Boston: Little, Brown, 1995.

As she struggles to make ends meet while maintaining her family's dignity, eleven-year-old Genevieve faces the possibility of turning in a slave for the bounty. Grades 5-8.

Hopkinson, Deborah. *Sweet Clara and the Freedom Quilt.* New York: Alfred A. Knopf, 1993.

This is a story about a black girl's escape from slavery on a Southern plantation. She stitches a quilt with a map pattern and guides herself to freedom in the North. Grades K-5.

Hughes, Langston. *Don't You Turn Back: Poems by Langston Hughes.* Lee Bennett Hopkins, selector. New York: Alfred A. Knopf, 1969.

This book contains several poems that illustrate the experience of slaves. Grades 5-8.

Hunt, Irene. *Across Five Aprils.* Chicago: Follett, 1964.

Nine-year-old Jethro runs his Illinois farm almost alone, with dangers as exciting as those in battle. Runner-up for the Newbery Medal. Grades 6-9.

Hurmence, Belinda. *A Girl Called Boy.* New York: Clarion Books, 1982.

Blanche Overtha Yancy, a rebellious girl who cares nothing about her family's history, finds herself a slave in 1850s North Carolina after she rubs a carved soapstone conjure bird. Grades 3-6.

Johnson, Dolores. *Seminole Diary: Remembrances of a Slave.* New York: Macmillan, 1994.

This book is written in diary form by Libbie, a young slave. It tells of her family's escape from slavery in 1834. *Seminole Diary* reveals a seldom told story of slaves who escaped and joined Native American groups, where they found safety and acceptance. Grades K-3.

Johnson, Neil. *The Battle of Gettysburg.* New York: Four Winds Press, 1989.

The author has written a detailed photo essay that captures a reenactment of the Battle of Gettysburg held in 1988 on the 125th anniversary of the conflict. Grades 5 and up.

Keith, Harold. *Rifles for Watie.* New York: Thomas Y. Crowell, 1957.

Jeff Bussey was tired of being called "freed state scum" when he left Kansas in 1861 to join the Union Volunteers. The story follows Jeff through a lesser-known aspect of the Civil War—the western battles. The information for this book was gathered from the diaries of western veterans. Winner of the Newbery Award. Grades 6 and up.

Lester, Julius. *To Be a Slave.* New York: Dial Books for Young Readers, 1968.

This book contains firsthand accounts of the auction block, plantation life, resistance to slavery, emancipation, and post-emancipation times that were taken from nineteenth-century slave narratives. Grades 6-9.

Levine, Ellen. *If You Traveled on the Underground Railroad.* New York: Scholastic, 1988.

Levine uses a question-and-answer format to explain the Underground Railroad. Grades 2-4.

Lunn, Janet. *The Root Cellar.* New York: Charles Scribner's Sons, 1981.

Twelve-year-old Rose discovers that she can travel back to the 1860s when she climbs through the door of her aunt's root cellar. An exciting time-travel fantasy that is also rich in historical detail, particularly in its portrayal of the part Canada played in the U.S. Civil War. Grades 5 and up.

Lyon, George Ella. *Cecil's Story.* New York: Orchard Books, 1991.

A boy thinks about the possible scenarios that exist for him at home if his father goes off to fight in the Civil War. Grades K-3.

———. *Here and Then.* New York: Orchard, 1994.

Through ghostly visitation and a diary that seems mysteriously to write itself with twelve-year-old Abby's hands, a Civil War nurse asks for help with medical supplies across an abyss of 133 years. Grades 4-7.

Lyons, Mary E. *Letters from a Slave Girl.* New York: Charles Scribner's Sons, 1992.

This is a fictionalized account of the life of Harriet Jacobs, told in the form of letters that she might have written during her slavery in North Carolina and as she prepared for escape to the North in 1842. It is full of struggle and survival. Grades 4-8.

Marrin, Albert. *Unconditional Surrender: U. S. Grant and the Civil War.* New York: Atheneum, 1994.
This is a biography of Grant's life and his role in the Civil War. Grades 5 and up.

———. *Virginia's General: Robert E. Lee and the Civil War.* New York: Atheneum, 1994.
This is a biography of Robert E. Lee, concentrating on the Civil War years. Grades 5 and up.

McCurdy, Michael, ed. *Escape from Slavery: The Boyhood of Frederick Douglass in His Own Words.* New York: Alfred A. Knopf, 1994.
This is a shortened autobiography presenting the early life of the slave who became an abolitionist, journalist, and statesman. Grades 4-8.

McGovern, Ann. *"Wanted Dead or Alive": The True Story of Harriet Tubman.* New York: Scholastic, 1965.
This book is a reprint of *Runaway Slave.* It gives an account of Harriet Tubman, who led more than 300 slaves north to freedom on the Underground Railroad between 1850 and the start of the Civil War. Grades 2-5.

McKissack, Patricia, and Fredrick McKissack. *Christmas in the Big House, Christmas in the Quarters.* New York: Scholastic, 1994.
This book describes the customs, recipes, poems, and songs used to celebrate Christmas in the slave owners' plantations and in the slaves' quarters just before the Civil War. Grades 3 and up.

———. *Sojourner Truth: Ain't I a Woman?* New York: Scholastic, 1992.
A slave named Isabella was born in New York in 1797. After she was freed in 1827, she chose the name Sojourner Truth, for which she became widely known. She was a preacher, an abolitionist, and an activist for the rights of blacks and women. This is a biography of her life. Grades 8-12.

McMullan, Kate. *The Story of Harriet Tubman, Conductor of the Underground Railroad.* New York: Dell, 1991.
In this biography of Harriet Tubman, events were carefully researched and taken from authentic autobiographies, writings, and commentaries. Grades 3-7.

McPherson, Stephanie Sammartino. *I Speak for the Women: A Story About Lucy Stone.* Minneapolis, MN: Carolrhoda Books, 1992.
McPherson chronicles the life of the outspoken nineteenth-century abolitionist and supporter of women's rights. Grades 4-7.

Meltzer, Milton. *Underground Man.* San Diego, CA: Harcourt Brace Jovanovich, 1990.
A courageous young white man aids slaves escaping from Kentucky in pre–Civil War days. Grades 3-7.

———. *Voices from the Civil War: A Documentary History of the Great American Conflict.* New York: Thomas Y. Crowell, 1989.
Life and events of the Civil War are depicted through letters, diaries, memoirs, interviews, ballads, newspaper articles, and speeches. Grades 5 and up.

Mettger, Zak. *Reconstruction: America After the Civil War.* New York: Lodestar, 1994.
This book, based on first-person accounts, is illustrated with vintage photographs and drawings. Grades 5 and up.

———. *Till Victory Is Won: Black Soldiers in the Civil War.* New York: Lodestar, 1994.
This book tells of the contributions of black Americans and their bravery and dedication to the country. Photographs, excerpts from letters, and personal accounts reveal how black soldiers influenced the outcome of the Civil War. Grades 5 and up.

Monjo, F. N. *The Drinking Gourd.* New York: Harper & Row, 1970.
This is the suspenseful story of a young boy who helps a slave family escape to Canada and to freedom. PreK-3.

Moore, Kay. *If You Lived at the Time of the Civil War.* New York: Scholastic, 1994.
In a question-and-answer format, Moore explains what life was like during the Civil War. Grades 2-5.

Murphy, Jim. *The Long Road to Gettysburg.* New York: Clarion Books, 1992.
This book focuses on two young men—John Dooley, a Confederate soldier, and Thomas Galway, a Union soldier—who were present at one of the war's bloodiest and most famous battles. Included are maps, photographs, and the text of Abraham Lincoln's "Gettysburg Address." Grades 4-7.

Nixon, Joan Lowery. *A Dangerous Promise.* New York: Bantam Books, 1994.
After being taken in by Captain Taylor and his wife in Kansas, twelve-year-old Mike Kelly and his friend Todd Blakely join the Union army as musicians and see the horrors of the war in Missouri. Grades 4-7.

Paulsen, Gary. *Nightjohn.* New York: Delacorte, 1993.
Twelve-year-old Sarny's brutal life as a slave becomes even more dangerous when a newly arrived slave offers to teach her how to read. Grades 6-9.

Porter, Connie. *Addy Learns a Lesson: A School Story.* Middleton, WI: Pleasant, 1993.
Addy, a young slave in the South, escapes with her mother to Philadelphia through the Underground Railroad. Grades 3-5.

———. *Happy Birthday, Addy! A Springtime Story*. Middleton, WI: Pleasant, 1994.

Addy finds inspiration from a new friend while trying to shape a new life of freedom in Philadelphia after having been a slave. Grades 3-5.

———. *Meet Addy: An American Girl*. Middleton, WI: Pleasant, 1993.

Nine-year-old Addy Walker escapes from a cruel life of slavery to freedom during the Civil War. Grades 3-5.

Rappaport, Doreen. *Escape from Slavery: Five Journeys to Freedom*. New York: HarperCollins, 1991.

The author's narratives recount the traumatic experiences of five slaves who managed to escape to freedom before the Civil War. Grades 3-6.

Ray, Delia. *Behind the Blue and Gray: The Soldier's Life in the Civil War*. New York: Lodestar, 1991.

This is a sequel to *A Nation Torn: The Story of How the Civil War Began*. The author reveals how ordinary Union and Confederate soldiers experienced the Civil War. She describes how soldiers felt in battle and looks inside the makeshift hospitals and disease-ridden prison camps. She also tells of the diversity of recruits from elderly soldiers to all-black Northern regiments. Grades 4 and up.

———. *A Nation Torn: The Story of How the Civil War Began*. New York: Lodestar, 1990.

This is the story of the events leading to the war that tore apart the nation. It is well researched, with letters, diaries, and eyewitness accounts, as well as many vintage photographs. Grades 5 and up.

Reit, Seymour. *Behind Rebel Lines: The Incredible Story of Emma Edmonds, Civil War Spy*. San Diego, CA: Harcourt Brace Jovanovich, 1988.

This book tells the story of Emma Edmonds, who disguised herself as a man and spent two years as a battlefront nurse and a spy for the Union Army. Grades 5-6.

Rinaldi, Ann. *In My Father's House*. New York: Scholastic, 1993.

This story, based on actual events, centers on a family's divided loyalties during the Civil War. Grades 5-7.

———. *The Last Silk Dress*. New York: Holiday House, 1988.

During the Civil War, Susan finds a way to help the Confederate Army and uncovers a series of mysterious family secrets. Grades 7-10.

Ringgold, Faith. *Aunt Harriet's Underground Railroad in the Sky*. New York: Crown, 1993.

Cassie Lightfoot imagines herself back in the time of the Underground Railroad. While flying, she meets Harriet Tubman, who tells her about the hardships of slavery. Cassie's journey re-creates what it was like for a slave to travel on the Underground Railroad, moving from one helping hand to another until reaching freedom in Canada. Grades 1-5.

Russell, Sharman Apt. *Frederick Douglass*. New York: Chelsea House, 1988.

This is a thorough biography of Frederick Douglass, the abolitionist editor. Grades 5 and up.

Shore, Laura Jan. *The Sacred Moon Tree: Being the True Account of the Trials and Adventures of Phoebe Sands in the Great War Between the States, 1861–1865*. New York: Bradbury Press, 1986.

A twelve-year-old girl disguised as a boy travels behind enemy lines with a friend to try to rescue her brother from a Confederate prison. Grades 5-8.

Shura, Mary Francis. *Gentle Annie: The True Story of a Civil War Nurse*. New York: Scholastic, 1991.

This is a biography of Anna Blair Etheridge, a nurse during the Civil War, from childhood through her four years of service with the Army of the Potomac. Grades 4-7.

Stepto, Michele, ed. *Our Song, Our Toil: The Story of American Slavery as Told by Slaves*. Brookfield, CT: Millbrook Press, 1994.

This book recounts the story of American slavery from African captivity to emancipation, through excerpts from slave autobiographies and slavery documents. Grades 4 and up.

Sterling, Dorothy. *Freedom Train: The Story of Harriet Tubman*. New York: Scholastic, 1954.

This is a simple, easy-to-read biography with information about the Underground Railroad. Grades 3-6.

Stevens, Bryna. *Frank Thompson: Her Civil War Story*. New York: Macmillan, 1992.

This is the true story of Emma Edmonds, a Canadian woman who disguised herself as a man, joined the Union army, and served as a nurse and a spy during the Civil War. Grades 5 and up.

Stolz, Mary. *Cezanne Pinto: A Memoir*. New York: Alfred A. Knopf, 1994.

This is a narrative of the life of a slave who becomes a free man. According to a review in *Booklist*, this novel "combines fast-paced adventure with a compelling sense of history." Grades 6 and up.

Trump, Fred. *Lincoln's Little Girl*. Honesdale, PA: Boyds Mills, 1977.

This is a biography of Grace Bedell, who as a young girl wrote to Abraham Lincoln suggesting he grow whiskers. The book is documented by diaries, letters, and newspaper accounts. Grades 5-8.

Weiner, Eric. *Facts America: The Civil War*. New York: Smithmark, 1992.

This nonfiction book discusses the causes, major events, and the aftermath of the Civil War. The inviting format and excellent photographs make this an excellent addition to your Civil War library. Grades 5 and up.

Whittier, John Greenleaf. *Barbara Frietchie.* Green-willow Books, 1992.

This is an authentically illustrated version of Whittier's famous Civil War poem about the heroic deed of a staunchly patriotic ninety-year-old woman. Grades 2-5.

Winter, Jeanette. *Follow the Drinking Gourd.* New York: Alfred A. Knopf, 1988.

An old white sailor gives directions to the Underground Railroad in a song he teaches to the slaves. Grades 2-6.

Wisler, G. Clifton. *Mr. Lincoln's Drummer.* New York: Lodestar, 1995.

This book is based on the true story of an eleven-year-old Union drummer boy and his courage and bravery on the battlefield. This young soldier was awarded the Congressional Medal of Honor by Abraham Lincoln after his historic deeds came to the president's attention. Grades 6 and up.

——. *Red Cap.* New York: Lodestar, 1991.

During the Civil War, thirteen-year-old Ransom J. Powell runs away to become a drummer boy in the Union Army. Grades 5-8.

Wright, Courtni C. *Journey to Freedom: A Story of the Underground Railroad.* New York: Holiday House, 1994.

Joshua and his family are runaway slaves from a tobacco plantation in Kentucky. They follow the Underground Railroad to freedom. Grades 2-4.

Theme Resources

Commercial Resources

Albert, Toni. *Novel Ties: Charley Skedaddle.* New Hyde Park, NY: Learning Links, 1992.

This resource contains pre-reading and post-reading activities, vocabulary skills, comprehension questions, and writing activities in a chapter-by-chapter format for *Charley Skedaddle.* Use with students in grades 6-9.

Carratello, John, and Patty Carratello. *Thematic Unit: Civil War.* Huntington, Beach, CA: Teacher Created Materials, 1991.

This resource provides many theme-based activities for all areas of the curriculum, including math, science, language arts, and social studies. For use with students in grades 5 and up.

Cassidy, Janet. *The Civil War: Literature Units, Projects, and Activities.* New York: Scholastic, 1991.

This resource includes grades 4-8 literature activities for *Across Five Aprils, Lincoln: A Photobiography, The Boys' War, Behind Rebel Lines, Undying Glory,* and *Bull Run.*

Cobblestone: The History Magazine for Young People. Peterborough, NH: Cobblestone.

The focus of the April 1981 issue for students in grades 4 and up is "Highlight of the Civil War 1861–1865." Articles include "Brady of Broadway: First Press Photographer" and "First Prisoner of the Civil War."

The subject of the May 1987 issue for students in grades 4 and up is the aftermath of the Civil War and Reconstruction. Articles include "Reconstruction: Putting the Union Back Together" and "The Civil War and Reconstruction."

The topic of the July 1988 issue for students in grades 4 and up is the Battle of Gettysburg. Articles include "Gettysburg from Farmland to Battlefield" and "News from the Battlefield."

"Frederick Douglass: Fighter for Freedom" is the topic of February 1989 issue for students in grades 4 and up. Articles include "The Underground Railroad: The Beginning of Douglass's Journey" and "Frederick Douglass, Abolitionist Writer."

The subject of the September 1993 issue for students in grades 4 and up is Robert E. Lee. Articles include "Soldier of Honor: Lee's Early Military Career" and "The Civil War Years."

The subject of the May 1994 issue for students in grades 4 and up is Abraham Lincoln. Articles include "Slavery Debated: A Play" and "The Lincoln Assassination."

Ulysses S. Grant is the subject of the October 1995 issue for students in grades 4 and up. Articles include "At the Battle of Shiloh" and "What Kind of General Was He?"

The Civil War News. Arlington, VA: Cuter and Locke.

For a free sample of a 56-page monthly paper with news of preservations, reenactments, national parks, collector shows, and a calendar of Civil War events, call 1-800-222-1861. Use with students in grades 7 and up.

Copycat Magazine. Racine, WI: Copycat Press.

The January-February 1994 issue contains several ideas for use with the book *Aunt Harriet's Underground Railroad in the Sky.* For use with students in grades 2-4.

Davis, Ossie. *Escape to Freedom: A Play About Young Frederick Douglass.* New York: Viking, 1978.

This play brings to life the young Frederick Douglass. The 85-page drama is written for six students, grades 4-9, to perform. It contains stage directions and a short bibliography.

Hine, William C., compiler. *Jackdaw: Slavery in the United States.* Amawalk, NY: Jackdaw Publications, 1975.

This is a portfolio of primary source material featuring nine reproductions of historical documents. They include a slave sale poster from 1835, an 1838 bill of sale for a slave, a letter from a slave in 1838 with a transcript, and the Emancipation Proclamation, 1863, with a transcript. Comprehensive notes on the documents, along with a reading list and critical thinking questions, are also included. For use with students in grades 5 and up.

Inquiring into the Theme of Civil War Battles. Logan, IA: Perfection Learning.

This resource provides activities for *Thunder at Gettysburg*, background information for the theme, and much more. Grades 6-8.

Johnson, David, compiler. *Jackdaw: The Civil War.* Amawalk, NY: Jackdaw Publications, 1994.

This is a portfolio of primary source material featuring nine reproductions of historical documents. They include President Lincoln's Emancipation Proclamation, January 1st, 1863, which freed slaves in rebel areas; a message from Confederate General Howell Cobb to Governor Brown of Georgia after Sherman's men set fire to Atlanta; and the Civil War in photographs. Comprehensive notes on the documents along with a reading list and critical thinking questions are also included. Use with students in grades 5 and up.

Kennedy, Frances H., ed. *The Civil War Battlefield Guide.* Boston: Houghton Mifflin, 1990.

This resource brings the history of the Civil War to life in words, maps, and pictures. Sixty-five battles and campaigns are described by distinguished historians. For use with students in grades 5 and up.

Kids Discover: Lincoln. New York: Kids Discover.

The focus of the December 1995 issue is Abraham Lincoln. Articles include "The Path to the White House," "Slavery Splits the Nation," and "Lincoln Through the Ages." Use with students in grades 4 and up.

Kleinman, Estelle. *Novel Ties: Freedom Crossing.* New Hyde Park, NY: Learning Links, 1994.

This resource contains pre-reading and post-reading activities, vocabulary skills, comprehension questions, and writing activities in a chapter-by-chapter format for *Freedom Crossing.* For use with students in grades 4-7.

Laughlin, Mildred Knight, Peggy Tubbs Black, and Margery Kirby Loberg. *Social Studies Readers Theatre for Children.* Englewood, CO: Teacher Ideas Press, 1991.

The authors include suggested scripts for *Charley Skedaddle; Turn Homeward, Hanalee; Across Five Aprils; The Drinking Gourd; Nettie's Trip South;* among others, that students in grades 3-8 can perform.

Medland, Mary. *Novel Ties: The Red Badge of Courage.* New Hyde Park, NY: Learning Links, 1990.

This resource contains pre-reading and post-reading activities, vocabulary skills, comprehension questions, and writing activities in a chapter-by-chapter format for *The Red Badge of Courage.* Use with students in grades 5 and up.

Reeves, Barbara. *Historical Ties: The Civil War.* New Hyde Park, NY: Learning Links, 1991.

This guide includes activities for *Across Five Aprils, Charley Skedaddle, The Perilous Road,* and *Rifles for Watie.* For use with students in grades 5 and up.

Witt, Sandra, and Janice Petrovich. *Novel Ties: Across Five Aprils.* New Hyde Park, NY: Learning Links, 1990.

This resource contains pre-reading and post-reading activities, vocabulary skills, comprehension questions, and writing activities in a chapter-by-chapter format for *Across Five Aprils.* Use with students in grades 6-9.

Inquiring into the Theme of Civil War Battles: Based on Patricia Lee Gauch's Thunder at Gettysburg. Logan, IA: Perfection Learning, 1994.

This guide offers many activities and suggestions for using trade books with students in grades 6-8 to expand on the theme.

Computer Resources

American Heritage: The Civil War. [CD-ROM]. New York: Bryon Press, 1995.

This multimedia CD-ROM is based on *The American Heritage Pictorial History of the Civil War* by Bruce Catton. It includes video footage of reenactments of major Civil War battles with animated maps of the battles. Audio clips, vintage photographs, historical documents, and a time line are also included.

The Civil War: Two Views. [CD-ROM]. Chicago: Clearvue, 1994.

This CD-ROM presents the issue from both sides of the Civil War. Students will be able evaluate political, economical, social, regional, and moral considerations that led to the war.

Videos

Across Five Aprils. Los Angeles: World Entertainment, 1990. (82 minutes)

This video is based on the Newbery Award–winning book *Across Five Aprils* by Irene Hunt.

America: A Firebell in the Night. New York: British Broadcasting/Time-Life Video, 1973. (52 minutes)

This episode, for grades 7 and up, investigates the roots of conflicts that remain embedded in American society today and explores the causes and miseries of the Civil War.

The Black Americans of Achievement Video Collection: Harriet Tubman. Bala Cynwyd, PA: Schlessinger Video Productions, 1992. (30 minutes)
This is a biographical video of Harriet Tubman, an antislavery activist.

The Black Americans of Achievement Video Collection: Sojourner Truth. Bala Cynwyd, PA: Schlessinger Video Productions, 1992. (30 minutes)
This is a biographical video of Sojourner Truth, an antislavery activist.

Frederick Douglass: An American Hero Whose Vision Transcended Race, Gender and Time. Atlanta, GA: Turner Home Entertainment, 1994. (30 minutes)
This is a biographical video of Frederick Douglass, an abolitionist.

Gettysburg. Atlanta, GA: Turner Pictures, 1993. (254 minutes)
This film, rated PG and best suited for students in grades 7 and up, features authentic Civil War battle scenes. It depicts the events, battles, and personal struggles of valor on both sides of the war.

Great Events and People in New York State History: New York State in the Civil War. Burlington, VT: Young People's Historical Society, 1987. (10 minutes)
This video was originally a filmstrip, produced in 1984. It was transferred to video in 1987. It illustrates New York state before the Civil War, conditions and events that led to the war, slavery and the Underground Railroad, and the effect of the Civil War on New York state. People highlighted include: Henry Ward Beecher, Gerrit Smith, Arthur Tappan, Sojourner Truth, Harriet Tubman, Lewis Tappan, and Frederick Douglass.

The House of Dies Drear. Chicago: Public Media Video, 1984. (116 minutes)
This video is based on the book by Virginia Hamilton.

The Red Badge of Courage. Chicago: Questar Video, 1988. (60 minutes)
This is a screen translation of the novel by Stephen Crane.

Songs of the Civil War. New York: Sony Music Videos, 1991. (60 minutes)
This documentary, for students in grades 5-8, captures the passion and turbulence of America's most critical hour through songs. Twenty-five popular songs of the time are featured, each introduced with a narrative. Featuring Hoyt Axton, Judy Collins, Richie Havens, and Waylon Jennings.

Touring Civil War Battlefields. Chicago: Questar Video, 1988. (60 minutes)
This film takes you to the actual Civil War battlefields to view reenactments of battles fought at Manassas, Antietam, Fredericksburg, and Gettysburg.

Trumpet Video Visits: Gary Paulsen. Holmes, PA: Trumpet Club, 1993. (24 minutes)
Gary Paulsen tells about the exciting adventures he has had.

United States History Video Collection: Causes of the Civil War. Bala Cynwyd, PA: Schlessinger Video Productions, 1996. (35 minutes)
The industrial North, the agricultural South and the Cotton Belt, plantation slavery, black resistance to slavery, free blacks and the abolition movement, the Underground Railroad, Abraham Lincoln, and the secession of the Southern States are presented.

End-of-Unit Celebration

A Soldier's Daily Camp Ration

Capture the "flavor" of the Civil War days by sharing this list of soldier's rations with your class, then prepare the recipes that follow.

12 ounces of pork or bacon or 20 ounces of fresh beef
22 ounces soft bread or flour or 16 ounces hard bread or 20 ounces corn meal

With every hundred rations, there should be:

1 peck beans or peas
10 pounds of rice or hominy
10 pounds of green coffee or 8 pounds
   of roasted and ground coffee or
     1½ pounds of tea
20 ounces of candles

4 pounds of soap
2 quarts of salt
4 quarts of vinegar
4 ounces pepper
½ bushel potatoes
1 quart molasses

Marching Ration

1 pound hard bread	Sugar
¾ pound salt pork or 1¼ pound	Coffee
fresh meat	Salt

Recipes

Hardtack (a staple of the Civil War soldier)

INGREDIENTS

3 cups flour   1 cup water

2 teaspoons salt

PROCEDURE

1. In a large bowl, mix flour and salt.

2. Add water and stir or work with hands to blend.

3. Knead dough, adding more flour if mixture becomes sticky. Turn out onto a floured board.

4. Roll the dough into a rectangle ½-inch thick.

5. Using a sharp knife, cut the dough into 3-inch squares.

6. Using a large, clean nail, poke 16 holes through each square.

7. Bake at 375 degrees for 25 minutes or until brown.

8. Store in an airtight container.

    Makes 12.

Source: Barchers, Suzanne I., and Patricia C. Marden. *Cooking Up U.S. History: Recipes and Research to Share with Children.* Englewood, CO: Teacher Ideas Press, 1991.

Appleade

INGREDIENTS

2 large apples   Sugar to taste

1 quart water

PROCEDURE

1. Core and cut apples into slices. Do not peel. Place in a pan.

2. Boil the water.

3. Pour boiling water over apple slices.

4. Let sit for 30 minutes.

5. Strain well.

6. Sweeten to taste.

7. Chill.

    Serves 6.

Source: Barchers, Suzanne I., and Patricia C. Marden. *Cooking Up U.S. History: Recipes and Research to Share with Children.* Englewood, CO: Teacher Ideas Press, 1991.

Other Activities

1. Involve your school in your study of the Civil War by having students relay interesting facts they have learned or present book reviews or book talks during the announcements.

2. Hold a Civil War encampment in your classroom for a day. Have students dress in clothing of the time period. If possible, invite local Civil War enthusiasts to attend, dressed in Confederate and Union uniforms. Make hardtack and appleade ahead of time for the event.

3. Divide your class into two groups for a debate about slavery. The groups should meet before the debate to decide what they will say to defend their positions. One group will be Northerners who feel strongly that slavery is wrong. The other group will be Southerners who feel that there is a need for slavery and that Northerners should mind their own business.

4. If your school is near a Civil War battlefield, arrange a field trip to the site. If a field trip is not possible, allow students to visit the site themselves for extra credit and to bring back information for the class.

5. Arrange to have the town or city historian, or a local Civil War buff, visit your class to share what he or she has learned about this period of United States history.

6. Send a letter to your students' parents about your study of the Civil War. Invite them to share any family stories about the war or slavery with your class.

7. Have students research their family tree to find out who was living at that time and find out anything they can about them.

8. Create a "Nation Torn Apart by War" bulletin board (see fig. 4.1, p. 98).

9. Learn about the infirmities that prevented certain individuals from going to war. Reasons for medical exemption from military service in the Civil War were numerous. Documents from Marion, in the county of Wayne in New York state in 1864, noted the following reasons:

fermoral hernia	bronchial affliction
dislocated right knee	chronic disease of the heart
varicose veins	ulcerated leg
blind in left eye	disease of the lungs
broken leg	asthma
cataract of right eye	fever sore on right lower leg
right thigh injury from fall off horse	has but three teeth in upper jaw
larengitis (sic) and rheumatism—left some of the time quite helpless	

See figure 4.2 (p. 99) for an actual exemption from service document.

10. Have students work individually or in groups to solve the "Famous Women of the Civil War" crossword puzzle (see fig. 4.3, p. 100).

Fig. 4.1. **Nation torn apart by war bulletin board.**

MATERIALS

>Blue, gray, white, and red construction paper
>
>Small Union flag
>
>Small Confederate flat

PROCEDURE

1. Cover the entire bulletin board with red construction paper.

2. On white construction paper, list the causes of the Civil War as your students study them. Place this list under the title on your bulletin board.

3. Use blue construction paper (2 sheets) for listing facts about the Union as your students learn them. The blue paper is used to represent the Union's color.

4. Use gray construction paper (2 sheets) to list facts about the Confederacy as your students learn them. The gray paper is used to represent the Confederacy's color.

5. Leave space on each side of the bulletin board for student-prepared reports about famous people of the Civil War.

6. Facts to compare: uniforms, position on slavery, economics, government, major victories, casualties.

FAMOUS PEOPLE	A NATION TORN APART BY WAR	FAMOUS PEOPLE
	Causes of the Civil War	
	Union Facts **Confederate Facts**	

Fig. 4.2. **Exemption from service document.**

I Franklin S. Dean of the town of
Marion Wayne County N.Y. claim exemption from Military Duty in the
National Guard. I assign the following reasons for such exemption.

When a mere child the elbow of
my left arm was put out of joint
& never properly set, or set at all,
causing a permanent bad joint which
as I grow older is continually growing worse,
& a stiffening of the joint: it prevents me
at times from performing the ordinary business
on a farm.
I also have a bad knee joint, which
at times slips out of joint causing great
pain & entirely disabling me.

Franklin S. Dean

Wayne County: SS.

Franklin S. Dean of
the town of Marion in said County being
duly sworn deposes & says that the facts
set forth in the above statement by him
made are in all respects true.
Subscribed & affirmed to this
12th day of August 1864 before me.
Henry R. Taber Justice of the Peace

Surgeon's Certificate of Exemption.

This is to Certify, That I have Examined........................
of the Town of .... and find that he is suffering from

and therefore totally unfit for Military Duty.

Examining Surgeon for Wayne County.

1862

From *U.S. History Through Children's Literature.* © 1997. Teacher Ideas Press. (800) 237-6124.

Fig. 4.3. **Famous women of the Civil War.**

Across

5. An abolitionist known for her speech "And aren't I a woman?"

6. First woman to earn a medical degree; started the Women's Central Association of Relief (WCAR).

7. Spied for the Union army from a mansion in Richmond, Virginia.

8. Volunteer nurse at the Union Hotel Hospital; author of *Little Women*.

10. Disguised herself as Franklin Thompson; became a Union nurse and a spy.

Down

1. A wealthy widow who spied for the South in Washington, D.C.

2. Author of *Uncle Tom's Cabin*.

3. Known as "Moses"; made nineteen trips on the Underground Railroad.

4. Posed as Harry Buford, recruited own battalion for the Confederacy.

6. Founder of the American Red Cross.

9. Confederate spy from Virginia who was jailed twice for spying.

11. The Union Army's Superintendent of Women Nurses.

WORD LIST

ALCOTT	DIX	TRUTH
BARTON	EDMONDS	TUBMAN
BLACKWELL	GREENHOW	VANLEW
BOYD	STOWE	VELAZQUEZ

ANSWERS: Famous Women of the Civil War

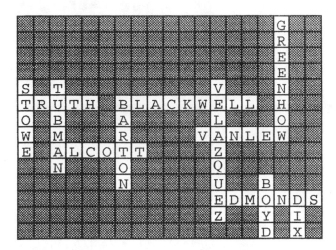

Civil War Research Project

Divide your class into groups of three to five students. Together, each group should research one of the following topics, write a report on it, and prepare a presentation for the class.

Boys' Roles in the Civil War   Slavery

Causes of the Civil War   The Underground Railroad

Reconstruction   Women's Roles in the Civil War

These topics could be narrowed down further to specific women, military figures, or specific battles of the war. The research could be done in social studies class with the aid of your school librarian. The writing of the paper could be done in English class.

Chapter 5

Pioneer Life and Westward Expansion

Introduction

Americans began moving westward before the American Revolution. In 1862, the passing of the Homestead Act spurred on this westward movement even more. This law gave 160 acres of land free to anyone who settled on it for five years and improved the land by building a house and planting crops.

Life on the prairie was very difficult at times. The pioneers traded conveniences for new challenges when they went West. Included in this chapter are some excellent trade books that can be used to help students better understand life on the prairie.

Read the following selection to your class and discuss to begin your study of pioneer life and westward expansion:

Pioneers

Clothed in buckskin, clothed in homespun,
Clothed in strength and courage, too.
They pressed westward ever westward,
Where the land was wild and new.
Pioneers!

Wearing coonskin, Wearing gingham,
Wearing patience mile on mile,
They crossed rivers, prairies, mountains,
Pressing westward all the while.
Pioneers!

Toting rifles, toting kettles,
Toting faith and hardihood,
They left comfort far behind them
For a future they thought good.
Pioneers!

They took little of the riches
That a wealthy man can boast,
But their courage, patience, vision,
Were the coins that matter most.
Pioneers!

Aileen Fisher and Olive Rabe, 1956

Whole Group Reading

Brink, Carol Ryrie. *Caddie Woodlawn*. New York: Macmillan, 1935.
This is a collection of adventures that eleven-year-old Caddie has from the fall of 1864 to the fall of 1865 in western Wisconsin. Caddie's father convinces her mother to allow her to grow up a tomboy because she had been a frail child. As a result, Caddie and her brothers have many exciting adventures. The book is based on the author's grandmother's childhood, and it emphasizes the delights of being an American pioneer. Winner of the 1936 Newbery Medal. *Caddie Woodlawn* was chosen to read with the whole class because it is based on real-life experiences and gives students a real feeling for what life was like for the pioneers. Grades 5 and up.

102

Author Information

Carol Ryrie Brink was born December 28, 1895 in Moscow, Idaho. She was given the family name of Caroline, which had been shortened to Kitty, Carrie, and Caddie in other generations. Because her birthday came near Christmas, her mother decided to call her Carol. By the time she was eight years old she had lost both of her parents, so she was sent to live with her grandmother and aunt. Her grandmother, Caddie Woodhouse, told fine stories, and it is on these stories that *Caddie Woodlawn* is based. When her children were young, Brink began to write stories for them, stories that grew and eventually turned into books. All of her writing stems from personal experience. Brink wrote a total of twenty-seven books for both children and adults. She died in 1981 at the age of eighty-five.

Activities

1. Have students draw pictures of Caddie, Tom, and Warren, using the descriptions on page 2.

2. Have students make small birch bark canoes according to the description on pages 9 and 10.

3. Have students make a comparison chart of Caddie or Tom and themselves. They should compare clothing, schooling, chores, food gathering, food preparation, and recreational activities.

4. Hold a spelling bee (or "spelldown" as Caddie called it) with your class. You could use recent spelling words, or vocabulary from the novel.

5. On a map of the United States, have students locate the following:
   Boston, MA   Menomonie, WI
   Chippewa River   Mississippi River
   Idaho   St. Louis, MS
   Menomonie River

6. Hold a recitation as discussed on pages 180 and 181. Each student should choose a short poem to memorize and then recite it to the class.

7. Have students list advantages and disadvantages of the Woodlawns going to England.

8. Encourage students who would like to read more about Caddie and the other Woodlawn children to read *Magical Melons*, also written by Carol Ryrie Brink. It is a sequel to *Caddie Woodlawn*.

Discussion

Give the class the following instruction: As we read this book, we will be discussing the following questions. Write down your ideas about the questions and add to them as needed.

1. Describe Caddie Woodlawn. Do you know anyone who is like her today?

2. What is Caddie's seven-year-old sister Hetty like?

3. Why does Caddie wish she could wear boys' clothes?

4. Why are Indians so anxious to look at the Woodlawns?

5. What is Caddie's relationship with Indian John?

6. Why did Mr. Woodlawn convince Caddie's mother to let Caddie run wild with the boys?

7. Why doesn't Mr. Tanner, the circuit rider, trust the Indians?

8. What does Mr. Tanner do?

9. How does Mr. Woodlawn feel about the Civil War and slavery?

10. How does Caddie compare Indians to pigeons?

11. Describe Uncle Edmund.

12. Why does Uncle Edmund want to take Nero home with him?

13. Why wasn't Mrs. Woodlawn able to sell her turkeys?

14. Compare the Woodlawns' clothing to your own.

15. What does Caddie like most about school?

16. Why did Mrs. Woodlawn say to Caddie, "You'll be the death of me if not yourself!"?

17. How did Caddie feel after fixing Mr. Tanner's clock?

18. Discuss the disowning of Mr. Woodlawn's father by his grandfather.

19. How does Caddie's father feel about not being the nobleman he was entitled to be?

20. Why does Caddie wish she were a boy?

21. How did Caddie react to the news that Nero was lost?

22. What news did Melvin Kent bring to the Woodlawns?

23. Why were the Woodlawns' neighbors so afraid of Indians?

24. What did Melvin Kent and the other men plan to do?

25. What did Caddie do to save Indian John and his people? If you were Caddie, what would you have done?

26. What did Indian John trust Caddie with before he went away?

27. How did Caddie spend her silver dollar? What did she receive from it?

28. Describe the recitation that Miss Parker held at school.

29. Why did the arrival of The Little Steamer bring such excitement? What news did it bring?

30. What news did Mr. Tanner bring when he returned?

31. How did Indian John's dog save Caddie and the others at the schoolhouse?

32. Why did Miss Parker call Obediah a hero?

33. What do you think Tom has planned for Annabelle?

34. How did Caddie feel about her punishment for playing tricks on Annabelle?

35. Discuss your feelings about Caddie's father's explanation of the importance of women.

36. What decision do you think Mr. Woodlawn should make about whether or not to become the next Lord Woodlawn?

37. How does Caddie feel about going to England?

38. Whose return to the Woodlawn home made everyone so happy?

39. Discuss what Caddie meant when she said, "I'm the same girl and yet not the same." How has she changed?

Vocabulary

pioneer (p1)
one of the first explorers, settlers, or colonists of a new country or region

massacre (p2)
a brutal killing of a large number of people or animals

intrusion (p3)
the act of intruding; to come in without being invited or wanted

irresolute (p3)
not firm in acting or making up one's mind

cove (p6)
a small, sheltered bay or inlet in a shoreline

crude (p6)
lacking refinement or good taste

savage (p7)
a person living in a wild or primitive condition

pliable (p9)
easily bent, twisted, or molded

buckskin (p9)
a soft, strong, grayish yellow leather made from skins of deer or sheep

squaw (p10)
an American Indian woman or wife

venison (p10)
deer meat

pitch (p10)
the sticky sap of certain pines

dismay (p12)
a feeling of alarm, uneasiness, and confusion

sedate (p13)
calm and steady in manner

lull (p13)
to quiet or put to sleep by soothing sounds or motions

fervor (p14)
very strong emotion or enthusiasm

brooch (p14)
an ornamental pin worn near the neck of a garment

escapade (p16)
a reckless or mischievous act or prank

piously (p16)
religiously

incite (p17)
to urge into action

victuals (p17)
food

flintlock (p18)
a gunlock in which a piece of flint is struck against steel to light the gunpowder

enthralled (p18)
fascinated

parish (p19)
in certain religious groups, a district, having its own church and clergy

irksome (p21)
tiresome; tedious

unfathomable (p21)
impossible to understand

Sabbath (p23)
a day of the week set aside for rest and worship

devoutly (p24)
religiously

aristocrat (p25)
a member of an aristocracy; a nobleman or noblewoman

reproach (p38)
to blame for some wrong

infamy (p45)
a notoriously bad reputation; public disgrace

haughty (p46)
satisfied with oneself and scornful of others; arrogant

silhouette (p47)
the outline of a person or object against a light or a light background

homespun (p49)
cloth made of homespun yarn or a strong, loose fabric

comrade (p53)
a close companion or friend

quagmire (p54)
an area of deep, soft mud

marshes (p54)
areas of low, wet land; swamp

hummock (p54)
a low mound

loon (p54)
a web-footed diving bird resembling a duck, but with a pointed bill and a weird, laughing cry

enterprise (p56)
a project, undertaking, or venture requiring effort, ability, or daring

dauntless (p58)
fearless; brave; daring

vigor (p64)
active strength or force of mind or body; healthy energy

contemptuously (p67)
scornfully

skeptical (p86)
not believing readily; inclined to question or doubt

moat (p89)
a ditch, usually full of water, around a castle, fortress, or other structure, used as a defense against attackers

forsake (p91)
to leave completely; to desert; to give up

vice (p94)
an evil or immoral habit

virtue (p94)
right living; morality; goodness

pensive (p98)
quietly and seriously thoughtful, often with a touch of sadness

indolent (p106)
habitually lazy

eclipse (p121)
a complete or partial hiding of the sun (solar eclipse) as the moon passes between the sun and an observer on the earth

impassive (p141)
not affected by emotion; showing no feeling

portage (p145)
the carrying of boats and goods overland between two bodies of water

arbutus (p178)
a trailing evergreen plant that bears clusters of fragrant pink or white flowers in very early spring

sledge (p179)
a vehicle mounted on low runners, used for carrying people or loads over snow and ice

consternation (p185)
>great fear or dismay that makes one feel helpless

industrious (p189)
>hardworking and diligent

keel boat (p202)
>a shallow freight boat with no sails, propelled by poles or oars

abolitionist (p202)
>an individual who wanted to end slavery in the United States

languid (p204)
>lacking energy or spirit

wistful (p208)
>wishful; longing

stealthy (p214)
>done in a secret or underhanded way

vicissitude (p216)
>any sudden, unexpected change, whether good or bad, that occurs during a person's life or career

quaint (p224)
>pleasantly odd or old-fashioned

pandemonium (p234)
>great disorder and uproar

hoyden (p240)
>a bold, boisterous girl; a tomboy

sacred (p252)
>of or having to do with, or intended for, religion or religious use

porridge (p261)
>a soft food made by boiling oatmeal or some other grain in water, milk, or other liquid

Small Group Reading

📖 Conrad, Pam. *Prairie Songs*. New York: Harper & Row, 1985.

This is a story about life on the Nebraska prairie in the mid-1800s. The vastness and loneliness is seen through the eyes of Louisa, who loves the beautiful, quiet space it offers. The harshness of daily life is experienced through Emmeline, the doctor's wife who has recently moved from the East to the prairie. Grades 6-8.

Author Information

Pam Conrad was born June 18, 1947 in New York, New York. She began writing in February of 1957 when she became bedridden with the chicken pox. Her mother gave her paper to draw on, but she began writing poetry instead. For many years—during college, early in her marriage, and in early motherhood—she did not write. She returned to college and to writing when her youngest daughter was three years old. She wrote many books and has received many awards for her writing.

Pam Conrad died in 1996.

Activities

1. On a map of the United States, have students locate the following:

   Central City, NE
   Grand Island, NE
   Howard County, NE
   Kansas City, MS
   Philadelphia, PA

2. To learn more about Nebraska pioneers and Solomon Butcher, have students read *Prairie Visions: The Life and Times of Solomon Butcher*, also by Pam Conrad. This could be an extra-credit activity.

3. Have students write diary entries as if they were Mrs. Berryman. They should include her feelings about life on the prairie. Students can then share these entries with the rest of the class.

4. Have students gather sod to make a soddy based on Louisa's description. Have them explain to the rest of the class what a soddy is and how it is made.

Discussion

Give the small group the following instruction: As your group reads this book, discuss the following questions.

1. Who are Louisa and Lester waiting for?

2. What was it about Emmeline Berryman that Louisa said will stay in her memory for all eternity?

3. Why were the people of Howard County so glad to have Dr. Berryman and his wife move there?

4. How was their new home different than Mrs. Berryman expected?

5. What made Mrs. Whitfield think that the doctor and his wife would leave?

6. How did J.T. describe poetry to Louisa?

7. Why did Louisa and Lester collect cow chips?

8. What was the plan that Louisa's mother had?

9. What was Solomon Butcher doing on his travels across the prairie?

10. Why did the cottonwood trees mean so much to Louisa's mother?

11. Do you think Mrs. Berryman will survive in Nebraska?

12. Why do you think Paulie threatened his mother with the rifle?

13. What happened to the Berrymans' baby?

14. How has Mrs. Berryman changed since she first came to Nebraska?

15. What did the Indians do when they came to Louisa's sod house?

16. What finally happened to Mrs. Berryman?

17. How did Louisa feel when she saw the photoprint of her family at the Independence Day celebration?

Vocabulary

prairie (p1)
a large tract or area of more or less level, grassy land having few or no trees, especially the broad, grassy plain of central North America

prairie dog (p2)
a small rodent of the plains of North America that lives in large communities and is very destructive to vegetation

gunnysack (p7)
a sack made from a coarse, heavy material such as burlap

sod (p7)
the top layer of the earth, especially when covered with grass

parasol (p8)
a small, light umbrella carried to protect oneself from the sun

frivolous (p20)
not important or worthwhile

gingham (p27)
a cotton fabric woven in solid colors, stripes, checks, or plaids

intricate (p29)
complicated or involved

coverlet (p29)
a bedspread

savage (p33)
wild, untamed, and often fierce

expedition (p43)
a journey made for a definite purpose

vast (p53)
of very large size; enormous; huge

papoose (p53)
a North American Indian baby or small child

absurd (p53)
unreasonable; ridiculous

brooch (p59)
an ornamental pin, worn near the neck

awry (p83)
not right

phantom (p86)
ghostlike

mangy (p91)
in animals characterized by having mange, a skin disease marked by itching and loss of hair

lament (p104)
to feel or to express great sorrow

treacherous (p121)
dangerous

recitation (p123)
  the reciting of a memorized piece before an
  audience
garment (p125)
  an article of clothing
torrent (p125)
  a stream of water flowing with great speed and
  violence
hodgepodge (p141)
  a confused mixture

larder (p142)
  a place where food is stored; a pantry
vulnerable (p145)
  capable of being hurt, injured, or wounded
defiant (p146)
  resisting
silhouette (p154)
  the outline of a person or object seen against a
  light or a light background

Small Group Reading

Fritz, Jean. *The Cabin Faced West*. New York: Coward, 1958.

In this story based on the life of Fritz's great-great-grandmother, Ann learns the hardships and pleasures of life in a cabin in the western Pennsylvania wilderness. Grades 4 and up.

Author Information

The daughter of missionary parents, Jean Fritz spent her first twelve years in China. As a child, she often wondered about America and what it meant to be an American.

After she had married and had two children, Fritz began writing for magazines such as *The New Yorker* and *Redbook*.

Each of Fritz's historical novels grew from her personal interest in the subject. Her enthusiasm for her subjects brings the past to life in an entertaining, informative, and detailed fashion.

Fritz was the 1986 recipient of the Laura Ingalls Wilder Award of the American Library Association, which is given once every three years to an author whose work has made a "substantial and lasting contribution to literature for children."

Activities

1. Have students write letters from Ann to her best friend back in Gettysburg telling her what life is like in her new home on the prairie.

2. On a map of the United States, have students locate Valley Forge, Pennsylvania, and Gettysburg, Pennsylvania.

3. Ask your students this question: If you were Ann and could only take five personal items West with you, what would they be? Have them make small posters called "The Possessions I Would Take West." The posters should include an illustration of each item with a caption telling why the item was chosen. Display these in your classroom.

4. As a group, have students choose a short scene from the book that they think best illustrates pioneer life. They can then write a short script for the scene and perform it for the whole class.

Discussion

Give the small group the following instruction: As your group reads this book, discuss the following questions.

1. Why did Ann's father build their cabin so that it faced west?

2. What is Ann's most precious possession and why?

3. What was the most important job Ann had to do while her mother was at the McPhales'?

4. How did Arthur Scott bring so much excitement to Ann's world?

5. What did Arthur Scott tell Ann about why he had come to this part of the country?

6. What did Andy want for payment for helping Ann's father on their farm?

7. As Andy was learning, what changes in him did Ann notice?

8. What does Ann miss most about Gettysburg?

9. What did Ann's mother do to help cheer her up?

10. How did the storm make Ann feel?

11. Who had taken Ann's diary and why?

12. Who was the Hamiltons' special dinner guest?

13. Why did General Washington tell Ann that he envies her?

14. At the end of the story, how does Ann feel about the west?

Vocabulary

squatter (p11)
a person who settles on land without owning it, paying for it, or having a right to it

exasperation (p28)
the feeling of being annoyed or irritated almost to the point of anger

johnnycake (p31)
a flat, cornmeal cake baked on a griddle

conspirator (p48)
a person involved in a conspiracy (a secret plan of two or more persons)

cringe (p56)
to shrink, cower, or crouch in fear or submission

earnest (p58)
very serious, determined, or sincere

forsake (p70)
to leave completely; to desert; to give up

flax (p74)
a plant with blue flowers and a slender stem that yields the fiber used in making linen

gratitude (p80)
thankfulness for a gift or favor; appreciation

glowering (p83)
staring angrily

calico (p94)
cotton cloth printed with a figured design

herald (p107)
a bearer of important news; a messenger

dignified (p114)
having dignity; proud

frolic (p120)
an occasion full of playful fun

Small Group Reading

Harvey, Brett. *My Prairie Year, Based on the Diary of Elenore Plaisted.* New York: Holiday House, 1986.

This is a true account of life on the prairie in the 1800s based on the diary of the author's grandmother when she was ten years old. As the family members become homesteaders, traveling from their home in Maine, the reader experiences how Elenore adjusts to the changed seasons, geography, and lifestyle of the prairie states. Grades 1-4.

Author Information

Brett Harvey was born April 28, 1936 in New York, New York. She has worked as a drama and literature director, a publicity and promotion director, a freelance journalist, a book critic, and a children's book author.

Of her writing, Harvey says, "Although I never met her, it was my grandmother who was indirectly responsible for my career as a children's book author. She wrote down her reminiscences of her journey to the Dakotas as a child, and I made her story into my first book for children. Curiously, she herself became a children's book illustrator. And her daughter, my mother, was a cookbook writer. So we have a family history of writers and illustrators."

Activities

1. Have students write in their own diaries as Elenore did, describing all of their activities for three to four days.

2. Have students spend one or two class periods in the library doing further research on prairie life. Was Elenore's life on the prairie typical of that time period? The students can present what they have learned to the rest of the class.

3. Along with their research, have students search for photographs of the prairie. These could then be displayed for the whole class to see.

4. Have students locate Lincoln, Maine, and the Dakota Territory on a map of the United States.

5. Elenore described their house using the following simile: "Our house on the prairie was like a little white ship at sea." Have students write four or five similes to describe their own homes, your school, a nearby landmark, and so on.

Discussion

Give the small group the following instruction: As your group reads this book, discuss the following questions.

1. Why was Elenore's house covered by a high bank of earth up to the windowsills?

2. Compare life on the prairie with the Plaisteds' life in Maine.

3. What were Elenore and her mother's chores on the prairie?

4. Why didn't the children go to school?

5. What did Elenore mean when she said they "put up" the vegetables?

6. Describe summer on the prairie.

7. What did Elenore compare tornadoes to?

8. How do you think the square patch of land kept Elenore's house and barns from burning in the prairie fire?

9. Why did Mr. Plaisted stretch a rope from the barn to Elenore's front door?

10. How did Elenore feel when a box arrived from her Aunt Addie?

11. Compare and contrast Elenore's life on the prairie with your own life.

Vocabulary

prairie (p4)
a large tract or area of more or less level, grassy land having few or no trees, especially the broad, grassy plain of Central North America

billow (p4)
anything that swells or surges like a wave

anchor (p4)
to fix firmly; to make secure

tornado (p4)
a violent, destructive, whirling wind, forming a funnel-shaped cloud that extends downward from a mass of clouds and moves along a narrow path

homesteaders (p6)
people who were given a piece of land by the United States government to farm, improve, and eventually own

moat (p8)
a ditch, usually full of water, around a castle, fortress, or other structure, used as a defense against attackers

drills (p11)
shallow trenches

proprietor (p13)
> the legal owner of something, such as a store or business

knead (p15)
> to mix and work into a mass by pressing or squeezing

coulee (p18)
> a stream that runs through the prairie

mirage (p20)
> an optical illusion, such as of a lake and palm trees in a desert or an upside-down ship at sea, that appears quite close but is actually an image of a distant object reflected by the atmosphere

thrashing machine (p25)
> a machine used on farms for separating grains or seeds from chaff

transfixed (p26)
> made motionless, as with horror or fear

silhouette (p26)
> the outline of a person or object seen against a light or a light background

crimson (p29)
> deep red

cylindrical (p33)
> shaped like a cylinder

swathed (p33)
> binded or wrapped

Small Group Reading

MacLachlan, Patricia. *Sarah, Plain and Tall*. New York: Harper & Row, 1985.

Life on the prairie and mail-order brides are featured in this 1800s story. Two children anxiously await the arrival of their potential mother, Sarah, who experiences some melancholy moments as she reflects on the differences between life by the ocean and life on the prairie. Sarah misses her brother, the sea, and her life in Maine. The children worry that Sarah will leave. However, a strong bond develops between Sarah and her new family, and she decides that she would miss them even more. Winner of the 1986 Newbery Medal. Grades 3-5.

Author Information

Patricia MacLachlan was born in Cheyenne, Wyoming. Before beginning her writing career, she worked as an English teacher and a social worker. She is a guest lecturer at colleges, and a teacher of creative writing workshops for both children and adults.

Most of MacLachlan's books are about families. Sarah was a real person from pioneer days who came from Maine to marry one of Patricia's mother's relatives.

Activities

1. Have students write a letter from Sarah to a friend in Maine telling her friend about her new life on the prairie.

2. Have students illustrate Sarah's new home, including the house and barn.

3. Have students go to the library to research some of the flowers Sarah loved so much. The following flowers were mentioned in the story:

Bride's bonnet	Indian paintbrush	tansy
columbine	marigolds	wild asters
dahlias	nasturtiums	wild feverfew
flax	prairie violets	woolly ragwort
goldenrod	Russian olive	zinnias

The students should share this information with the class by putting information about each flower on a 5-by-7-inch card along with an illustration. These can then be placed on a bulletin board titled "Sarah's Flowers."

4. Have students write a diary entry from Papa, Caleb, or Anna, telling his or her reaction to Sarah's arrival. These diary entries should then be shared orally with the rest of the class.

5. When Sarah leaves Maine for the prairie, she takes seashells with her to remind her of Maine. Ask your students to tell what they would take with them from their home if they were to go away on a long trip.

Discussion

Give the small group the following instruction: As your group reads this book, discuss the following questions.

1. According to Anna, what was the worst thing about her brother Caleb?

2. Why do you think Papa really stopped singing?

3. Why did Papa place an advertisement in the newspaper?

4. When Sarah answered Papa's advertisement, what did Caleb want him to ask her?

5. When Papa received the letter from Sarah saying she would come to visit, what was it that made him smile?

6. Why does Anna wish that they had a sea of their own?

7. What did Sarah do with Caleb's hair after she cut it, and why?

8. What did Papa use to make a dune for Sarah, Anna, and Caleb?

9. Why is Caleb becoming more hopeful that Sarah will stay with them?

10. How did Anna know that the chickens Matthew and Maggie brought wouldn't be for eating?

11. After the storm, why was Caleb afraid Sarah would leave them?

12. What did Sarah bring from town? What did it really mean?

Vocabulary

prairie (p5)
a large tract or area of more or less level, grassy land having few or no trees, especially the broad, grassy plain of central North America

feisty (p7)
full of spirit; frisky

dune (p29)
a hill or bank of loose sand heaped up by the wind

tumbleweed (p35)
a plant that, when withered, breaks from its roots and is blown about by the wind, scattering its seed

killdeer (p37)
a North American wading bird related to the plover, having a loud cry

sly (p45)
clever in a secret, sneaky way

pungent (p47)
sharp or piercing to the taste or smell

eerie (p48)
causing or arousing fear; strange

hail (p49)
drops of ice that fall during a storm; hailstones

Small Group Reading

Nixon, Joan Lowery. *A Family Apart*. New York: Bantam Books, 1987.
This is the story of Frances Mary and the other Kelly children, who are sent on the Orphan Train to St. Louis in the mid-nineteenth century to live with frontier families. This book was chosen as a National Council for Social Studies—Children's Book Council Outstanding Trade Book in the Field of Social Studies. Grades 4-7.

Author Information

Joan Lowery Nixon was born February 3, 1927 in Los Angeles, California. She taught elementary school in Los Angeles from 1947 to 1950 and has taught creative writing at the University of Houston and at Midland College in Texas. Nixon has also taught creative writing at many public schools in Texas.

When Nixon entered ninth grade, she became interested in journalism and soon became editor of the school newspaper. The following year at Hollywood High School, she met her favorite teacher, Miss Bertha Steadfast. Through the rest of high school she took every English class Miss Steadfast taught. Steadfast was the one who told Nixon that she had talent and would be a writer. Nixon has since written dozens of books for children, and her popularity as an author continues.

Activities

1. Have students in this group act out chapter 9—the choosing of the children. A narrator should first summarize the book, and then the group can perform it for the rest of the class.

2. On a map of the United States, have students trace the route of Frances and her brothers and sisters to their new families in the following order:

    1. New York City
    2. Hudson River
    3. Albany, NY
    4. Hannibal, MO
    5. Mississippi River
    6. St. Joseph, MO

    Also, have students locate the following places discussed in the novel:

    Fort Leavenworth, KS   Pennsylvania
    Iowa   St. Louis, MO
    Nebraska

3. Students who want to read about Mike's story should read *Caught in the Act*. Danny and Peg's story is told in *A Place to Belong*, and Megan's story can be found in *In the Face of Danger*. These are all written by Joan Lowery Nixon.

4. Have students create posters advertising the arrival of more orphan children in a Midwest town. They should attempt to persuade townspeople to adopt these children by telling of the hardships the children have faced and how they can provide a loving home for them.

5. Encourage students who would like to read about another child who found a new home through the Orphan Train, to read *An Orphan for Nebraska* by Charlene Joy Talbot. Ask the students to compare and contrast the two novels. This could be an extra-credit activity.

6. Have students contact The Orphan Train Society of America to find out more about how some of these children made out later in life. For a free packet of materials, write to:

    Director
    The Orphan Train Society of America
    Route 4, Box 565
    Springdale, AR 72764

Discussion

Give the small group the following instruction: As your group reads this book, discuss the following questions.

1. How did Jennifer and Jeff end up learning about Frances Mary Kelly, their great-great-great-grandmother?

2. Why was Frances treated so badly on the streets of New York City?

3. Where was Frances's friend Mara to be taken after she recovered in the hospital?

4. What did Frances catch Mike doing?

5. How do you think Frances felt when she had to tell her mother where Mike was?

6. Why was Frances alarmed at meeting Mr. Charles Loring Brace?

7. Why did Mrs. Kelly decide to send her children out west with Reverend Brace?

8. Discuss how the children must have felt in the courtroom when they heard that they would be leaving.

9. Why did Frances decide to pretend to be a boy?

10. Why were the children so excited to see farm animals from the train?

11. What was the Fugitive Slave Act that Captain Taylor told the children about?

12. When the train reached Missouri, how did Frances and Mike feel?

13. How did Mike risk his life to help the others on the train?

14. Discuss your reactions to Mr. Crandon's feelings about Mike.

15. How would you feel if you were one of the orphans waiting to be chosen?

16. Why did Mr. and Mrs. Cummings come to Kansas?

17. What happened to make Frances realize that she would have to be more careful in her new home?

18. Discuss how Frances and Petey feel about their new home.

19. What do you think the noise was that woke Frances during her first night in her new room?

20. How does Frances feel about helping Janus and Odette?

21. Do you agree with what Frances said to Mr. Mueller about obeying and breaking the law regarding slaves? Explain your opinion.

22. What made Frances finally understand what her mother had done for them?

23. What kept Frances from being arrested?

Vocabulary

sepia (p3)
    reddish brown

ornate (p7)
    fancy or showy

cornice (p7)
    a molding high on the walls of a room

precariously (p7)
    dangerously

pungent (p7)
    sharp or piercing to the taste or smell

obliged (p8)
    forced

urchin (p9)
    a poor, usually ragged child

regally (p10)
    stately; splendidly

humiliation (p11)
    stripped of pride or self-respect; disgraced

baluster (p13)
    one of the small posts that supports the handrail, as of a staircase

woebegone (p15)
    overcome with or showing woe or sadness

haberdasheries (p19)
    shops that sell men's clothes, such as shirts, ties, and hats

teem (p19)
    to be full and almost overflowing

tenement (p19)
    an apartment house that is poorly built or maintained, usually overcrowded, and often in a slum

porridge (p22)
    a soft food made by boiling oatmeal or some other grain in water, milk, or other liquid

indignation (p33)
    anger aroused by something that is not right, just, or fair

bravado (p35)
    a show of bravery without much courage or confidence underneath

parcel (p37)
    something that is wrapped up; a package

confer (p42)
 to hold a discussion; to talk together

gavel (p42)
 a small wooden mallet used by the person in charge of a meeting to call attention or order

ragamuffin (p43)
 a dirty, ragged person, especially a child

sidle (p44)
 to move sideways, especially in a cautious or sly manner

falter (p45)
 to hesitate, be uncertain, or give way

eternally (p45)
 forever

sacrifice (p47)
 a giving up of something cherished, usually for the sake of something else

astonishment (p54)
 amazement

pantalets (p57)
 long, ruffled, or embroidered underpants showing below the skirt, worn in the nineteenth century

somber (p60)
 gloomy; sad

kin (p61)
 relatives; family

recede (p62)
 to move back; to withdraw

meager (p62)
 lacking in quality or quantity; inadequate; inferior

bolster (p73)
 to support, prop, or make stronger

scarlet (p75)
 brilliant red with a bit of orange

trestle (p77)
 an open, braced framework used to support a road for railroad tracks

flounces (p78)
 gathered or pleated ruffles

parasol (p78)
 a small, light umbrella carried to protect oneself from the sun

clout (p82)
 a heavy blow

subdue (p86)
 to gain power over, as by force; to conquer

wistful (p87)
 wishful; longing

valise (p87)
 a suitcase

prominent (p88)
 well known

porter (p89)
 a person hired to carry luggage, such as in an airport or station

homespun (p91)
 cloth made of homespun yarn or a strong, loose fabric

jaunty (p95)
 having a lively or self-confident air or manner

valiant (p97)
 having or showing courage; brave

rotund (p101)
 rounded; plump

drought (p109)
 a lack of rain for a long period; a severe dry spell

homestead (p110)
 a piece of land given to a settler by the United States government to farm, improve, and eventually own

dubious (p115)
 arousing doubt, doubtful

tantalize (p116)
 to torment by making something that one desires almost but never quite available

ornate (p120)
 fancy or showy

tarry (p122)
 to stay for a while; to linger

passel (p128)
 a large number or amount

contemptuous (p129)
 full of contempt or scorn; disdainful

chagrin (p136)
 a feeling of embarrassment or distress caused by a disappointment or failure

diphtheria (p138)
 a serious contagious disease of the throat, usually associated with a high fever, that blocks air passages and makes breathing difficult

camphor (p143)
 a white, crystalline substance with a strong odor, used in medicine, plastics, lacquers, and mothballs

ford (p146)
 to cross (such as a river) at a shallow place

serene (p155)
 peaceful; calm

abolitionist (p157)
 an individual who wanted to end slavery in the United States

Small Group Reading

📖 Paulsen, Gary. *Mr. Tucket*. New York: Delacorte Press, 1994.

In 1848, while on a wagon train headed for Oregon, fourteen-year-old Francis Tucket is kidnapped by Pawne Indians and then falls in with a one-armed trapper who teaches him how to live in the wild. Grades 5 and up.

Author Information

Gary Paulsen was born May 17, 1939 in Minneapolis, Minnesota.

Paulsen has been a writer since the 1960s. He has also worked as a teacher, field engineer, editor, soldier, director, farmer, rancher, truck driver, and trapper.

Dogsong (1986), *Hatchet* (1988), and *The Winter Room* (1990) received Newbery Honor Book citations. Many of his books have been selected as American Library Association (ALA) Best Books for Young Adults and as ALA Notable Children's Books, as well as receiving other prestigious honors. His books are definite favorites among middle-school students.

Paulsen writes from first-hand knowledge of the outdoors, and from his experiences as a hunter, trapper, and even as a dogsledder in the Alaska Iditarod race.

In an interview for *Something About the Author*, Paulsen tells of a turning point in his life. On a subzero winter day he went into a library to warm himself. "To my absolute astonishment the librarian walked up to me and asked if I wanted a library card. When she handed me the card, she handed me the world. I can't even describe how liberating it was."

Activities

1. Have students write an epilogue for *Mr. Tucket*. It should take place five years after the end of the story and tell what has happened to Mr. Grimes and to Francis Tucket.

2. Encourage students who enjoyed *Mr. Tucket* to read its sequel—*Call Me Francis Tucket*, also by Gary Paulsen.

3. On a map of the United States, have students locate the following:
   Kansas   Rocky Mountains
   Missouri   St. Louis, MO
   Oregon

4. Have students write character sketches for Francis Tucket and Jason Grimes. They should include physical characteristics as well as character traits.

5. As a group, have students prepare and present to the class a book talk for *Mr. Tucket*. Their book talk should attempt to persuade others in the class to read this book. If they choose, they could dress to fit the time period for their presentation.

Discussion

Give the small group the following instruction: As your group reads this book, discuss the following questions.

1. What present did Francis get for his fourteenth birthday?

2. How was Francis treated when he was captured by the Indians?

3. What made Francis believe that the people from the wagon train would not come looking for him?

4. What did Braid bring for Francis that made him want to scream?

5. Do you think the mountain man will help Francis?

6. How did Francis escape from the Pawnees?

7. Why did the mountain man decide to call Francis Mr. Tucket?

8. Where did the mountain man take Francis?

9. How did Francis win the mare?

10. Why did Francis decide to stay with Jason Grimes through the winter?

11. What dangers did Mr. Grimes and Jason face during the winter?

12. What happened to Spot Johnnie and the trading post?

13. How did Francis feel when Mr. Grimes took off after Braid?

14. Why did Francis decide to leave Mr. Grimes and head for Oregon?

Vocabulary

Conestoga wagon (p2)
a heavy covered wagon with broad wheels, used by early American freight haulers and pioneers

muslin (p3)
a strong cotton cloth, often used for sheets or curtains

Quakers (p4)
members of the Society of Friends, a religious group who got their name because their founder told them to tremble at the word of the Lord

caliber (p6)
the diameter of the inside of a tube, especially of the barrel of a gun, such as a revolver or rifle

travois (p20)
a simple vehicle without wheels, once used by American Indians on the Great Plains, that consisted of two poles trailing from a draft animal with the load slung on a platform between them

squaw (p23)
an American Indian woman or wife

venison (p36)
the flesh of the deer, used as food

savvy (p45)
to understand

grouse (p48)
a plump bird, often hunted for sport

mulish (p49)
like a mule; stubborn

clamor (p56)
a loud and continuous noise, especially a loud protest or outcry

prestige (p57)
fame, importance, or respect based on a person's reputation, power, or past achievements

hue (p109)
a color, or shade of a color

purify (p110)
to make or become pure or clean

nettle (p117)
to annoy or irritate

contrary (p127)
entirely different; opposite

veer (p131)
to shift or change direction

canter (p132)
a slow, gentle gallop

dominate (p136)
to control or rule over

skittish (p139)
easily frightened; likely to shy, as a horse

tether (p150)
a rope or chain used to tie an animal so that it can go only so far

carnage (p153)
a bloody killing of great numbers of people, as in war

headstrong (p157)
stubbornly set upon having one's own way; obstinate

corral (p161)
an enclosed space or pen for livestock

vengeance (p162)
with great force or violence

prairie (p165)
a large tract or area of more or less level, grassy land having few or no trees, especially the broad, grassy plain of central North America

Small Group Reading

Woodruff, Elvira. *Dear Levi: Letters from the Overland Trail.* New York: Alfred A. Knopf, 1994.
Twelve-year-old Austin writes letters home to his brother Levi in Pennsylvania and tells him about the danger, sorrow, and excitement he encounters on the way to settle the family claim in Oregon. Grades 4-7.

Author Information

Elvira Woodruff was born June 19, 1951 in Somerville, New Jersey. Besides being a writer, Woodruff has worked as a janitor, gardener, baker, and window decorator.

According to Woodruff, becoming a writer has been one of her most pleasant surprises. Her cousin, Frank Asch, was instrumental in helping her get started. Upon selling her second manuscript, *The Wing Shop*, to Holiday House, she realized that she could make writing a career.

Activities

1. On a map of the United States, have students locate:

California	Oregon
Columbia River	Platte River
Indiana	Rocky Mountains
Nebraska	Snake River
Ohio	Sudbury, PA

2. Have students write letters to Austin from Levi. They could choose any point in the novel and respond to what Austin has said, as well as tell what Levi has been doing.

3. For extra credit, have students in the group read *Cassie's Journey: Going West in the 1860's* by Brett Harvey and compare the two books.

4. To share what they have learned about some of the hardships pioneers faced on their journeys west, have students role-play one or more of the main characters and tell the class the highlights of their journey. Characters to be presented are Austin, Reuben, Hiram, Frank, and Mr. and Mrs. Morrison.

Discussion

Give the small group the following instruction: As your group reads this book, discuss the following questions.

1. What was Levi's most prized possession that was given to his first grandchild?

2. Why is Austin going to Oregon?

3. How does Austin describe the prairie to Levi?

4. What kind of problems are Austin and the rest of the people on the wagon train having on their journey to Oregon?

5. Why did Reuben trade buttons with Austin and Hiram?

6. What happened when the wagon train met up with some Indians?

7. What did Mr. Morrison tell Austin that made him so excited?

8. Why did Frank run away?

9. How did Austin react to the news of Mr. Morrison's death?

10. What did Reuben mean about the militia being more savage than the Indians?

11. Discuss the killing of the Indians in the Sioux village. What are your feelings about it?

12. What do you think will become of Austin now that Mrs. Morrison is gone?

13. How did Reuben come to the rescue of Austin and Levi?

Vocabulary

cholera (p15)
an infectious bacterial disease that attacks the intestines, often causing death

dysentery (p19)
a disease of the intestines

concoction (p26)
something made by the mixing of ingredients

rheumatism (p27)
a painful inflammation and stiffness of the joints

prairie dog (p39)
a small rodent of the plains of North America that lives in large communities and is very destructive to vegetation

fray (p43)
a noisy quarrel; a fight; a brawl

hardtack (p44)
a hard, unsalted, crackerlike biscuit

malady (p48)
a disease, sickness, or illness

desolate (p54)
dreary; barren

militia (p59)
a body of citizens given military training outside the regular armed forces and called up in emergencies

saber (p59)
a heavy cavalry sword with a curved blade

savage (p59)
wild, untamed, and often fierce

kinship (p61)
relationship, especially by blood

alkali (p68)
a substance, such as potash, soda, or ammonia, that neutralizes acids by combining with them to form salts

inconsolable (p86)
unable to be comforted or cheered; broken-hearted

comrade (p91)
a close companion or friend

infernal (p109)
horrible; terrible

scoundrel (p113)
a mean or dishonest person

Bibliography

Individual Titles

Ackerman, Karen. *Araminta's Paintbox*. New York: Atheneum, 1990.

When Araminta and her parents' wagon breaks down on the journey from Boston to California in the mid-nineteenth century, the young girl loses her beloved paint box, which then makes its own way west. The map at the front, showing both Araminta's route and that of the paint box, provides graphic reinforcement. Grades 2-5.

Bial, Raymond. *Frontier Home*. Boston: Houghton Mifflin, 1993.

Sacrifice was a big part of pioneer life, but the rewards of freedom, independence, and a better life drew many families west. This book examines pioneer tools, homes, and daily life. Grades K-3.

Blos, Joan W. *A Gathering of Days: A New England Girl's Journal, 1830–32*. New York: Charles Scribner's Sons, 1979.

This novel written in diary form is an account of the fourteenth year of Catherine Cabot Hill's life as a nineteenth-century pioneer girl. Grades 4-7.

Brenner, Barbara. *Wagon Wheels*. New York: Harper & Row, 1978.

This book is based on a true story about a black pioneer family who takes advantage of the Homestead Act in 1878 to settle land in Kentucky. Besieged by the difficulties facing the pioneers, they must overcome hunger, cold, prairie fire, and fear of Indians while coping with the death of their mother to survive. Grades K-3.

Brink, Carol Ryrie. *Magical Melons.* New York: Macmillan, 1944.

This sequel to *Caddie Woodlawn* presents fourteen escapades of the Woodlawn children, who lived on the Wisconsin border in 1860. Grades 3-7.

Coerr, Eleanor. *Chang's Paper Pony.* New York: Harper & Row, 1988.

In San Francisco during the 1850s gold rush, Chang, the son of Chinese immigrants, wants a pony but cannot afford one until his friend Big Pete finds a solution. Grades K-3.

———. *The Josefina Story Quilt.* New York: Harper & Row, 1986.

Josefina the hen is considered a nuisance on the Faith family's trip west until her squawking saves them from robbers. Grades 2 and up.

Conrad, Pam. *Prairie Visions: The Life and Times of Solomon Butcher.* New York: HarperCollins, 1991.

Through this book, students can experience the lives of Nebraska pioneers at the turn of the century. Grades 3-7.

Field, Rachel. *Calico Bush.* New York: Dell, 1966.

This is a pioneer story of Marguerite, a young French orphan in the New World who promises to serve the Sargent family for six long years in return for food, shelter, and clothing. A Newbery Honor Book. Grades 4-7.

Freedman, Russell. *Children of the Wild West.* New York: Clarion Books, 1983.

Fascinating photographs depict what it would be like to be a child in the 1800s. From housing to celebrations and school life, the authentic photographs are a lesson all by themselves. Grades 3-6.

Greenwood, Barbara. *A Pioneer Sampler: The Daily Life of a Pioneer Family in 1840.* New York: Ticknor & Fields, 1995.

This is an excellent resource for students to use in researching pioneer life. Grades 4 and up.

Harvey, Brett. *Cassie's Journey: Going West in the 1860's.* New York: Holiday House, 1988.

This book is based on actual accounts of mid-nineteenth-century wagon-train journeys west. Grades 2-4.

———. *My Prairie Christmas.* New York: Holiday House, 1990.

In this book, set in the Dakota Territory at the turn of the century, the children and their mother are hoping that a blizzard won't keep Papa from getting home in time for Christmas. This is a companion volume to *My Prairie Year.* Grades PreK-3.

Henry, Joanne Landers. *A Clearing in the Forest: A Story About a Real Settler Boy.* New York: Four Winds Press, 1992.

In this is companion book to *Log Cabin in the Woods: A True Story About a Pioneer Boy*, Elijah Fletcher is a settler boy growing up in Indianapolis during the 1830s. The book is based on the unpublished manuscript of Elijah Fletcher and on the diaries of Calvin Fletcher, his father. Grades 3-6.

———. *Log Cabin in the Woods: A True Story About a Pioneer Boy.* New York: Four Winds Press, 1988.

The year is 1832 and Oliver, age eleven, lives with his family in a log cabin on a clearing farm in the woods. Grades 2-5.

Holland, Isabelle. *Journey Home.* New York: Scholastic, 1990.

Two orphan sisters in the late 1800s leave New York on the orphan train to find a new home in the West. Grades 4-7.

Hooks, William H. *Pioneer Cat.* New York: Random House, 1988.

While moving west on the Oregon Trail, nine-year-old Kate Purdy and her family ward off a buffalo stampede and deal with a stowaway cat and her kittens. Grades 2-4.

Knight, Amelia Stewart. *The Way West: Journal of a Pioneer Woman.* Illustrated by Michael McCurdy. New York: Simon & Schuster, 1993.

This story is adapted from the journal Knight kept while she, her husband, and their seven children journeyed from Iowa across the Oregon Trail to the West Coast. Grades 3-6.

Kudlinski, Kathleen V. *Facing West: A Story of the Oregon Trail.* New York: Viking, 1944.

Young Ben wonders whether he will have more trouble with his debilitating asthma as his family sets out from Missouri for Oregon. Grades 4-7.

Lasky, Kathryn. *Beyond the Divide.* New York: Macmillan, 1983.

The trip from Pennsylvania to California that fourteen-year-old Meribah Simon and her father undertake during the heyday of the Oregon Trail encompasses his death and her transformation from an ingenuous girl to a mature woman. Grades 7-12.

Lasky, Kathryn, and Meribah Knight. *Searching for Laura Ingalls.* New York: Macmillan, 1993.

Lasky recounts a personal family vacation to see the childhood homes of Laura Ingalls Wilder. She and her family visited the settings for most of the "Little House" books. While Lasky and daughter Meribah wrote the book, husband Christopher took the photographs. The result is a wonderful record of the sights that Wilder described in her books. Grades 2-6.

Lavender, David. *The Santa Fe Trail.* New York: Holiday House, 1995.

Lavender tells of the succession of traders who made the trip on the Santa Fe Trail between 1822 and 1879. Grades 4-7.

Lawlor, Laurie. *Addie Across the Prairie.* Niles, IL: Whitman, 1986.

Nine-year-old Addie learns about sod houses and curious Indians as her family travels cross-country to the Dakota Territory. Grades 3-5.

———. *Addie's Long Summer.* Morton Grove, IL: Whitman, 1992.

Addie is disappointed to find that her cousins do not fit into pioneer farm life. Grades 5-7.

Levine, Ellen. *If You Traveled West in a Covered Wagon.* New York: Scholastic, 1992.

This book recounts from a child's perspective what it was like to travel the Oregon trail. Grades 2-5.

Little, Leslie Jones. *Children of Long Ago.* New York: Philomel, 1988.

This book contains poems of simpler days, with grandmothers who read aloud and children who walk barefoot on damp earth and pick blueberries for their paper dolls to eat.

Love, D. Anne. *Bess's Log Cabin Quilt.* New York: Holiday House, 1995.

With her father away and her mother ill with fever, ten-year-old Bess works hard on a log cabin quilt to save the family farm. Grades 3-5.

MacBride, Roger Lea. *Little House on Rocky Ridge.* New York: HarperCollins, 1993.

In 1894, Laura Ingalls Wilder, her husband, and her seven-year-old daughter Rose leave the Ingalls family in Dakota and make the long and difficult journey to Missouri to start a new life. Grades 3-7.

MacLachlan, Patricia. *Skylark.* New York: HarperCollins, 1994.

This is a sequel to *Sarah, Plain and Tall.* When a drought comes to the plains, Sarah takes Anna and Caleb back to her family in Maine, where the land is green and the ocean is nearby. The children fear that Sarah will never return to their father and the dry, dusty farmland he loves. Grades 3 and up.

Moeri, Louise. *Save Queen of Sheba.* New York: E. P. Dutton, 1981.

Young David survives a wagon massacre but now must take care of his young sister. Grades 5-7.

Nixon, Joan Lowery. *Caught in the Act.* New York: Bantam Books, 1988.

In the mid-nineteenth century, eleven-year-old Michael Kelly is sent to a foster home, a Missouri farm with a mean owner, a bullying son, and a number of secrets. Grades 4-7.

———. *A Deadly Promise.* New York: Bantam Books, 1992.

This companion volume to *High Trail to Danger* concludes Sarah Lindley's adventures west as she vows to clear her father's name after he is wrongly accused of murder. Dying in her arms, he whispers evidence that could solve the crimes, but Sarah must first unravel his message. Grades 6 and up.

———. *High Trail to Danger.* New York: Bantam Books, 1991.

Sarah, befriended by a young reporter and a stagecoach driver, is nevertheless surrounded by dangers that worsen as she discovers what has become of her father. Grades 6 and up.

———. *In the Face of Danger.* New York: Bantam Books, 1988.

Megan gradually finds contentment and purpose in her new home on the Kansas prairie with her adoptive family. Grades 4-7.

———. *Keeping Secrets.* New York: Delacorte Press, 1995.

In 1863, eleven-year-old Peg Kelly is drawn into the dangerous activities of a mysterious young woman who has come to her home in Missouri after fleeing the raid of William Quantrill and his raiders on Lawrence, Texas. Grades 4-7.

———. *A Place to Belong.* New York: Bantam Books, 1989.

In 1856, having traveled with his young sister from New York to a foster home on a farm in Missouri, ten-year-old Danny plots to get his foster father to send for and marry his mother. Grades 4-7.

Paulsen, Gary. *Call Me Francis Tucket.* New York: Delacorte Press, 1995.

Having separated from the one-armed trapper who taught him how to survive in the wilderness of the Old West, fifteen-year-old Francis gets lost and continues to have adventures involving dangerous men and a friendly mule. Grades 5 and up.

Rounds, Glen. *Sod Houses on the Great Plains.* New York: Holiday House, 1995.

This book tells of our country's first homesteaders who moved across the Missouri River and onto the Great Plains. They found themselves in an almost treeless land, where the only building material was the prairie sod itself. Grades K-3.

Russell, Marion. Adapted by Ginger Wadsworth. *Along the Santa Fe Trail.* Morton Grove, IL: Whitman, 1993.

In 1852, seven-year-old Marion Sloan Russell travels with her brother in a wagon train along the Santa Fe Trail, experiencing hardship and wonder. Grades 2-4.

Sanders, Scott Russell. *Aurora Means Dawn.* New York: Bradbury Press, 1989.

After traveling from Connecticut to Ohio in 1800 to start a new life in the settlement of Aurora, the Sheldons find that they are the first family to arrive there and realize that they will be starting a new community themselves. Grades K-4.

———. *Here Comes the Mystery Man.* New York: Bradbury Press, 1993.

The Goodwin family's pioneer home is visited by the traveling peddler, who brings wondrous things and amazing tales from far away. Grades K-4.

———. *Warm as Wool.* New York: Bradbury Press, 1992.

When Betsy Ward's family moves to Ohio from Connecticut in 1803, she brings along a sockful of coins to buy sheep so that she can gather wool, spin cloth, and make clothes to keep her children warm. Grades K-4.

Sandin, Joan. *The Long Way Westward.* New York: Harper & Row, 1989.

This is an easy-to-read book that tells the story of a family that left Sweden and moved from New York to Minnesota. Grades 1-3.

———. *Pioneer Bear.* New York: Random House, 1995.

Andrew and his family are excited when a photographer comes to take a picture of their dancing bear, but then Bearly can't be found. Grades K-3.

Sandler, Martin W. *Pioneers: A Library of Congress Book.* New York: HarperCollins, 1994.

This book contains photographs from the archives of the Library of Congress that document this account of Americans moving west. Grades 3 and up.

Schlissel, Lillian. *Women's Diaries of the Westward Journey.* Schocken, 1982.

This book provides information on the dozens of women who recorded their journey across the American West in the nineteenth-century. Grades 8 and up.

Shaw, Janet. *Changes for Kirsten.* Middleton, WI: Pleasant, 1988.

A harsh Minnesota winter brings many changes to Kirsten's frontier life, including the new responsibility of helping her brother Lars set his traps and helping her family move into a new house. Grades 3-7.

———. *Kirsten Learns a Lesson: A School Story.* Middleton, WI: Pleasant, 1986.

After immigrating from Sweden to join relatives in a American prairie community, Kirsten endures the ordeal of a strange school through a secret friendship with an Indian girl. Grades 3-7.

———. *Kirsten Saves the Day: A Summer Story.* Middleton, WI: Pleasant, 1988.

Kirsten is proud and excited when she finds a bee tree full of honey, but she exposes herself to great danger by trying to harvest the honey by herself. Grades 3-7.

Shub, Elizabeth. *The White Stallion.* Greenwillow Books, 1982.

This book is a mixture of homespun charm and fairy tale. It is 1845 and Gretchen finds herself separated from her family, pioneers on their way west.

Fortunately, a magnificent white stallion comes to her rescue. An ALA Notable Children's Book. Grades 2-4.

Steedman, Scott. *A Frontier Fort on the Oregon Trail.* New York: Peter Bedrick Books, 1993.

The authors describe life on a frontier fort on the Great Plains in the nineteenth century. Grades 4 and up.

Stein, R. Conrad. *The Story of the Homestead Act.* Chicago: Childrens Press, 1978.

From 1863 until about 1890, thousands of people moved west to claim free land on the prairies of the Great Plains. Stein explains the historical background behind this government act that gave millions of acres of American soil to farmers willing to settle the new lands. Grades 3-6.

Turner, Ann. *Dakota Dugout.* New York: Macmillan, 1985.

A tall, vigorous woman describes her experiences as a young bride living in a sod house on the Dakota prairie. Grades K-3.

———. *Sewing Quilts.* New York: Macmillan, 1994.

A pioneer girl sees pieces of her life sewn into the quilts that she, her sister, and her mother make. Grades K-3.

Van Leeuwen, Jean. *Bound for Oregon.* New York: Dial Books for Young Readers, 1994.

This is a fictionalized account of the journey made by nine-year-old Mary Ellen Todd and her family from their home in Arkansas westward over the Oregon Trail in 1852. Grades 5 and up.

———. *Going West.* New York: Dial Books for Young Readers, 1992.

This story follows a family's emigration by prairie schooner from the East and across the plains to the West. Grades K-4.

Welch, Catherine. *Clouds of Terror.* Minneapolis, MN: Carolrhoda Books, 1994.

Living on a farm in southwestern Minnesota in the 1870s, a brother and sister try to help their family cope with plagues of locusts. Grades 2-4.

Whelan, Gloria. *Next Spring an Oriole.* New York: Random House, 1987.

This pioneer story, narrated by ten-year-old Libby Mitchell on her journey from Virginia to Michigan in a covered wagon in 1837, is well written and easy to read. Grades 2-4.

Wilder, Laura Ingalls. *By the Shores of Silver Lake.* New York: Harper & Row, 1939.

Laura's family spends the winter on a Dakota homestead miles from the nearest neighbor. Newbery Award Runner-Up. Grades 3-7.

———. *Dance at Grandpa's.* New York: Harper & Row, 1994.

This book was adapted from the "Little House" books. A young pioneer girl and her family attend a wintertime party at her grandparents' house in the Big Woods of Wisconsin. Grades K-3.

———. *Farmer Boy.* New York: Harper & Row, 1933.
Farmer Boy tells the story of the ninth year in the New York farm childhood of Laura Ingalls Wilder's husband, Almanzo. It paints a detailed picture of farm life and schools in the 1870s. Grades 3-7.

———. *The First Four Years.* New York: Harper & Row, 1971.
The Wilder family discovers that frontier homesteading is a rough but rewarding experience. Grades 3-6.

———. *A Little House Christmas: Holiday Stories from the Little House Books.* New York: Harper & Row, 1994.
Christmas stories from the original books are gathered together and published in one volume. Grades 3-7.

———. *Little House in the Big Woods.* New York: Harper & Row, 1932.
This is the first in an autobiographical series about a pioneer family in 1870s Wisconsin. It details their day-to-day customs and seasonal activities, family stories, and songs. Grades 3-7.

———. *Little House on the Prairie.* New York: Harper & Row, 1935.
In this book, Laura and her family journey by covered wagon into Indian territory. Grades 3-7.

———. *Little Town on the Prairie.* New York: Harper & Row, 1941.
Pa's homestead thrives, Laura gets her first job in town, blackbirds eat the crops, Mary goes to college, and Laura gets into trouble at school but becomes a certified schoolteacher. Newbery Award Runner-Up. Grades 3-7.

———. *The Long Winter.* New York: Harper & Row, 1961.
Almanzo Wilder makes a dangerous trip to save the village from starvation. Newbery Award Runner-Up. Grades 3-7.

———. *On the Banks of Plum Creek.* New York: Harper & Row, 1937.
The Ingalls family encounter a terrible blizzard and a grasshopper plague after moving to Minnesota. Newbery Award Runner-Up. Grades 3-7.

———. *These Happy Golden Years.* New York: Harper & Row, 1943.
Laura is courted by Almanzo, and they marry and move into their own little house on a homestead claim. Newbery Award Runner-Up. Grades 5-9.

Wisler, G. Clifton. *Jericho's Journey.* New York: Lodestar, 1993.
Jericho Wertherby and his family leave Tennessee for Texas in 1852. The hazardous trip tests his ability to survive, while his courage and determination serve him well. Although he is short in stature, he discovers that there are many ways to grow tall. Grades 5-9.

Theme Resources

Commercial Resources

Anderson, William. *Laura Ingalls Wilder Country.* New York: HarperCollins, 1990.
Color photographs of the Ingalls family's homesites are the highlight of this book, appropriate for grades 5 and up. The text focuses on the difference between Wilder's real life and her fictionalized version of it.

Anderson, William, ed. *The Horn Book's Laura Ingalls Wilder.* Horn Book, 1987.
This is a revised edition of the December 1953 *Horn Book* devoted to Laura Ingalls Wilder, suitable for grades 7 and up. It includes articles by Garth Williams, Virginia Kirkus, Anne Carroll Moore, and Marcia Dalphin, and a letter written by Wilder.

Artman, John. *Pioneers: An Activity Book.* Carthage, IL: Good Apple, 1987.
This resource includes information and activities for students in grades 3-6 on several well-known people of the pioneer period. They include Daniel Boone, Andrew Jackson, Lewis and Clark, Davy Crockett, and Sam Houston.

Clayton, Dina. *Novel Ties: The Cabin Faced West.* New Hyde Park, NY: Learning Links, 1990.
This resource contains pre-reading and post-reading activities, vocabulary skills, comprehension questions, and writing activities in a chapter-by-chapter format for *The Cabin Faced West.* For use with students in grades 4 and up.

Cobblestone: The History Magazine for Young People. Peterborough, NH: Cobblestone.
The February 1986 issue for students in grades 4 and up highlights the life of Laura Ingalls Wilder. Articles include "A Laura Ingalls Wilder Chronology" and "The Ingallses' Good, Plain Food." It also includes a quilting project, a Little House crossword, and a previously unpublished story by Wilder.

Friedland, Joyce, and Rikki Kessler. *Historical Ties: Westward Expansion and Frontier Life.* New Hyde Park, NY: Learning Links, 1985.
This resource provides activities for *Caddie Woodlawn* and *Light in the Forest.* Use with students in grades 5 and up.

Fuhler, Carol. *Novel Ties: Caddie Woodlawn.* New Hyde Park, NY: Learning Links, 1991.

This resource contains pre-reading and post-reading activities, vocabulary skills, comprehension questions, and writing activities in a chapter-by-chapter format for *Caddie Woodlawn.* Use with students in grades 5 and up.

Garson, Eugenia, compiler. *The Laura Ingalls Wilder Songbook.* New York: Harper & Row, 1968.

The words and music for many of the songs mentioned by Wilder in the "Little House" books are arranged thematically, with citations from the appropriate book included. A good book to use with students in grades 4-8.

Hackett, Christine. *Little House in the Classroom.* Carthage, IL: Good Apple, 1989.

Music, art, cooking, math, reading, and writing activities are included for seven of the "Little House" books. Suitable for use with students in grades 3-8.

Hatch, Lynda. *Pathways of America: The Oregon Trail.* Carthage, IL: Good Apple, 1994.

This book includes detailed background information, emigrant journal quotations, activities, and more that cover the 2,000-mile journey the emigrants faced as they traveled the Oregon Trail. Suitable for use with students in grades 5 and up.

Kelly, Joanne. *On Location: Settings from Famous Children's Books, #1.* Englewood, CO: Teacher Ideas Press, 1992.

This resource contains setting location information, actual photographs, extension activities for *Little House in the Big Woods*, *On My Honor*, *Caddie Woodlawn*, and *Across Five Aprils.* Suitable for use with students in grades 5 and up.

King, David C. *Connect, A Literature/Social Studies Program: A Family Apart.* Littleton, MA: Sundance, 1991.

This resource contains activities for the novel *A Family Apart* by Joan Lowery Nixon for students in grades 4-7.

Laughlin, Mildred Knight, Peggy Tubbs Black, and Margery Kirby Loberg. *Social Studies Readers Theatre for Children.* Englewood, CO: Teacher Ideas Press, 1991.

This book provides a section on combining a set of scripts using a pioneer theme and featuring books by Laura Ingalls Wilder. It also includes suggested scripts for *Caddie Woodlawn*, *Pioneer Cat*, *Addie Across the Prairie*, and *A Family Apart*, among others. Use with grades 3-8.

Macon, James. *Novel Ties: Little House on the Prairie.* New Hyde Park, NY: Learning Links, 1989.

This resource contains pre-reading and post-reading activities, vocabulary skills, comprehension questions, and writing activities in a chapter-by-

chapter format for *Little House on the Prairie.* Appropriate for use with students in grades 3-7.

Marsh, Norma. *Novel Ties: Sarah, Plain and Tall.* New Hyde Park, NY: Learning Links, 1994.

This resource contains pre-reading and post-reading activities, vocabulary skills, comprehension questions, and writing activities in a chapter-by-chapter format for *Sarah, Plain and Tall.* Use with students in grades 3-5.

Myers, Kathleen, ed. *Inquiring into the Theme of Pioneer Life: Based on Pam Conrad's Prairie Songs.* Logan, IA: Perfection Learning, 1994.

This resource, designed for use with grades 6-8, provides activities for *Prairie Songs*, background information for the theme, and much more.

Parish, Peggy. *Let's Be Early Settlers with Daniel Boone.* New York: Harper & Row, 1967.

Parrish gives instructions for creating more than forty pioneer models, including a quill pen, a dunce cap, a log cabin, and a covered wagon. She also gives directions for making costumes. Use with students in grades 3-5.

Perl, Lila. *Hunter's Stew and Hangtown Fry: What Pioneer America Ate and Why.* New York: Seabury Press, 1977.

In this upper elementary book the author explores the role of food throughout the westward movement. She describes the adaptations of food made necessary by the conditions as well as the contributions of immigrant groups. Selected recipes are included.

Pofahl, Jane. *United States History: The Westward Movement.* Grand Rapids, MI: T. S. Dennison, 1994.

This resource book for grades 3-6 includes cross-curricular activity pages on the Westward Movement.

Sterling, Mary Ellen. *Thematic Unit: Westward Ho.* Huntington Beach, CA: Teacher Created Materials, 1992.

This resource includes a variety of theme-based activities for all curriculum areas. Appropriate for use with students in grades 4 and up.

Walker, Barbara M. *The Little House Cookbook: Frontier Foods from Laura Ingalls Wilder's Classic Stories.* New York: Scholastic, 1979.

Walker includes recipes and explanations for many foods mentioned by Laura Ingalls Wilder and cites references to the novels in which these foods appear. Use this book with students in grades 4-8.

Wilder, Laura Ingalls. *The Laura Ingalls Wilder Country Cookbook.* New York: HarperCollins, 1995.

Intermingled with Laura's recipes are anecdotes about Laura's life on Rocky Ridge Farm by Wilder historian William Anderson. Photographs of Rocky Ridge Farm by Leslie Kelly allow readers to see all aspects of Laura's homestead. This book is best suited for use with students in grades 4 and up.

——. *My Little House Songbook.* New York: Harper-
Collins, 1995.

The songs in this book are adapted from the
"Little House" books. Use with students in grades 2-5.

The World Almanac Info Power: Pioneers. Sundance,
1992.

This is a magazine-style publication that includes
stories on "American Trailblazers," "A Pioneer Gal-
lery," the "Great Pioneer Debate," "Log Cabins:
Homes on the Range," and more. For use with students
in grades 4 and up.

Computer Resources

The Oregon Trail. Minneapolis, MN: MECC.

This program will take students for a trip on the
Oregon Trail. They'll hunt wild buffalo, raft down
rivers, and trade for essential supplies while trying to
survive. Grades 3 and up.

The Oregon Trail II. [CD-ROM]. Minneapolis, MN:
MECC.

The Oregon Trail II gives students new challenges to face on their trek across the American frontier. There is more decision making, more random
events, and more inclement weather, hazards, and
health complications. There is also a built-in journal
for students to use.

Videos

Caddie Woodlawn. Los Angeles: Churchill Films,
1989. (104 minutes)

This video is based on the book by Carol Ryrie
Brink. It dramatizes the story of Caddie Woodlawn, a
frontier girl who makes peace between the Indians and
the settlers in frontier Wisconsin.

Home at Last. Chicago: Public Media Video, 1988. (58
minutes)

This video is based on the real Orphan Trains,
which resettled children in the Midwest at the turn of
the century.

*Little House on the Prairie: Centennial and The Camp-
Out.* Alexandria, VA: Time-Life Video, 1993. (90
minutes)

This video contains two episodes from the *Little
House on the Prairie* television series, starring Michael
Landon. "Centennial" focuses on the one hundredth
birthday of the United States. In "The Camp-Out," the
Oleson family joins the Ingalls on a camp-out.

*Little House on the Prairie: Christmas at Plum Creek
and The Christmas They Never Forgot.* Alexandria, VA: Time-Life Video, 1994. (90 minutes)

This video contains two episodes from the *Little
House on the Prairie* television series, starring Michael
Landon. "Christmas at Plum Creek" shows what it was
like for the Ingalls family to be short on cash at Christmas. In "The Christmas They Never Forgot," a sudden
snowstorm traps the Ingalls family inside their house
on Christmas eve, where they exchange stories of their
favorite Christmases.

*Little House on the Prairie: A Harvest of Friends and
At the End of the Rainbow.* Alexandria, VA: Time-
Life Video, 1993. (90 minutes)

This video contains two episodes from the *Little
House on the Prairie* television series, starring Michael

Landon. "A Harvest of Friends" focuses on the difficulty of surviving on a small farm in Minnesota. In "At
the End of the Rainbow," Laura and a friend think they
have found gold and dream about being rich.

O Pioneers! Los Angeles: Hallmark Hall of Fame,
1992. (99 minutes)

Jessica Lange stars in this adaptation of the novel
by Willa Cather. *O Pioneers!* brings to life the story of
men and women who fought to turn the wilderness into
a home.

Sarah, Plain and Tall. Los Angeles: Hallmark Hall of
Fame, 1990. (98 minutes)

This video is based on the novel by Patricia
MacLachlan. Glenn Close stars as a mail-order bride
who journeys to the frontier and wins the love of a
widower and his children. Grades 2 and up.

Skylark: The Sequel to Sarah, Plain and Tall. Los Angeles: Hallmark Hall of Fame, 1992. (98 minutes)

This video is based on *Skylark* by Patricia
MacLachlan. It takes place two years after Sarah, a
mail-order bride, married Jacob Witting. They live a
simple life on the Kansas prairie until a draught destroys the land.

Trumpet Video Visits: Gary Paulsen. Holmes, PA:
Trumpet Club. (24 minutes)

Gary Paulsen tells about the exciting adventures
he has had.

*United States History Video Collection: Expansion-
ism.* Bala Cynwyd, PA: Schlessinger Video Productions, 1996. (35 minutes)

Territorial expansion and the Louisiana Purchase,
the Lewis and Clark expedition, the War of 1812,
Native American resistance, the Trail of Tears, and the
Oregon Trail are presented.

End-of-Unit Celebration

Recipes

Get a taste of what the frontier life was all about by preparing the following recipes. Depending on the age of the students, prepare these ahead of time or make them with your class.

Butter

INGREDIENTS

Heavy whipping cream

Salt, to taste

PROCEDURE

1. Take cream out of refrigerator about 1 hour before making butter.

2. Pour cream into a glass jar that has a tight-fitting lid. Fill only half full.

3. Shake jar until curd (solid) separates completely from whey (liquid).

4. Pour whey into a separate container (this is buttermilk and is drinkable).

5. Pour curd into a strainer and let drain for several minutes until all liquid is drained off.

6. Place curd into a bowl and stir in salt.

7. Use the butter as desired.

Source: Barchers, Suzanne I., and Patricia C. Marden. *Cooking Up U.S. History: Recipes and Research to Share with Children.* Englewood, CO: Teacher Ideas Press, 1991.

Corn Fritters

INGREDIENTS

1 #2 can corn (20 ounces)	1 teaspoon salt
2 eggs	1 teaspoon sugar
½ cup milk	Vegetable oil for frying
1 cup flour	Optional: syrup, butter, or confectioners' sugar
1 teaspoon baking powder	

PROCEDURE

1. Strain corn and put it into a large mixing bowl.

2. Add eggs, milk, flour, baking powder, salt, and sugar. Stir until blended.

3. Heat oil in large frying pan or deep fat fryer over medium heat.

4. When oil is hot, drop 1 tablespoon of batter into the frying pan.

5. Cook 3 minutes and then turn and cook 3 minutes on the other side or until light brown.

6. Drain fritters on paper towels.

7. Serve with butter or maple syrup or roll fritters in confectioners' sugar.

   Makes 25 to 30.

Source: Barchers, Suzanne I., and Patricia C. Marden. *Cooking Up U.S. History: Recipes and Research to Share with Children.* Englewood, CO: Teacher Ideas Press, 1991.

Baked Beans

INGREDIENTS

1½ cups dried beans	½ cup brown sugar
Water	1 tablespoon mustard
½ cup chopped onion	1 teaspoon salt
4 tablespoons molasses	¼ pound bacon
3 tablespoons catsup	

PROCEDURE

1. Put beans into a large pot and cover with water.
2. Soak beans for 1 hour.
3. Add 3 more cups of water.
4. Boil over low heat for 1 hour.
5. Preheat oven to 250 degrees.
6. Strain beans, but save the water.
7. Put beans into a casserole dish.
8. Add onion, molasses, catsup, brown sugar, mustard, salt, and bacon. Stir well.
9. Cover casserole dish and bake 6 to 9 hours or until beans are soft. (Check beans often and add some of the water used to soak the beans if they become dry.)

   Serves 4.

Source: Barchers, Suzanne I., and Patricia C. Marden. *Cooking Up U.S. History: Recipes and Research to Share with Children.* Englewood, CO: Teacher Ideas Press, 1991.

Other Activities

1. Have students complete webs of pioneer life. Figure 5.1, page 128, features a reproducible web. The web can be used for review purposes at the end of the unit or as an organizer for a written assignment.

2. Have students select five special items (other than food or clothing) that they would want to take with them on a wagon trip out West. Have them tell why each item was chosen. This can be a written or oral assignment.

3. Based on what students have learned in their study of pioneer life, have them create a guide to help people on their journey West. It could contain maps, a packing list, medical supplies needed, and information about possible destinations.

4. Provide *The Oregon Trail, The Oregon Trail II*, and *Writing Along the Oregon Trail* computer programs for student use in your classroom or computer lab throughout your study of pioneer life.

Fig. 5.1. **Web of pioneer life.**

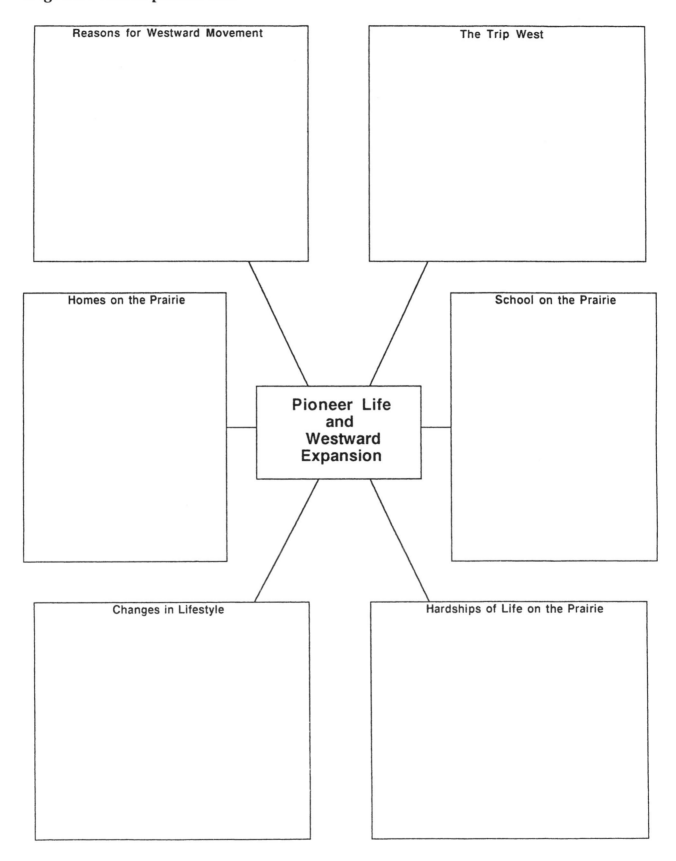

Pioneer Life and Westward Expansion
Research Project

Divide your class into groups of two to research the following topics. When the projects are completed, hold a presentation day.

The Orphan Train

The Oregon Trail

Housing on the Prairie

A Day in the Life of a Wagon Train

Hardships Faced by Pioneers

Reasons for Westward Movement

Life for Pioneer Women
  Responsibilities of Women
  What restrictions were female teachers
    required to follow?
  What other occupations could women
    have?

The Homestead Act of 1862
  Who was eligible to settle a homestead?
  Who was not eligible?
  Which lands did the U.S. set aside so that
    they would not be settled?
  What did the U.S. government promise to
    the people who settled homesteads?
  What did the U.S. government promise to
    the Native American tribes?

Daily Life on the Prairie

Laura Ingalls Wilder

Pioneer Tools

Pioneer Homes

Students may also select their own topic but should obtain your approval before they begin.

Chapter 6

Immigration

Introduction

For immigrants to the United States, freedom was worth more than anything else. It meant the opportunity to practice the religion of their choice. It meant living free of fear of government persecution. It meant being able to keep their families together under one roof. It also meant the possibility of a better future for their children. The titles in this chapter were selected in an effort to help students understand the reasons for immigration, the hardships faced by immigrants, and the value of freedom in general.

To begin your study of immigration, read the following selection to your class. The poem was written by Emma Lazarus in 1883 to aid the fund-raising campaign for a pedestal for the Statue of Liberty. The last five lines are inscribed on the base of the statue. Discuss what this poem means to your students.

The New Colossus

Not like the brazen giant of Greek fame,
With conquering limbs astride from land to
    land;
Here at our sea-washed, sunset gates shall
    stand
A mighty woman with a torch, whose flame
Is the imprisoned lighting, and her name
Mother of Exiles. From her beacon-hand
Glows world-wide welcome; her mild eyes
    command
The air-bridged harbor that twin cities
    frame.

"Keep, ancient lands, your storied pomp!"
    cries she
With silent lips. "Give me your tired, your
    poor,
Your huddled masses yearning to breathe
    free,
The wretched refuse of your teeming shore.
Send these, the homeless, tempest-tost to
    me—
I lift my lamp beside the golden door!"

Emma Lazarus

Whole Group Reading

📖 Nixon, Joan Lowery. *Land of Hope*. New York: Bantam Books, 1992.

Rebecca, a fifteen-year-old Jewish immigrant arriving in New York City to live in the Lower East Side, almost abandons her dream of getting an education when she is forced to work in a sweatshop seven days a week. Grades 5 and up. This book was chosen as the class set title because Nixon's text illustrates well the hardships faced by the majority of immigrants to the United States.

Author Information

Joan Lowery Nixon was born February 3, 1927 in Los Angeles, California. She taught elementary school in Los Angeles from 1947 to 1950 and has taught creative writing at the University of Houston and at Midland College in Texas. Nixon has also taught creative writing at many public schools in Texas.

When Nixon entered ninth grade, she became interested in journalism and soon became editor of the school newspaper. The following year at Hollywood High School, she met her favorite teacher, Miss Bertha Steadfast. Through the rest of high school she took every English class Miss Steadfast taught. Steadfast was the one who told Nixon that she had talent and would be a writer. Nixon has since written dozens of books for children.

Activities

1. Have students illustrate the scene Rebekah and the other passengers saw when they reached the United States, using the description on pages 75 through 77.

2. Have the class act out what it was like for immigrants to be processed at Ellis Island (see descriptions on pages 82 through 90). Four or five students should act as the doctors and inspectors; the rest of the class can play immigrants passing through the inspection process. Figure 6.1 is an inspection sheet with questions for the inspectors to ask.

Fig. 6.1

IMMIGRANT INSPECTION SHEET

What is your name?_____

What is your age? What is your nationality?_____

What is your destination? _____

Who paid your fare?_____

What is your occupation? _____

How much money do you have? Show it to me. _____

Have you ever been in prison or in the poorhouse?_____

---

3. As Joan Lowery Nixon states at the end of *Land of Hope*, four out of ten Americans have family who passed through Ellis Island, the "Gateway to America." My own father, Arnold Jacob Jansen, came here from Holland in 1909. Have students research their own family histories to find out if they have family who came through Ellis Island. They should find out as much information as they can about these immigrants to share with the class. Those who do not have family who came through Ellis Island could interview other community members or teachers who do have such family members.

4. Students who wish to find out how Kristin and Rose made out in America should read two of Joan Lowery Nixon's other books, *Land of Dreams* (New York: Bantam Books, 1994), which centers on Kristin, and *Land of Promise* (New York: Bantam Books, 1993), which centers on Rose.

Discussion

Give the class the following instruction: As we read this book, we will be discussing the following questions. Write down your ideas about these questions and add to them as needed.

1. What had Rebekah's grandfather read about the United States?

2. What did Rebekah's Uncle Avir tell her family about the United States in his letters?

3. Why did Rebekah's grandfather make the decision that it was time for them to leave Russia for the United States?

4. Where did Rebekah's mother put the family's travel money?

5. What did her grandfather mean when he told Rebekah, "You should have been a boy. What a fine scholar you would have made"?

6. Rebekah wondered if their fear had weighed more than their possessions. What did she mean?

7. What were some of the reasons the United States turned immigrants away?

8. Why was the family questioned and examined before leaving for the United States?

9. Why was the spelling of Rebekah's name changed? How did it make her feel?

10. Why did some of the steerage passengers hang clusters of garlic around their quarters?

11. Discuss Rebekah's dream for the future. Do you have any dreams for yourself?

12. Why would Jacob's opinion be treated with more respect than Rebekah's?

13. Discuss the differences between the cultures from which Rebekah, Kristin, and Rose came.

14. Why did her brother Nessin tell Rebekah that Aaron Mirsch had no chance with her?

15. What made Rebekah suddenly look forward to arriving in the United States?

16. Why are freedom and independence so important to Rebekah?

17. How did Rebekah feel upon reaching New York City?

18. Why were immigrants warned not to draw attention to themselves at Ellis Island?

19. What happened to Mordecai at Ellis Island?

20. What did the Levinskys find out about what Uncle Avir told them?

21. Do you think Rebekah will ever see Kristin and Rose again?

22. How would you have felt in Rebekah's place when her mother said an education for her would be a waste of money?

23. How did Elias feel about the work he would be doing?

24. In what way were the Levinskys forced to change their lifestyle?

25. What happened that made Rebekah feel a new surge of hope?

26. What did the death of her grandfather mean to Rebekah?

27. How did Rebekah's parents come to realize the importance of her dream?

Vocabulary

peasant (p2)
in Europe, a country person of humble birth, such as a small farmer

loot (p2)
to rob

retaliate (p2)
to get even, as for an injury or wrong

emigrate (p3)
to move from one country or section of a country to settle in another

steerage (p3)
a part of a passenger ship open to passengers paying the lowest fares, which offered little or no comfort or privacy

cossacks (p5)
one of the people of southern Russia noted as horsemen and soldiers

scholar (p8)
a school pupil or student

refugee (p9)
a person who flees from persecution or danger

trundled (p9)
rolled

interminable (p10)
never ending or seeming never to end

quarantine (p10)
the keeping of persons or things that have been infected or exposed to contagious diseases away from other people or things

persecution (p16)
the act or practice of oppression or harassing with ill-treatment on the basis of race, religion, or beliefs that differ from those of the persecutor

fray (p27)
a noisy quarrel; a fight; a brawl

kosher (p29)
clean or proper, according to Jewish religious laws

piety (p29)
reverence, strictness, and devotion in practicing one's religion

gait (p33)
a way of walking, stepping, or running

noncommittal (p44)
not binding one to an opinion, attitude, or plan of action

scandalous (p51)
disgraceful; shocking

funnel (p53)
a smokestack or chimney on a ship or steam locomotive

gruel (p55)
a thin, liquid food made by boiling cereal in water or milk

stateroom (p63)
a private cabin on a ship or a sleeping room on a train

pallor (p74)
paleness of the face

manifest (p76)
a list, as of cargo or passengers, for a ship or airplane

cholera (p76)
a infectious bacterial disease that attacks the intestines, often causing death

smallpox (p76)
a highly contagious viral disease causing a high fever and skin eruptions that usually leave permanent scars

yellow fever (p76)
an infectious disease of warm countries caused by a virus transmitted to humans by the bite of certain mosquitoes

boisterous (p82)
noisy and wild

disdain (p85)
scorn or contempt, especially toward someone or something considered inferior

polygamy (p86)
the condition or practice of having more than one wife or husband at a time

sweatshop (p89)
a place where work is done under poor conditions, for very little pay and for long hours

discordant (p111)
not agreeing or fitting together; clashing

drudgery (p111)
dull, hard, unpleasant work

acrid (p113)
burning; bitter; irritating, such as a taste or odor

motley (p123)
a mixture of very different and often clashing elements

malice (p133)
an intention or desire to hurt or injure someone

suffragette (p136)
a woman who fought for women's right to vote

heathen (p141)
    a person who is regarded as irreligious, uncivilized, or unenlightened

shirtwaist (p153)
    a tailored blouse that looks something like a shirt

alderman (p155)
    in some cities and towns, a member of the local government or city council

arduous (p159)
    difficult to do; strenuous

dowry (p168)
    the money or property a wife brings to her husband when they marry

Small Group Reading

Cohen, Barbara. *Molly's Pilgrim*. New York: Bantam Books, 1983.

This is the story of a young Jewish immigrant who is having trouble adjusting to life in America and her first Thanksgiving when her mother makes her a unique pilgrim doll. Grades 2-5.

Author Information

Barbara Cohen was born March 15, 1932 in Ashbury Park, New Jersey.

Cohen was a high school English teacher as well as an author of more than thirty books since 1972. Her books have won numerous awards, including American Library Association Notable Children's Book citations for *Thank You Jackie Robinson*, *I Am Joseph*, and *Seven Daughters and Seven Sons*. She also won the Sydney Taylor Award for lifetime work.

Cohen became interested in books as a young child and wanted to write books like those she loved. She attributed her writing ability to time she spent as a child listening to relatives tell stories.

Barbara Cohen died November 22, 1992.

Activities

1. Have students locate Plymouth, Massachusetts on a map of the United States.

2. Have students in this group make pilgrim dolls that resemble members of their family who came to America. Students should then present their dolls to the class and explain where the dolls would have come from and why.

3. Have students write a short script for *Molly's Pilgrim* and perform it for the class.

Discussion

Give the small group the following instruction: As your group reads this book, discuss the following questions.

1. Why did the other children at school laugh at Molly?

2. Why can't Molly and her family return to their home in Russia?

3. What opportunity does Molly have in America that she wouldn't have in Russia?

4. Why didn't Molly want her mother to talk to her teacher?

5. What project did Miss Stickley decide to have the class do for Thanksgiving?

6. Why was Molly afraid to take her pilgrim doll to school?

7. How did Molly's pilgrim help the rest of the class better understand pilgrims and Thanksgiving?

Vocabulary

tenement (p10)
   an apartment house that is poorly built or maintained, usually overcrowded, and often in a slum

cossack (p13)
   one of a people of southern Russia noted as horsemen and soldiers

synagogue (p13)
   a place of meeting for Jewish worship and religious instruction

Small Group Reading

Freedman, Russell. *Immigrant Kids*. New York: E. P. Dutton, 1980.

Children can compare their lives today with those of children who immigrated to America from Europe at the turn of the century. Period photographs show these children at home, at school, at work, and at play. Grades 3-7.

Author Information

Russell Freedman was born October 11, 1929 in San Francisco, California. He has worked as a newsman, a television publicity writer, an editor, an instructor of writing workshops, and a freelance writer, particularly of works related to young people.

Freedman has written at least one book a year and has built a solid reputation among teachers, librarians, and the reading public for his craftsmanship, reliability, and intellectual integrity. He has written nonfiction books on a wide variety of topics, although now he mostly writes biographies. When he prepares to write a biography he immerses himself in his subject. He does this by reading numerous books, conducting meticulous research, and visiting historical sights important to his subject.

Activities

1. Have students do further research on Ellis Island and Lewis Hine's crusade against child labor. The following resources will be helpful:

   Fisher, Leonard Everett. *Ellis Island: Gateway to the New World*. New York: Holiday House, 1986.

   Freedman, Russell. *Kids at Work: Lewis Hine and the Crusade Against Child Labor*. New York: Clarion Books, 1994.

   Jacobs, William Jay. *Ellis Island: A New Hope in a New Land*. New York: Charles Scribner's Sons, 1990.

   Levine, Ellen. *If Your Name Was Changed at Ellis Island*. New York: Scholastic, 1993.

   This information should be shared with the class.

2. Have students make small posters containing information on any one of the following subjects:
   Ellis Island
   Immigrant Children at Play
   Immigrants at Work
   Reasons for Coming to America
   School Life of Immigrants

   Students should then use these posters to share with the rest of the class what they learned by reading this book.

Discussion

Give the small group the following instruction: As your group reads this book, discuss the following questions.

1. What child labor reform did Lewis Hine help to bring about?

2. What common belief did immigrants hold in the late eighteenth and early nineteenth centuries?

3. Describe the conditions that many immigrants faced on their journey to the United States.

4. Where did the majority of immigrants land in the United States?

5. Why was Ellis Island known as "Heartbreak Island"?

6. Describe what took place at Ellis Island.

7. Why did most turn-of-the-century immigrants settle in big cities?

8. Describe the living conditions many immigrants faced in large cities in the United States.

9. What made people consider immigrant families a success?

10. How were immigrant children treated in schools?

11. For what jobs were boys trained in vocational schools?

12. For what jobs were girls trained in vocational schools?

13. Describe the main cause of conflict between immigrant children and their parents.

14. Discuss the working conditions immigrant workers faced in factories.

15. What is a sweatshop?

16. What type of games did immigrant children play?

Vocabulary

tenement (p2)
an apartment house that is poorly built or maintained, usually overcrowded, and often in a slum

sweatshop (p2)
a place where work is done under poor conditions, for very little pay and for long hours

steerage passengers (p4)
passengers of a ship paying the lowest fare and occupying the steerage, which lay deep down in the hold of the ship

indomitable (p13)
not easily defeated or overcome

teeming (p14)
full to almost overflowing

monotonous (p21)
boring because of lack of variety or change

dank (p21)
unpleasantly cold and wet

ultimatum (p26)
a final proposal or offer, whose refusal may lead to an act of force or punishment

heritage (p39)
something, such as a tradition, belief, or attitude, handed down from the past

knickerbockers (p46)
loose-fitting, short trousers, gathered in below the knee

alcove (p46)
a recess or small section of a room opening out from the main section

orator (p54)
a person who delivers a speech

itinerant (p54)
a person who travels from place to place, especially one who moves from job to job

hurdy-gurdy (p60)
another name for a hand organ

Small Group Reading

Lord, Bette Bao. *In the Year of the Boar and Jackie Robinson*. New York: Harper & Row, 1984.
Shirley Temple Wong has no friends when she first arrives in the United States from China, but she soon develops a passion for baseball. Named a 1984 Notable Book by the American Library Association. Grades 3-7.

Author Information

Bette Bao Lord was born November 3, 1938 in Shanghai, China. In 1946 she emigrated to the United States with her family, and in 1964 she became a naturalized citizen. Lord was Assistant to the Director of the East-West Cultural Exchange in Hawaii from 1961 to 1962. She has taught and performed modern dance and was also Conference Director of the National Conference for the Associated Councils of the Arts from 1970 to 1971.

According to Lord, she wrote *In the Year of the Boar and Jackie Robinson* because she wanted to remember "the fun and the fright of being a Chinese Immigrant dumped into the fifth grade at P.S. 8 [a New York City public school] without speaking a word of English, without knowing another soul."

Activities

1. Shirley is so amazed by some of the modern conveniences that many of us take for granted. Have students imagine that Shirley were to travel to the 1990s. What would she think of the advances in modern technology? Have students choose an item (such as a microwave oven, computer, etc.) and describe what they think Shirley's reaction to it would be.

2. Have students research modern Chinese customs, comparing their findings with customs mentioned in the novel.

3. Ask students to find out more about Jackie Robinson, then discuss him in their group. Why was Robinson such an inspiration to many people, including Shirley? Have students think about who is an inspiration in their lives today and why, then write essays about these people. The essays could be bound together in a book called "The People Who Inspire Us."

4. Have students write letters from Shirley to Fourth Cousin, telling about Shirley's experiences in America. These letters can be shared orally with the class as a way of presenting the novel.

Discussion

Give the small group the following instruction: As your group reads this book, discuss the following questions.

1. What made Fourth Cousin and Bandit think that Bandit's father was bringing a dog home?

2. Why is Bandit going to be sent away?

3. What does Bandit's family think about Americans?

4. Why didn't anyone sleep on the final day of the Year of the Dog?

5. How did Bandit come to choose Shirley Temple Wong for her name?

6. How does Shirley feel about her father?

7. What will be different about Shirley's mother's life in America?

8. What did Shirley think the washing machine was for?

9. What happened when Shirley went to the store for her father?

10. Why did Mrs. Rappaport think something might be wrong with Shirley's eyes?

11. Discuss Shirley's feelings about her new life in America.

12. How did Shirley and Mabel become friends?

13. How is life in America like baseball?

14. What is Shirley's favorite summer pastime?

15. What does Shirley do to help her piano teacher?

16. Why does Shirley soon wish she had never heard of Nonnie?

17. According to Shirley's father, what is the most valuable treasure a person can have?

18. Why did Shirley miss the game that won the pennant for the Dodgers?

19. Discuss the effect the Dodgers loss in the World Series had on Shirley.

20. What dream of Shirley's came true at the end of the book?

Vocabulary

Confucian (p2)
people who follow the philosophy of Confucius, who stressed personal good conduct, devotion to one's family and ancestors, social harmony, justice, and peace

patriarch (p2)
a man who is the ruler or head, such as of a family or tribe

brazier (p4)
an open pan for holding hot coals or burning charcoal

matriarch (p7)
a woman who is the ruler or head, such as of her family, tribe, or community

dictum (p7)
something said with authority; a formal pronouncement

harmony (p7)
agreement

bureau (p7)
a chest of drawers, usually with a mirror

Buddha (p9)
the founder of a religion that holds that freedom from pain, suffering, and desire can be reached by right living, meditation, and self-control

abacus (p9)
a device for adding, subtracting, multiplying, and dividing that uses beads that slide on rods

ebony (p10)
a hard, heavy wood, usually black

clan (p13)
a group of families claiming descent from a common ancestor

brocade (p14)
a fabric woven with a raised design, often in gold or silver threads

peasant (p16)
in Europe, a country person of humble birth, such as a small farmer

melodious (p18)
pleasant to hear; musical

mettle (p32)
spirit, courage, or resolution

emphatic (p35)
spoken or done with emphasis

ambassador (p44)
a representative or messenger

forlorn (p57)
sad or pitiful as a result of being alone or neglected

illustrious (p58)
very famous; distinguished

hoary (p58)
very old; ancient

odious (p58)
arousing hate or disgust; offensive

gossamer (p66)
a flimsy, delicate material or fabric

sashay (p66)
to walk in a swaggering or conspicuous way; to strut

reverent (p70)
feeling or showing reverence and great respect

regale (p71)
to give pleasure or delight; to entertain

interrogate (p75)
to question, usually in a formal examination

cloakroom (p85)
a room where such items as coats, hats, and luggage are left for a short time

civics (p90)
the study of citizenship and government

fraught (p91)
> filled; loaded

timbre (p92)
> the quality of a sound, aside from its pitch or loudness, that distinguishes it from another sound

creed (p92)
> a set of personal beliefs or principles

pauper (p92)
> a very poor person, especially one who receives public charity

hue (p93)
> a color, or shade of a color

desolate (p96)
> dreary; barren

mayhem (p98)
> the crime of hurting someone very badly, so that he or she is disabled or maimed

plague (p98)
> anything troublesome or distressing

maiden (p100)
> of or having to do with the first use, trial, or experience

tyranny (p102)
> a cruel act

jaunty (p108)
> having a lively or self-confident air or manner

alchemy (p110)
> any power that changes or transforms

ingenuity (p110)
> skill or cleverness, as shown in inventing or solving things

adept (p111)
> skillful

talisman (p114)
> an item, such as a ring or stone, that bears symbols believed to bring good luck

molt (p118)
> to shed (such as feathers, horns, or skin) in preparation for a new growth

progressives (p124)
> people who believe in progress or reform

valor (p136)
> great courage or bravery, especially in war

commemorate (p150)
> to honor or keep fresh the memory of

filial (p154)
> suitable to or expected of a son or daughter

Small Group Reading

Surat, Michele Maria. *Angel Child, Dragon Child*. Milwaukee, WI: Raintree, 1983.

This is the story of little Ut (pet name for smallest child), whose family has come to the United States from Vietnam. Ut has some initial difficulty with her American schoolmates but finally wins them over through kindness and sensitivity. Grades 3-6.

Author Information

Michele Maria Surat is a graduate of Bread Loaf School of English in Vermont. She has taught at the high school level and worked as a freelance writer.

Ut's story began when a Vietnamese child with a tear-streaked face shared a photograph of her mother with "Miss Teacher." Surat was compelled to tell the tale of these beautiful and courageous children. She hoped to create a story that would promote understanding between Vietnamese children and their American peers.

Activities

1. With the help of your school's art teacher or parent volunteers, have students create a paper dragon to be hung in the classroom. Instructions for a Serpent Kite, and a Caterpillar Kite, which are much like paper dragons, can be found in:

   Dixon, Norma. *Kites: Twelve Easy-to-Make High Fliers*. New York: Morrow Junior Books, 1996. Grades 3 and up.

2. Have students bring in small cardboard jewelry gift boxes. Inside these boxes, students can glue a picture of whatever they feel will make them smile when they feel sad. It could be a picture of a family member, a special pet, or a good friend. The students can decorate these boxes and keep them in their desks to be brought out when needed.

3. Have students research other Vietnamese customs, their way of life, Vietnamese foods, the climate in Vietnam, and other aspects of Vietnam.

4. Have students write a letter from Ut to her mother in Vietnam telling her about her new life in America. The students can then share these letters with the class.

Discussion

Give the small group the following instruction: As your group reads this book, discuss the following questions.

1. Where is Ut from?

2. Why did the American children laugh at Ut and Chi Hai?

3. What surprised Ut about how the children were taught in American schools?

4. What does the nickname Ut mean?

5. What is it that helps Ut to be brave?

6. How does Ut describe snow? Brainstorm some of your own descriptions of snow.

7. What did the principal have Ut and Raymond do after he stopped their snowball fight?

8. Why did Ut's mother stay behind in Vietnam?

9. When the principal read Ut's story to the class, what idea did Raymond have?

10. Discuss how Ut and her family must have felt when her mother joined them in America.

11. In the afterword, what did you discover about Vietnam's legend of the Angelic Fairy and the Dragon King?

12. Why do Vietnamese people put their family name first?

13. What did you learn from reading this story?

Vocabulary

twitter (p9)
to utter light, chirping, birdlike notes

screech (p9)
to scream or shriek in a harsh way

gleam (p12)
to shine

noble (p16)
of or having to do with a high rank or title; aristocratic

fairy (p35)
an imaginary being, often tiny with a graceful human form, able to work magic

descendant (p35)
anyone proceeding from an ancestor, such as a child or grandchild; offspring

Small Group Reading

Talbot, Charlene Joy. *An Orphan for Nebraska*. New York: Atheneum, 1981.
Kevin O'Rourke lives a newsboy's street life after his mother dies on the journey across the ocean to New York City in the 1870s. He and others like him are sent out West by the Children's Aid Society. Grades 4-6.

Author Information

Charlene Joy Talbot was born November 14, 1928, in Frankfort, Kansas. After college, she traveled to New York, California, Mexico, and Europe, working as a typist, secretary, waitress, and classified ad-taker. In 1958 she worked part-time as a secretary and began to write.

According to Talbot, "The wonderful thing about writing for children is that they're interested in everything. You can do all the things you wanted to do as a child, and then write about them as though you were still there."

Activities

1. Have students act out for the class the choosing of children by the people of Cottonwood City as described beginning on page 84.

2. On a map of the United States, have students locate the following:
    Michigan   New Jersey
    Nebraska   Staten Island, NY

3. Encourage students who are interested in reading more about children who were sent out West by the Children's Aid Society to read books from The Orphan Train series by Joan Lowery Nixon.

4. As a group, have students write a letter from Kevin to a friend back in Ireland, telling him what has happened since his journey across the ocean. This letter should be shared with the rest of the class.

Discussion

Give the small group the following instruction: As your group reads this book, discuss the following questions.

1. How did the people on the steerage deck react to the sight of land?

2. Why was it so unusual that Kevin could read?

3. Why was Kevin going to America?

4. What did the immigrants have to go through before being admitted to the United States?

5. What did Kevin find out about his uncle, Michael O'Halloran?

6. What do you think will become of Kevin, all alone in New York City?

7. What did Kevin's uncle suggest that he do?

8. Discuss Kevin's new life as a newsboy.

9. What did the people at the lodging house do to help newsboys like Kevin?

10. Where does the Children's Aid Society want to send Kevin, and why?

11. What did homesteaders receive?

12. How did the land change as the emigrant train traveled west?

13. How did the children feel after they arrived in Cottonwood City?

14. What was Kevin's reaction to being taken in by Euclid Smith?

15. Why was taking a bath a new experience for Kevin?

16. Describe Yuke's shanty on his claim.

17. Why was Kevin worried about Yuke being engaged?

18. What took place at the literary?

19. How did Kevin feel when Yuke returned after the spring blizzard?

20. What happened when Kevin, Hannah, and the others went snipe hunting?

21. Do you think Kevin will leave Yuke to go with his Uncle Michael?

22. Did Sally come to Cottonwood City to marry Yuke?

23. What solution to Kevin's problem of leaving or staying did Hannah suggest?

24. What damage did the grasshoppers cause?

25. What did Kevin and Yuke decide to do together?

26. Discuss how Kevin's life changed since arriving in America.

Vocabulary

fetid (p3)
: having a bad odor, as of rot or decay

steerage (p3)
: the part of a passenger ship open to passengers paying the lowest fares

aft (p5)
: at, near, or toward the stern or rear part of a ship

prodigy (p6)
: a child or young person with amazing talent or brilliance

prairie (p7)
: a large tract or area of more or less level, grassy land having few or no trees, especially the broad, grassy plain of central North America

dismay (p8)
: a feeling of alarm, uneasiness, and confusion

smallpox (p11)
: a highly contagious viral disease causing a high fever and skin eruptions that usually leave permanent scars

scurvy (p14)
: (as adjective) nasty; mean; low

warren (p16)
: any crowded place where people live

dilapidated (p21)
: ruined by neglect; falling to pieces

privy (p21)
: an outdoor toilet; an outhouse

clamorous (p23)
: noisy

penitentiary (p23)
: a prison, especially one run by a state or federal government

covertly (p25)
: secretly

turret (p25)
: a small tower, often at the corner of a large building or castle

industrious (p45)
: hard-working and diligent

urchin (p48)
: a poor, usually ragged child

chilblain (p64)
: a painful itching, swelling, and redness of the hands or feet, caused by exposure to extreme cold

hackney (p66)
: a carriage for hire

emigrant (p66)
: a person who leaves a place or country to settle in another

homestead (p73)
: a piece of land given to a settler by the United States government to farm, improve, and eventually own

sorghum (p81)
: a tall plant that looks like corn, is filled with sweet juice, and is grown as food for livestock and to make syrup

docile (p84)
: easy to teach, manage, or handle; obedient

guffaw (p85)
: a burst of laughter

pauper (p85)
: a very poor person, especially one who receives public charity

livery stable (p86)
: a place where horses and vehicles are cared for or kept for hire

diphtheria (p89)
: a serious contagious disease of the throat, usually associated with high fever, that blocks air passages and makes breathing difficult

sod (p95)
: the top layer of the earth, especially when covered with grass

forlorn (p99)
: sad or pitiful because of being alone or neglected

banshee (p99)
: in Gaelic myths, a female spirit whose wailing was supposed to warn that someone was going to die

brogue (p103)
: speech characteristic of a certain accent in the pronunciation of English

shanty (p107)
a crude, hastily built shack or cabin

victuals (p110)
food

greenhorn (p113)
an inexperienced person; a beginner

haggard (p118)
looking as if ill, starved, exhausted, or in pain

hummock (p125)
a low mound

journeyman (p134)
a worker who has completed an apprenticeship in a skilled trade or craft

teamster (p138)
a person who drives a team or truck as an occupation

leaden (p143)
dark and gloomy

recitation (p143)
the oral presentation of a memorized piece of writing before an audience

frivolous (p143)
not important or worthwhile; trivial

judicious (p143)
having, showing, or using good judgment; wise

vestibule (p146)
an entrance hall or lobby

flourish (p150)
a showy display in doing something

sedately (p183)
calmly and steadily in manner

telegraph (p188)
a device for sending and receiving messages by means of a series of electrical or electromagnetic pulses

heyday (p196)
the time of greatest power

scythe (p200)
a long, curved blade fixed at an angle to a long bent handle and used to cut down grass or grain

condolence (p208)
an expression of sympathy

Bibliography

Individual Titles

Beatty, Patricia. *Lupita Mañana*. New York: Beech Tree Books, 1981.
The focus of this book is the problem of illegal immigration. Thirteen-year-old Lupita comes to the United States from Mexico to support her poverty-stricken family. Grades 5-8.

Bode, Janet. *New Kids on the Block: Oral Histories of Immigrant Teens*. New York: Franklin Watts, 1989.
Teenage immigrants from various countries recount the emotional experience of fleeing from their homelands and adjusting to a new life in the United States. Grades 5-9.

Buss, Fran, with Daisy Cubias. *Journey of the Sparrows*. New York: Lodestar, 1991.
This is a story of the secret lives of twentieth-century immigrants to the United States. Maria and her siblings are Salvadoran refugees who are smuggled into the United States inside crates. They try to make a living in Chicago with the help of a sympathetic family. Grades 5 and up.

Cech, John. *My Grandmother's Journey*. New York: Bradbury Press, 1991.
A grandmother shares with her granddaughter at bedtime their favorite story about Russia, gypsies, a field of butterflies, the revolution, and a young mother who journeys halfway around the world to freedom with her baby. Based on a true story. Grades PreK-4.

Cohen, Barbara. *Gooseberries to Oranges*. New York: Lothrop, Lee & Shepard, 1982.
This story about immigration and resettlement traces a Russian family's journey from their homeland to their new life in New York City. In addition to an account of their difficult voyage, the book describes life in the garment district of New York City. Grades 2-4.

Cummings, Betty Sue. *Now, Ameriky*. New York: Atheneum, 1979.
Brigid Ni Cleary comes to America from Ireland to raise passage money for the rest of the family. Grades 5-8.

Fährmann, Willi. *The Long Journey of Lukas B*. New York: Bradbury Press, 1985.
The journey of fourteen-year-old Lukas Bienmann takes him from his Prussian village to America and back again. Grades 7-10.

Fisher, Leonard Everett. *Ellis Island: Gateway to the New World*. New York: Holiday House, 1986.
This book about immigration to New York City in the nineteenth and twentieth centuries provides excellent information about this important period in American history. Grades 3-7.

Geras, Adèle. *Voyage.* New York: Atheneum, 1983.

In 1904, Jewish immigrants, harboring fears of the past and hopes for the future, board a ship in Hamburg. The crossing brings them together. Grades 6-8.

Harvey, Brett. *Immigrant Girl: Becky of Eldridge Street.* New York: Holiday House, 1987.

Through a first-person narrative, the main character, Becky, tells the reader about her family's life in New York City in 1910. Pencil drawings illustrate her neighborhood and daily routines as the reader experiences the early twentieth century in the city through Becky's eyes. Grades 1-4.

Hesse, Karen. *Letters from Rifka.* New York: Henry Holt, 1992.

In letters to her cousin, a young Jewish girl chronicles her family's flight from Russia in 1919 and her own experiences when she must be left in Belgium for a while when the others emigrate to America. Grades 4-8.

Hotze, Sollace. *Summer Endings.* New York: Clarion Books, 1991.

Twelve-year-old Christine is a Polish immigrant whose father was trapped in Poland by the Nazi invasion. During the summer of 1945 many things happen, including the end of the war and the finding of Christine's father. Grades 5 and up.

Hoyt-Goldsmith, Diane. *Hoang Anh: A Vietnamese-American Boy.* New York: Holiday House, 1992.

A Vietnamese boy celebrates the festival of TET—the season of new beginnings—in his American home. Grades 2-6.

Jacobs, William Jay. *Ellis Island: A New Hope in a New Land.* New York: Charles Scribner's Sons, 1990.

Written as if you were there, Jacobs writes of coming to Ellis Island. The second half of the book combines a history of immigration in the United States. Grades 2-5.

Knight, Margy Burns. *Who Belongs Here? An American Story.* Gardiner, ME: Tilbury House, 1993.

This picture story explores the oppression of immigrants and refugees who have come to the United States. Grades 3-7.

Kroll, Steven. *Mary McLean and the St. Patrick's Day Parade.* New York: Scholastic, 1991.

In this picture book, set in the 1850s, a recently arrived Irish girl determines to ride in the St. Patrick's Day Parade in New York City. Grades 2-6.

Lawlor, Veronica, selector. *I Was Dreaming to Come to America: Memories from the Ellis Island Oral History Project.* New York: Viking, 1995.

In their own words, immigrants recall their arrival in the United States. Hand-painted collage illustrations embellish the accounts. These are wonderful first impressions of Ellis Island and America to share with students. Grades 3 and up.

Leighton, Maxine. *An Ellis Island Christmas.* New York: Viking, 1992.

Having left Poland and braved ocean storms to join her father in America, Krysia arrives at Ellis Island on Christmas Eve. Grades 1-4.

Levine, Ellen. *I Hate English!* New York: Scholastic, 1989.

Levine presents the stages of learning the language of a new country with sympathy and humor. Grades 1-4.

———. *If Your Name Was Changed at Ellis Island.* New York: Scholastic, 1993.

This book conveys historical accounts of Ellis Island in a question-and-answer format. Grades 2-5.

Levinson, Nancy Smiler. *I Lift My Lamp: Emma Lazarus and the Statue of Liberty.* New York: Lodestar, 1986.

This is a biography of the American poet who authored the words that are inscribed on the Statue of Liberty. Grades 5 and up.

Levinson, Riki. *Soon Annala.* New York: Orchard, 1994.

While eagerly awaiting the arrival of her two younger brothers from the old country, Anna tries to speak more English and less Yiddish. Grades K-3.

———. *Watch the Stars Come Out.* New York: E. P. Dutton, 1985.

Grandma tells about mama's journey to America by boat many years ago. Grades K-3.

Maestro, Betsy. *The Story of the Statue of Liberty.* New York: Lothrop, Lee & Shepard, 1986.

This book celebrates the centennial of the Statue of Liberty in a simple, read-aloud text. Grades K-3.

Mayerson, Evelyn Wilde. *The Cat Who Escaped from Steerage.* New York: Charles Scribner's Sons, 1990.

This story revolves around the two weeks that Polish immigrants spent in steerage on their way to America. A scrawny cat is both a comfort and a risk for nine-year-old Chanah. Grades 4-6.

McGugan, Jim. *Josepha.* San Francisco: Chronicle Books, 1994.

Josepha, an immigrant boy, leaves school to begin working and says good-bye to his best friend. Grades K-3.

Meltzer, Milton. *The Chinese Americans.* New York: Thomas Y. Crowell, 1980.

The Chinese who first came to America faced racism and abuse, but they won their struggle for equality and made important contributions to American society. Grades 6-10.

Nixon, Joan Lowery. *Land of Dreams*. New York: Delacorte Press, 1994.

Kristen Swensen and her Swedish family settle into farm life in Minnesota. As the suffragette movement grows, Kristen is caught up in the struggle for women's rights. Grades 5 and up.

———. *Land of Promise*. New York: Bantam Books, 1993.

Rose Carney, a young girl from Ireland, befriends Rebecca (from Russia) and Kristen (from Sweden) during the long journey to America. They part ways at Ellis Island, and Rose continues to a new life in Chicago. Grades 5 and up.

O'Connor, Karen. *Dan Thuy's New Life in America*. Minneapolis, MN: Lerner, 1992.

This book describes the experience of thirteen-year-old Dan Thuy Huynh and her family, newly arrived Vietnamese immigrants in San Diego, California, as they adapt to life in a new country. Grades 3-7.

Robinet, Harriette Gillem. *Children of the Fire*. New York: Atheneum, 1991.

Chicago, six years after the Civil War, was a true melting pot, with more and more immigrants of all nationalities pouring in. In the fall of 1871, the weather is dry, and the prairie winds help spread fires that break out through the city. A young black girl named Hallelujah demonstrates courage and resourcefulness to live through the great Chicago fire. Grades 4-8.

Rosenberg, Maxine B. *Making a New Home in America*. New York: Lothrop Lee & Shepard, 1986.

This book takes a look at immigration today, focusing on the lives of children who have recently come from Japan, Guyana, India, Cuba, and Vietnam. This is a good book to use for stimulating discussion about problems facing immigrants today. Grades 1-4.

Sandin, Joan. *The Long Way to a New Land*. New York: Harper & Row, 1981.

This story is about Swedish immigration to the United States during the 1860s. Grades 1-4.

Sandler, Martin W. *Immigrants: A Library of Congress Book*. New York: HarperCollins, 1995.

More than 100 photographs and illustrations accompany this thorough text about immigration. Grades 5 and up.

Say, Allen. *Grandfather's Journey*. Boston: Houghton Mifflin, 1993.

This personal history of the author's family points out the emotions that are common to the immigrant experience. Winner of the 1993 Caldecott Medal. Grades K-3.

Siegel, Beatrice. *Sam Ellis's Island*. New York: Four Winds Press, 1985.

The author recounts the story of the colonial merchant Sam Ellis, his purchase of Ellis Island in New York Harbor, and its role in U.S. history as the major landing point for immigrants. Grades 4-6.

Szucs, Loretto Dennis. *Ellis Island: Gateway to America*. Salt Lake City, UT: Ancestry, 1986.

Szucs provides much factual information about Ellis Island and the immigrants who came through there. Grades 5 and up.

Wartski, Maureen Crane. *A Long Way from Home*. New York: New American Library, 1980.

Kien, a young Vietnamese refugee trying to make a new life for himself in America, finds himself caught in the middle of a battle between the local townspeople and the new immigrants. Grades 5 and up.

Weik, Mary Hays. *A House on Liberty Street*. New York: Atheneum, 1973.

This is an inspiring story, based on fact, about an immigrant's contributions to America. Grades 5-6.

Winter, Jeanette. *Klara's New World*. New York: Alfred A. Knopf, 1992.

This is a picture book re-creation of nineteenth-century immigration as seen through the eyes of a young Swedish girl. Grades 2-7.

Yep, Laurence. *Dragon's Gate*. New York: HarperCollins, 1993.

This 1994 Newbery Honor Book follows the life of a young Chinese railroad worker in the 1860s as he struggles to survive and maintain his dignity in the face of prejudice. Grades 5-7.

———. *Dragonwings*. New York: HarperCollins, 1975.

A young Chinese boy adjusts to life in San Francisco during the time of an earthquake in the spring of 1906. Grades 5-9.

Theme Resources

Commercial Resources

Bernardin, Tom. *The Ellis Island Immigrant Cookbook*. New York: Tom Bernardin, 1991.

This book is filled with recipes and letters from immigrants who passed through Ellis Island. Use with students in grades 5 and up.

Cavanaugh, Betty Gaglio. *Multicultural Art Activities*. Huntington Beach, CA: Teacher Created Materials, 1994.

This book includes directions and patterns for more than forty art projects from cultures around the world. Use at an intermediate level.

Cobblestone: The History Magazine for Young People. Peterborough, NH: Cobblestone.

The December 1982 issue is part one of a two-issue feature for grades 4 and up on American immigrants. Articles include "Steps in Time: Immigration to America" and "Our Most Famous Immigrant: The Statue of Liberty."

The January 1983 issue is part two of a two-issue feature for grades 4 and up on American immigrants. Articles include "The Immigration Stations: Ellis and Angel Islands" and "Lewis Hine and the Children of Ellis Island."

The subject of the November 1991 issue for grades 4 and up is "The Story of American Jews." Articles include "German Jews: Making a Place in America" and "Through the Golden Door."

The focus of the March 1991 issue for grades 4 and up is Chinese Americans. Articles include: "The Long Journey to Fu-Sang: Chinese Immigration to America Begins" and "Benevolent Associations: Aid for Immigrants."

Hill, Linda Burrell. *Using Multicultural Literature: Journeys.* Huntington Beach, CA: Teacher Created Materials, 1994.

This resource promotes historical, geographic, cultural, and social literacy with activities based on trade books, including *Molly's Pilgrim* and *In the Year of the Boar and Jackie Robinson.* Intermediate level.

Jasmine, Julia. *Multicultural Holidays: Share Our Celebrations.* Huntington Beach, CA: Teacher Created Materials, 1994.

This book provides background information on more than seventy-five holidays throughout the year and includes suggestions for ways to observe these holidays in classrooms, doing related activities. All grades.

Laughlin, Mildred Knight, Peggy Tubbs Black, and Margery Kirby Loberg. *Social Studies Readers Theatre for Children.* Englewood, CO: Teacher Ideas Press, 1991.

The authors include suggested scripts for *Molly's Pilgrim* and *An Orphan for Nebraska.* Use with students in grades 4 and up.

Perl, Lila. *The Great Ancestor Hunt: The Fun of Finding Out Who You Are.* New York: Clarion Books, 1989.

This book, best used with students in grades 4-7, shows how to trace one's ancestors through various means. An appendix describes how to use a number of available government resources.

Scriabine, Christine Brendel, Ph.D. *Jackdaw: Immigration: 1870–1930.* Amawalk, NY: Jackdaw Publications, 1995.

This portfolio of primary source material features fourteen reproductions of historical documents. They include: an Ellis Island photo poster with scenes from 1900–1914, a letter to President Theodore Roosevelt on shameful treatment of immigrants at Ellis Island—1906, and an information booklet titled "What Every Immigrant Should Know" from 1922. Notes on the documents, along with a reading list and critical thinking questions, are included. Suitable for use with students in grades 5 and up.

Sima, Patricia, Sharon Coan, Ina Massler Levin, and Karen Goldfluss. *Thematic Unit: Immigration.* Huntington Beach, CA: Teacher Created Materials, 1993.

This intermediate-level resource provides many theme-based activities for all areas of the curriculum, including math, science, language arts, and social studies.

Weitzman, David. *My Backyard History Book.* Boston: Little, Brown, 1975.

Activities and projects demonstrate that learning about the past begins at home. Grades 3 and up.

Wolfman, Ira. *Do People Grow on Family Trees? Genealogy for Kids and Other Beginners.* New York: Workman, 1991.

This is an excellent guide for finding out about one's own family history and how to formally record it. Grades 4 and up.

Videos

America: "Huddled Masses." British Broadcasting/Time Life Video, 1973. (52 minutes)

This video analyzes the history of immigration from the turn of the century to the present day. Use with students in junior high and up.

Meet the Newbery Author: Russell Freedman. New York: Houghton Mifflin-Clarion Author and Artist Videos. (18 minutes)

Viewers are taken on a journey to New York City and Washington, D.C., to meet Russell Freedman. The video gives students insight into the writing process and the research that Freedman puts into his books.

Molly's Pilgrim. New York: Phoenix/BFA Films and Video, 1985. (24 minutes)

This is a heartwarming story of a young immigrant schoolgirl who breaks through the prejudices of her classmates with the help of a "pilgrim" doll made for the Thanksgiving celebration. Use this video with elementary-age students and older.

United States History Video Collection: Immigration and Cultural Change. Bala Cynwyd, PA: Schlessinger Video Productions, 1996. (35 minutes)

Past and present immigration, the world of the immigrants, and the limits of mobility and ethnic diversity are presented.

End-of-Unit Celebration

Immigration Research Project

Select two or three countries from which many people in your area of the United States have emigrated. Divide your class into groups to research these countries. Depending on the size of the groups, individual students or groups of two would then research the following subtopics:

Clothing: Find examples of modern and traditional clothing from the country. Is the dress influenced by the climate of the region? Are there special costumes worn for certain ceremonies?

Customs: What are the customs of people from this country? How do they compare with customs in the United States? What symbols are important to people of this country, and why?

Food: What types of food are typical of this country? Collect recipes and type them into a booklet to share with the class. Choose one or two recipes to prepare and bring in for the class to share.

Geography: Locate your country on a world map. What countries border it? What is the climate of the country? How does the climate affect the inhabitants' day-to-day lives? What major landforms, rivers, and lakes can be found in this country?

Holidays: What holidays are celebrated, and why? What holidays are still celebrated by people who emigrated to the United States? How are these holidays celebrated?

Interviews: Interview immigrants from this country or their relatives to find out their stories to share with the class.

Language: What is the prominent language spoken in this country? Are symbols used in written language different from those used in written English? Compare how their language sounds to that of American English. Learn how to say "Hello, how are you?," "Goodbye," and another saying of your choice and teach them to the class.

Following completion of the research, each group can work cooperatively to prepare and present the information they have acquired to the rest of the class. Encourage students to be creative in their presentations. Specify that they may bring in items associated with the country and use photographs, illustrations, posters, and other media to share the essence of their researched country.

You may wish to invite other classrooms to attend your presentations. Your celebration could be titled "Celebrating Our Heritage." Parents could be invited as well. Immigration is an important part of United States history. This culminating experience following your unit study should be an exciting and memorable one.

The following figures (pages 148, 149, 150) are copies of original naturalization documents for my father. Share these with your students and discuss the meaning of these documents.

Fig. 6.2. The following is a Certificate of Arrival document for my father, Aarnout Jacobus Jansen. He immigrated to the United States from Holland on March 31, 1909, during the largest wave of immigration.

U. S. DEPARTMENT OF LABOR
BUREAU OF NATURALIZATION

No. 5 33665

CERTIFICATE OF ARRIVAL

I HEREBY CERTIFY that the Immigration records show that the alien named below arrived at the port, the date, and in the manner shown, and was lawfully admitted to the United States of America for permanent residence.

Port of entry: New York, NY
Name: Jansen, Aarnout
Date: March 31, 1909
Manner of arrival: SS Potsdam

I FURTHER CERTIFY that this certificate of arrival is issued under authority of, and in conformity with, the provisions of the Act of June 29, 1906, as amended, solely for the use of the alien herein named and only for naturalization purposes.

IN WITNESS WHEREOF, this Certificate of Arrival is issued

June 16, 1933

BY DIRECTION OF THE SECRETARY OF LABOR.

Raymond F. Crist
Commissioner of Naturalization.

Fig. 6.3. This is the Oath of Allegiance document that my father signed, after which he became a citizen of the United States.

OATH OF ALLEGIANCE

I hereby declare, on oath, that I absolutely and entirely renounce and abjure all allegiance and fidelity to any foreign prince, potentate, state, or sovereignty, and particularly to

Wilhelmina, Queen of the Netherlands

of whom (which) I have heretofore been a subject (or citizen); that I will support and defend the Constitution and laws of the United States of America against all enemies, foreign and domestic; that I will bear true faith and allegiance to the same; and that I take this obligation freely without any mental reservation or purpose of evasion: SO HELP ME GOD. In acknowledgment whereof I have hereunto affixed my signature.

Arnold Jacob Jansen
(Signature of petitioner)

Sworn to in open court, this 27 day of September A. D. 1937

_____, Clerk.

By _____ _____, Deputy Clerk.

NOTE.—In renunciation of title of nobility, add the following to the oath of allegiance before it is signed: "I further renounce the title of (give title or titles) an order of nobility, which I have heretofore held."

Petition granted: Line No. 7 of List No. 22 and Certificate No. 4 113 982 issued.

Petition denied: List No. _____

Petition continued from _____ to _____ Reason _____

Fig. 6.4. **This is a Declaration of Intention document, renouncing allegiance to Holland, and declaring my father's intention to become a United States citizen.**

TRIPLICATE
(To be given to declarant)

No. 2642

UNITED STATES OF AMERICA

DECLARATION OF INTENTION
(Invalid for all purposes seven years after the date hereof)

State of New York
County of Wayne
} ss:

In the Supreme Court
of Wayne County, N. Y. *at* Lyons, N. Y.

I, Aarnout Jacobus Jansen
now residing at Marion, Wayne County, New York
(Number and street) *(City or town)* *(State)*
occupation Farmer, aged 28 years, do declare on oath that my personal description is:
Sex Male, color White, complexion Light, color of eyes Blue
color of hair Light, height 5 feet 2 inches; weight 120 pounds; visible distinctive marks
None
race Dutch; nationality Netherlands
I was born in Biervliet, Holland, on April 15, 1907
(City or town) *(Country)* *(Month)* *(Day)* *(Year)*
I am not married. The name of my wife or husband is
we were married on , at ; she or he was
(Month) *(Day)* *(Year)* *(City or town)* *(State or country)*
born at , on , entered the United States
(City or town) *(State or country)* *(Month)* *(Day)* *(Year)*
at , on , for permanent residence therein, and now
(City or town) *(State)* *(Month)* *(Day)* *(Year)*
resides at I have no children, and the name, date and place of birth,
(City or town) *(State or country)*
and place of residence of each of said children are as follows:

I have not heretofore made a declaration of intention: Number , on
(Date)
at
(City or town) *(State)* *(Name of court)*
my last foreign residence was Biervliet, Holland
(City or town) *(Country)*
I emigrated to the United States of America from Rotterdam, Holland
(City or town) *(Country)*
my lawful entry for permanent residence in the United States was at New York, N. Y.
(City or town) *(State)*
under the name of Aarnout Jansen, on March 31, 1909
(Month) *(Day)* *(Year)*
on the vessel SS Potsdam
(If other than by vessel, state manner of arrival)

I will, before being admitted to citizenship, renounce forever all allegiance and fidelity to any foreign prince, potentate, state, or sovereignty, and particularly, by name, to the prince, potentate, state, or sovereignty of which I may be at the time of admission a citizen or subject; I am not an anarchist; I am not a polygamist nor a believer in the practice of polygamy; and it is my intention in good faith to become a citizen of the United States of America and to reside permanently therein; and I certify that the photograph affixed to the duplicate and triplicate hereof is a likeness of me: So HELP ME GOD.

Aarnout Jacobus Jansen
(Original signature of declarant without abbreviation, also alias, if used)

Subscribed and sworn to before me in the office of the Clerk of said Court,
at Lyons, New York this 15 day of Sept.
anno Domini 1935. Certification No. 5 33665 from the Commissioner of Naturalization showing the lawful entry of the declarant for permanent residence on the date stated above, has been received by me. The photograph affixed to the duplicate and triplicate hereof is a likeness of the declarant.

Chas A Noble
Clerk of the Supreme Court.
By *H Ralph Straus*, Deputy Clerk.
14—2023 U. S. GOVERNMENT PRINTING OFFICE: 1931

[SEAL]

Form 2202—L–A.
U. S. DEPARTMENT OF LABOR
NATURALIZATION SERVICE

Fig. 6.5. **The following is a Petition for Naturalization document, which was required of my father to become a United States citizen. Through this petition, my father changed his name from Aarnout Jacobus Jansen to Arnold Jacob Jansen.**

ORIGINAL
(To be retained by clerk)

UNITED STATES OF AMERICA
PETITION FOR NATURALIZATION

No. 1489

To the Honorable the __Supreme__ Court of __New York State__ at __Lyons, N. Y.__

The petition of __Aarnout Jansen__, hereby filed, respectfully shows:

(1) My place of residence is __R. D. 1, Marion, N. Y.__ (2) My occupation is __Farmer__

(3) I was born in __Biervliet, Holland__ on __April 15, 1907.__ My race is __Dutch__

(4) I declared my intention to become a citizen of the United States on __Sept. 15, 1933__ in the __Supreme__ Court of __New York State__, at __Lyons, New York__

(5) I am __not__ married. The name of my wife or husband is _____ we were married on _____ at _____; he was born at _____ on _____; entered the United States _____ on _____ for permanent residence therein, and now _____ I have __no__ children, and the name, date, and place of birth, and place of residence of each of said children are as follows: _____

(6) My last foreign residence was __Biervliet, Holland__ I emigrated to the United States of America from __Rotterdam, Holland__ My lawful entry for permanent residence in the United States was at __New York, N. Y.__, under the name of __Jansen, Aarnout__ __March 31, 1909__, on the vessel __SS Potsdam__ as shown by the certificate of my arrival attached hereto.

(7) I am not a disbeliever in or opposed to organized government or a member of or affiliated with any organization or body of persons teaching disbelief in or opposed to organized government. I am not a polygamist nor a believer in the practice of polygamy. I am attached to the principles of the Constitution of the United States and well disposed to the good order and happiness of the United States. It is my intention to become a citizen of the United States and to renounce absolutely and forever all allegiance and fidelity to any foreign prince, potentate, state, or sovereignty, and particularly to

__Wilhelmina, Queen of the Netherlands__

of whom (which) at this time I am a subject (or citizen), and it is my intention to reside permanently in the United States. (8) I am able to speak the English language. (9) I have resided continuously in the United States of America for the term of five years at least immediately preceding the date of this petition, to wit, since __March 31, 1909__ and in the County of __Wayne__ in this State, continuously next preceding the date of this petition, since __March 31, 1909__, being a residence within said county of at least six months next preceding the date of this petition.

(10) I have __not__ heretofore made petition for Naturalization: Number _____ on _____ and such petition was denied by that Court for the following reasons and causes, to wit: _____ and the cause of such denial has since been cured or removed.

Attached hereto and made a part of this, my petition for citizenship, are my declaration of intention to become a citizen of the United States, certificate from the Department of Labor of my said arrival, and the affidavits of the two verifying witnesses required by law. Wherefore, I, your petitioner, pray that I may be admitted a citizen of the United States of America, and that my name be changed to _____

__Arnold Jacob Jansen__

I, your aforesaid petitioner being duly sworn, depose and say that I have { read / heard read } this petition and know the contents thereof; that the same is true of my own knowledge except as to matters herein stated to be alleged upon information and belief, and that as to those matters I believe it to be true; and that this petition is signed by me with my full, true name.

Aarnout Jansen
(Complete and true signature of petitioner)

AFFIDAVITS OF WITNESSES

__Adrian DeFisher__, occupation __Farmer__ residing at __Marion, N. Y.__, and

__William DeFisher__, occupation __Farmer__ residing at __Marion, N. Y.__

each being severally, duly, and respectively sworn, deposes and says that he is a citizen of the United States of America; that he has personally known and has been acquainted in the United States with __Aarnout Jansen__, the petitioner above mentioned, since __June 1, 1932__ and that to his personal knowledge the petitioner has resided in the United States continuously preceding the date of filing this petition, of which this affidavit is a part, to wit, since the date last mentioned, and at __Marion__, in the County of __Wayne__, this State, in which the above-entitled petition is made, continuously since __June 1, 1932__ and that he has personal knowledge that the petitioner is and during all such periods has been a person of good moral character, attached to the principles of the Constitution of the United States, and well disposed to the good order and happiness of the United States, and that in his opinion the petitioner is in every way qualified to be admitted a citizen of the United States.

Adrian De Fisher
(Signature of witness)

William De Fisher
(Signature of witness)

Subscribed and sworn to before me by the above-named petitioner and witnesses in the office of the Clerk of said Court at __Lyons, New York__ this __23__ day of __June__, Anno Domini 19__37__ I hereby certify that certificate of arrival No. __5 33665__ from the Department of Labor, showing the lawful entry for permanent residence of the petitioner above named, together with declaration of intention No. __2642__ of such petitioner, has been by me filed with, attached to, and made a part of this petition on this date.

Chas G Noble
Clerk.

By *M Raefe Steen*
Special Deputy Clerk.

(SEAL)

From *U.S. History Through Children's Literature.* © 1997. Teacher Ideas Press. (800) 237-6124.

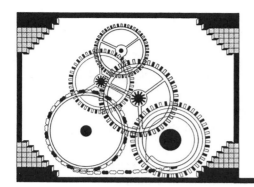

Chapter 7

Industrial Revolution

Introduction

The Industrial Revolution in the United States was a time of immense change. From Samuel Slater's mill in 1790 to the tenement sweatshops of New York City's garment industry in the early twentieth century, the age of manufacturing grew by leaps and bounds. In the closing decades of the nineteenth century, industrialization and labor reform took hold. Other aspects of this new industrial age, including improved manufacturing methods, the first transcontinental railroad, new inventions, and the growth of cities, all had major effects on the lives of the American people.

Working conditions, wages, safety, and health services were of great concern to workers. Poor working conditions, as well as low levels of pay, helped motivate workers to unite and form labor unions.

Trade books for this chapter were chosen to help students better understand these working conditions, the rise of labor unions, child labor, and the treatment of working women in the garment industry.

Read and discuss the following selection to begin your study of the Industrial Revolution.

There Is Power in a Union

Would you have freedom from wage-
    slavery?
Then join in the Grand Industrial Band.
Would you from misery and hunger be free?
Then come do your share like a man.

There is power, there is power
In a band of working men
When they stand
Hand in hand.
That's a power, that's a power
That must rule in every land
One Industrial Union Grand.

Would you have mansions of gold in the
    sky,
And live in a shack
Away in the back?
Would you have wings up in heaven to fly,
And starve here with rags on your back?

There is power, there is power
In a band of working men
When they stand
Hand in hand.
That's a power, that's a power
That must rule in every land,
One Industrial Union Grand.

If you've had enough of the Blood of the
    Lamb,
Then join in the Grand Industrial Band.
If, for a change, you would have eggs and
    ham,
Then come do your share like a man.

There is power, there is power
In a band of working men
When they stand
Hand in hand.
That's a power, that's a power
That must rule in every land,
One Industrial Union Grand.

151

If you like sluggers to beat off your head,
Then don't organize,
All unions despise.
If you want nothing before you are dead,
Shake hands with your boss and look wise.

There is power, there is power
In a band of working men
When they stand
Hand in hand.
That's a power, that's a power
That must rule every land,
One Industrial Union Grand.

Come all you workers from every land.
Come join the Great Industrial Band.
Then we our share of this earth shall
    demand.
Come on, do your share like a man.

There is power, there is power
In a band of working men
When they stand
Hand in hand.
That's a power, that's a power
That must rule in every land,
One Industrial Union Grand.

Attributed to Joe Hill

Whole Group Reading

Paterson, Katherine. *Lyddie*. New York: Lodestar, 1991.

Paterson tells the story of a young farm girl, Lyddie Worthen, who is determined to retain her pride, independence, and family in the face of the Industrial Revolution. In this story, set in the northeastern United States in the 1840s, Paterson explores the effect of industrialization on the existing social order of the time. Grades 5 and up. *Lyddie* was chosen to read with the whole class because it serves as an excellent springboard to the study of the Industrial Revolution.

Author Information

Katherine Paterson was born October 31, 1932 in the Jiangsu Province of China in the city of Qing Jiang; she spent her first four years in the nearby city of Hwaian. In the summer of 1937, she and her family went to the mountains of Jiangxi for a vacation. While there, war broke out between China and Japan. Her father crossed through combat zones to return to work in Hwaian, but Katherine, her mother, and three sisters never saw their home again. Since then, Paterson has lived in more than thirty homes in three countries.

Of her early years, she says, "My mother read to us regularly, and because it opened up such a wonderful world, I taught myself to read before I entered school. Soon afterwards I began to write. I can't remember wanting to become a writer, but I loved stories and poems so much that it was only natural to try my hand at them. My first published work appeared in the Shanghai American School newspaper when I was seven years old."

Following college, Paterson taught sixth grade in rural Virginia. She returned to school to study Bible and Christian Education before going to Japan in 1957. She studied the Japanese language for two years and then worked on the island of Shikoku as a Christian Education assistant.

Paterson's writing career began in 1964 after her first son was born. It was nine years before her first novel, *The Master Puppeteer*, was published. Since then, Paterson has won the Newbery Medal twice and has received many other awards in children's literature.

Activities

1. On a map of the United States, have students locate the following:

   Burlington, VT   Montpelier, VT

   Ferrisburg, VT   Woburn, MA

   Lowell, MA

2. Have students research how maple syrup is made. The following trade books are recommended for this purpose:

   > Burns, Diane. *Sugaring Season: Making Maple Syrup.* Minneapolis, MN: Carolrhoda Books, 1990.
   > This book describes, through text and photographs, the making of maple syrup from tapping the tree and collecting the sap to cooking and packaging. Grades 3 and up.

   > Lasky, Kathryn. *Sugaring Time.* New York: Macmillan, 1983.
   > Text and photographs show how a family taps the sap from maple trees and processes it into maple syrup. Grades 4 and up.

   Students could also make maple cream for all to taste on crackers or popcorn. To do this, whip maple syrup with a hand-mixer until it is light, like creamy honey.

3. Have students write an epilogue for *Lyddie*. It should take place ten years after Lyddie leaves home to go to college, and it should tell what has happened to Lyddie, Charlie, Rachel, and Luke Stevens.

4. Have the class create a comparison/contrast chart of Lyddie's life and life today. In what ways are the students' lives different? How are their lives similar to Lyddie's?

5. Luke Stevens was a Quaker. Have students find out more about Quaker life and beliefs.

6. Contact your local or county historian. Invite him or her to visit your class to provide information on what effect the Industrial Revolution had in your area of the United States.

Discussion

Give the class the following instruction: As we read this book, we will be discussing the following questions. Write down your ideas about these questions and add to them as needed.

1. What kind of sign did Lyddie's mother think the black bear represented?

2. Where had Lyddie's father gone?

3. What did Lyddie's mother want Lyddie and Charles to do?

4. How did the Quakers help Lyddie and Charles?

5. Discuss Lyddie's feelings when she and her brother were separated? How would you feel in that situation?

6. Why did people hire out their children?

7. How was Lyddie treated when she arrived at the tavern?

8. What did the author mean when she said, "Missing Charlie was like wearing a stone around her neck" to Lyddie?

9. Why was it hard for Lyddie to talk to Charlie when he came to visit her?

10. Whom did Lyddie find staying in her house?

11. What did Ezekial mean when he said, "A little reading is an exceedingly dangerous thing"?

12. Why do you think Lyddie decided to give Ezekial the calf money?

13. Why did Lyddie want to go work in the factory in Lowell?

14. Describe the city of Lowell, Massachusetts and Lyddie's reaction to it.

15. Why are Lyddie's roommates worried about her meeting with Dina Goss?

16. What was Lyddie's first full day as a factory girl like?

17. What was it on her second full day that made it easier for Lyddie?

18. What purchase did Lyddie make that seemed to be such a treasure to her?

19. How did Lyddie react to her mother's letter?

20. What is causing the tension between Betsy, Lyddie, and Amelia?

21. Discuss Lyddie's feelings about the petition. What would you do in her place, and why?

22. How did Lyddie get hurt?

23. Why didn't Lyddie want to help one of the new girls on the looms?

24. What did Luke Stevens bring to Lyddie?

25. How did Lyddie's uncle turn her life upside down?

26. Discuss some possible solutions for Lyddie, Rachel, and Charlie.

27. How do you feel about Rachel going to work at the factory as a doffer?

28. Why did Lyddie agree to let Charlie take Rachel to the Phinneys?

29. What do you think of the letter Lyddie received from Luke Stevens?

30. Why did Lyddie decide to go to one of Diana's meetings?

31. Was Lyddie right in defending Brigid? What do you think will happen now?

32. What did Lyddie find when she returned home?

33. Do you think Lyddie will ever go back home?

Vocabulary

adversary (p4)
an opponent, as in a contest; an enemy

heifer (p8)
a young cow that has not produced a calf

potash (p11)
a white substance made from wood ashes, used as a fertilizer and in making glass, soap, and other products

gunnysack (p12)
a sack made from a coarse, heavy material such as burlap

noxious (p13)
harmful to health or morals

Quaker (p14)
a member of the Society of Friends, a religious group (Quakers got their name because their founder told them to tremble at the word of the lord)

fallow (p16)
land allowed to remain unplanted so as to make it more fertile for future planting

ochre (p18)
an earthy material containing iron, varying in color from light yellow to deep orange or red and is used as a pigment

pendulum (p21)
a weight hung from a support and allowed to swing back and forth

exasperated (p22)
annoyed or irritated almost to the point of anger

flax (p23)
fibers of the flax plant when ready to be spun into thread

servitude (p23)
slavery

comrade (p25)
a close companion or friend

sod (p42)
the top layer of the earth

porridge (p42)
a soft food made by boiling oatmeal or some other grain in water, milk, or other liquid

impertinent (p44)
deliberately disrespectful

mortify (p48)
to deprive of self-respect or pride; to humiliate

gentry (p48)
people who are wellborn but not of nobility

slough (p49)
a place of deep mud or stagnant water, such as a bog or swamp

aristocratic (p55)
superior; exclusive; snobbish

scrivener (p58)
in olden days, a public clerk or scribe who prepared deeds, contracts, and other writings

smallpox (p60)
a highly contagious viral disease causing a high fever and skin eruptions that usually leave permanent scars

teeming (p61)
full to almost overflowing

abolitionist (p67)
an individual who wanted to end slavery in the United States

raucous (p75)
rough in sound; hoarse; harsh

laden (p75)
weighed down; loaded; burdened

ravenous (p78)
wildly hungry

blacklist (p81)
a list of persons or organizations regarded as bad or dangerous

feigning (p82)
pretending

doffer (p82)
a person whose function in a cotton mill is to remove the whirling bobbins when they are filled with thread and replace them with empty ones

vexed (p84)
irritated or annoyed

rapier (p87)
a long, narrow sword of light weight, used for thrusting

perdition (p90)
loss of one's soul

diphtheria (p94)
a serious, contagious disease of the throat, usually associated with high fever

banter (p98)
playful teasing; good-natured joking

cajoled (p98)
coaxed or persuaded by flattery or deceit

spinster (p107)
an unmarried woman, especially one no longer young; an "old maid"

tonic (p107)
anything, such as certain medicines, supposed to make a person feel better or more energetic

apothecary shop (p111)
a drugstore or pharmacy

garb (p114)
clothing

privy (p125)
an outdoor toilet; an outhouse

phrenologist (p138)
a supposed scientist who interprets what the bumps on a person's skull indicate about a person's intelligence, disposition, and character

paragon (p157)
a model of excellence

conundrum (p160)
a riddle whose answer depends on a pun

cravat (p164)
an old-fashioned word for a necktie

turpitude (p167)
wickedness

Small Group Reading

Bader, Bonnie. *East Side Story*. New York: Silver Moon Press, 1993.
A young girl and her older sister, working in the Triangle Shirtwaist factory, an early twentieth-century sweatshop on the Lower East Side of New York, join a protest to try to improve the miserable working conditions. Grades 4-7.

Author Information

Bonnie Bader was born May 27, 1961. She lives in Brooklyn, New York.
Bader received her Bachelor of Arts degree from the State University of New York at Binghampton, and her Master of Arts degree in Early Childhood and Elementary Education from Hunter College.

Bader has written and edited *Disney Book News*, written articles for *Info Power* magazine, and edited the Hardy Boys series, as well as other series for young adults. She wrote *Who's Afraid of Ghosts?*, *Golden Quest*, and coauthored (under a pseudonym) with Tracey West *Great-Uncle Dracula*.

By writing *Golden Quest* and *East Side Story* through the eyes of a child, Bader says, "I hope that readers will be able to better relate to the historic times of our country." Her goal is to write books that are educational and entertaining for children.

Activities

1. Have students write a letter from Rachel to Antonio. This letter should be written after the fire at the factory and the passing of the labor laws. It should tell what changes have been made and Rachel's plans for the future.

2. This group should compare *East Side Story* to *Lyddie*. What are the similarities and differences? Students can list these on charts and hang them in the classroom.

3. To find out more information about the Triangle Shirtwaist Company fire in 1911 and its role in labor reform, have students read these two books:

    Goldin, Barbara Diamond. *Fire! The Beginnings of the Labor Movement*. New York: Viking, 1992.

    Wertheimer, Barbara Mayer. *We Were There: The Story of Working Women in America*. New York: Pantheon Books, 1977.

4. Encourage the group to do an oral presentation for the class with the group that read *Fire! The Beginnings of the Labor Movement*. The groups can combine information on factory conditions from both books.

Discussion

Give the small group the following instruction: As your group reads this book, discuss the following questions.

1. Why was her pay so important to Rachel?

2. What was Rachel caught with that got her in trouble at the factory?

3. Do you think it is fair that the girls receive the same pay no matter how long they work?

4. Describe the working conditions at the Triangle Shirtwaist Company.

5. Why was Rachel roughly put into the crate?

6. Why do you think Rachel was treated so differently from her brothers?

7. What made Rachel envious of her brothers?

8. Why were Leah and other women picketing the shop?

9. What was it that caused Leah to be fired from her job?

10. How did Leah and Rachel's parents react to Leah's work with the union?

11. What was the union working for?

12. What is Rachel and Antonio's special project?

13. How did Antonio help Rachel see the possibility of a better future?

14. Why did Rachel and her family leave Russia?

15. How did Rachel feel when Antonio told her he was moving to Brooklyn?

16. How did the fire at the Triangle Shirtwaist Company in 1911 help bring about labor reform in 1914?

Vocabulary

shirtwaist (p2)
a tailored blouse that looks something like a shirt

oppressive (p5)
burdensome; harsh; cruel

sweatshop (p6)
a place where workers labor under poor conditions, for very little pay, and for long hours

eerie (p10)
causing or arousing fear; weird; strange

timid (p11)
fearful or shy

tenement (p13)
an apartment house that is poorly built or maintained, usually overcrowded, and often in a slum

strikebreaker (p21)
a person who contributes to a strike's failure by taking a striker's job

chaos (p23)
complete disorder and confusion

handbill (p34)
a small printed notice distributed by hand

dismal (p66)
dark, gloomy, and depressing

Small Group Reading

Fisher, Leonard Everett. *The Factories*. New York: Holiday House, 1979.

In this book, Fisher explores factories in the United States and how they made America a major industrial power, beginning with Samuel Slater's mill in 1790 and ending with the tenement sweatshops of New York City's garment industry. Grades 4 and up.

Author Information

Leonard Everett Fisher was born June 24, 1924 in the Bronx, New York. Fisher's career has included working as a painter, illustrator, author, and educator. He has been a visiting professor, artist, and consultant at several universities and colleges.

Fisher has won many awards for his work, including The New York Library Association/School Library Media Section Award for Outstanding Contributions in the Fields of Art and Literature, and the Regina Medal from the Catholic Library Association.

Leonard Everett Fisher has written and illustrated many children's books on American history.

Activities

1. On a map of the United States, have students locate the following places:

Albany, NY	Hartford, CT	Pittsburgh, PA
Boston, MA	Lowell, MA	Providence, RI
Bridgeport, CT	Merrimack River, MA	Rochester, NY
Buffalo, NY	Middletown, CT	Sacramento, CA
Chicago, IL	New Haven, CT	Waltham, MA
Concord, MA	Pawtucket, RI	Worcester, MA
Fairhaven, CT	Philadelphia, PA	

2. Have students create advertisements for skilled workers to come to the United States from England.

3. Encourage students to read *The Unions*, also written by Leonard Everett Fisher. It traces the growth and development of the labor movement during the nineteenth century.

4. Have students create a chart that lists working conditions, wages, safety standards, health services, and so on, for factory workers during the Industrial Revolution and today. The chart should then be used to present to the class what the group has learned.

Discussion

Give the small group the following instruction: As your group reads this book, discuss the following questions.

1. Why were American companies advertising in British newspapers for skilled workers to come to America?

2. Why were the British so worried about their skilled craftsmen going to America that they enacted laws restricting emigration and the exportation of British inventions and machinery?

3. What device did James Watt invent that sparked the Industrial Revolution? What did it do?

4. What did Sir Richard Arkwright invent?

5. Why did Samuel Slater leave England secretly? What did his coming to the United States mean to this country?

6. What was the first factory in America to operate successfully?

7. How do you feel about children working in the factories?

8. What did Francis Cabot Lowell bring to America?

9. Describe the inventions of Eli Whitney.

10. In what part of the United States was the manufacturing industry located in the early 1800s?

11. Why did teenage girls go to Lowell, Massachusetts to work in the factories?

12. How did working conditions change for the factory girls from 1830 to 1845?

13. By the mid-eighteenth century, what was the reason for factories being located in large cities?

14. Discuss the causes of the Civil War. What effect did the Industrial Revolution have on the war?

15. Discuss the advances in the Industrial Revolution following the Civil War. What were some of the highly sought after products that were manufactured?

16. Why did America become known as the land of "milk and honey" to the immigrants?

17. Under what kind of conditions did immigrants live and work?

18. Once it was finally enforced, how did the Tenement House Act help the people who lived in the tenements?

19. How did labor unions and politicians help provide better working conditions and benefits for factory workers?

Vocabulary

enraged (p7)
　　filled with rage; made angry or furious

resentful (p7)
　　full of or tending to feel resentment, anger, and ill-will based on real or imagined wrong or injury

aristocracy (p7)
　　a class of society inheriting by birth a high position or rank, certain powers and privileges, and usual wealth

despair (p7)
　　the heavy feeling that comes when all hope is lost or given up

tolerate (p7)
　　to allow or to permit without opposition

wary (p8)
　　watchful and suspicious; very careful; cautious

embark (p8)
　　to begin, such as an adventure or project; to set forth

prosperity (p8)
a prosperous condition, including material wealth and success

textile (p8)
of or having to do with weaving or woven fabrics

inducements (p9)
incentives designed to encourage desired actions

Parliament (p9)
the legislature of Great Britain, or of any of the self-governing members of the Commonwealth

emigrate (p9)
to move from one country or section of a country to settle in another

prohibit (p9)
to forbid, especially by authority or law

ambition (p11)
an eager desire to succeed or to achieve something, such as wealth or power

apprentice (p11)
a person who works for another to learn a trade or business

cumbersome (p11)
hard to move or manage; unwieldy

intricate (p11)
complicated or involved

ignorant (p12)
having little or no learning or knowledge

catalyst (p12)
something that speeds up change

colossal (p12)
beyond belief

blacksmith (p14)
a person who works with iron by heating it in a forge and then hammering it into shape

rival (p16)
to try to outdo or defeat; to compete with

supremacy (p16)
superior power or authority

hub (p18)
a center of great activity or interest

surrogate (p20)
a person having the authority to act in place of another

secular (p20)
of or for the world rather than the church; not sacred or concerned with religion

parasol (p27)
a small, light umbrella carried to protect oneself from the sun

vehement (p27)
marked by strong feeling or passion; intense

immigrant (p27)
a person who comes to a country or region where he or she was not born, with the intention of living there

idealism (p27)
the tendency to see things as one would like them to be rather than as they are

squalor (p28)
filth, wretched poverty, or degradation

dank (p30)
unpleasantly cold and wet

optimism (p30)
the tendency to see things in a positive light

divisive (p30)
causing people to disagree sharply

specter (p31)
a ghost

endure (p31)
to last for a long time; to continue to exist

skirmish (p32)
a brief fight between small groups of troops

subdue (p32)
to gain power over, as by force; to conquer

abundance (p32)
a full or plentiful supply; more than enough

artillery (p34)
large mounted guns; cannons

myriad (p38)
a vast, indefinite number

ravenous (p38)
extremely greedy

proliferation (p44)
rapid growth

conspicuous (p45)
attracting attention because remarkable

disenfranchise (p52)
to take away a right or privilege, especially the right to vote

hovel (p52)
a poor, dirty hut or small house in bad condition

tenement (p54)
an apartment house that is poorly built or maintained, usually overcrowded, and often in a slum

tuberculosis (p54)
a disease, caused by a certain bacterium and
marked by the formation of tubercles (lesions)
in various parts of the body, that chiefly affects
the lungs and is accompanied by a slow wasting away of strength and vitality

sweatshop (p54)
a place where workers labor under poor conditions, for very little pay, and for long hours

patent (p56)
a government document giving an inventor the
sole right to make and sell a new invention or to
use a new process for a certain number of years

infringement (p56)
a violation of someone's rights

agitated (p59)
aroused interest in changing something, as by
speaking or writing

unscrupulous (p60)
having no scruples, principles, or conscience;
dishonest

Small Group Reading

Freedman, Russell. *Kids at Work: Lewis Hine and the Crusade Against Child Labor*. New York:
Clarion Books, 1994.

This is a book about the children who, before World War I, labored in America's factories and
mines at substandard wages under poor conditions. Lewis Hine, a former schoolteacher, left his
teaching position in 1908 to take a full-time job as an investigative photographer for the National Child
Labor Committee, an organization that was conducting a major campaign against the exploitation of
children. Hine's photographs accompany Freedman's text and together present a vivid account of social
reforms that were urgently needed as industrialization changed American society. Grades 4 and up.

Author Information

Russell Freedman was born October 11, 1929 in San Francisco, California. He has worked as a
newsman, a television publicity writer, an editor, and an instructor of writing workshops, as well as a
freelance writer specializing in subjects of interest to young people.

Freedman has written at least one book a year and has built a solid reputation among teachers,
librarians, and the reading public for his craftsmanship, reliability, and intellectual integrity. He has
written nonfiction books on a wide variety of topics, although now he mostly writes biographies. When
he prepares to write a biography he immerses himself in his subject by reading numerous books,
conducting meticulous research, and visiting relevant historical sites.

Activities

1. On a map of the United States, have students locate the following:

Alexandria, VA	Cincinnati, OH	Lancaster, SC
Augusta, GA	Dunbar, LA	Loudon, TN
Bells, TX	Fall River, MA	Morgantown, WV
Biloxi, MS	Fayetteville, TN	Oshkosh, WI
Blufton, SC	Gastonia, NC	Sterling, CO
Browns Mills, NJ	Hastings-on-Hudson, NY	Wilmington, DE

2. Have students write essays about Lewis Hine's contributions to the enactment of child labor laws
    in the United States, including their own opinions of the importance of his work. These essays
    can be shared orally with the rest of the class.

3. Have students choose four or five photographs from the book, photocopy them, and put them on small pieces of poster board. Students should then write short summaries to place beneath the photos describing what is taking place in them. They can then display the posters in the classroom for all to see.

4. Encourage students who are interested in learning more about child labor to read Catherine A. Welch's *Danger at the Breaker* (Minneapolis, MN: Carolrhoda Books, 1992).

Discussion

Give the small group the following instruction: As your group reads this book, discuss the following questions.

1. Why had the number of child laborers been growing steadily before World War I?

2. What were some of the jobs these children did?

3. Why did many Americans demand an end to child labor in the early 1900s?

4. What did Lewis Hine do to help put an end to child labor?

5. How did Lewis Hine become a photographer?

6. What was Ellis Island called?

7. What happened to immigrants at Ellis Island?

8. How did Lewis Hine see his camera as a weapon against the exploitation of children?

9. What did Lewis Hine mean when he said, "I felt that I was merely changing my educational efforts from the classroom to the world"?

10. Why did factories hire children?

11. Why weren't the child labor laws that some states passed of much help?

12. Why was Lewis Hine sometimes in danger because of what he was doing?

13. What kind of things did Hine do to get into the factories, mines, sweatshops, and mills to take his photographs?

14. What industry was one of the worst offenders of child labor laws?

15. Describe some of the dangers to cotton mill workers.

16. What were the living conditions of immigrant cannery workers?

17. Why was Pennsylvania's child labor law almost useless in the coal mines?

18. What dangers did children face in the coal mines?

19. Why did most adult glassworks employees refuse to let their own children work in these factories?

20. Besides factory work, what other jobs did children in America's cities perform?

21. Why didn't any of the existing child labor laws in the early 1900s apply to farm workers?

22. Why did Lewis Hine say, "I am sure I am right in my choice of work"?

23. Following his ten years with the National Child Labor Committee, what did Lewis Hine do?

24. Upon his return to the United States, Hine chose to take positive photographs. What were they?

25. After all of Lewis Hine's contributions to society, how did he come to die in poverty?

26. Discuss the Declaration of Dependence.

27. Explain the purpose of the Fair Labor Standards Act, signed by President Franklin Delano Roosevelt in 1938.

Vocabulary

stenography (p8)
  the art of reading and writing in shorthand

pantomime (p12)
  to make gestures without speech

acrid (p15)
  burning; bitter; irritating, such as a taste or odor

teeming (p16)
  full to almost overflowing

sweatshop (p16)
  a place where workers labor under poor conditions, for very little pay, and for long hours

tenement (p16)
  an apartment house that is poorly built or maintained, usually overcrowded, and often in a slum

exploitation (p19)
  improper or selfish use

apprentice (p21)
  a person who works for another to learn a trade or business

militant (p22)
  taking or ready to take aggressive action, such as on behalf of beliefs or rights

itinerant (p26)
  a person who travels from place to place, especially one who moves from job to job

textile (p26)
  of or having to do with weaving or woven fabrics

wharf (p29)
  a structure, usually a platform built along or out from a shore, alongside which ships or boats may dock

sharecropper (p32)
  a farmer who lives on and farms land but does not own it and who gives the landowner a share of the crop as rent

tenant farmer (p32)
  one who lives on and farms land owned by someone else and pays rent either in cash or farm produce

doffers (p32)
  those cotton mill workers who remove the whirling bobbins when they are filled with thread and replace them with empty ones

emaciated (p35)
  abnormally thin, from hunger or disease

overseer (p35)
  a person who supervises laborers at their work

inquest (p52)
  a legal investigation, especially one held before a jury, that is conducted by a coroner to determine the cause of a death

migrants (p65)
  people who move regularly from place to place in search of work

abolition (p91)
  the act of putting an end to something

Small Group Reading

📖 Goldin, Barbara Diamond. *Fire! The Beginnings of the Labor Movement*. New York: Viking, 1992.

Fire destroys the Triangle Shirtwaist Company where Rosie's sister, Freyda, works. Rosie decides to join her sister and become involved in the union struggle for better working conditions in factories. Grades 3-6.

Author Information

Barbara Diamond Goldin lives in Northampton, Massachusetts and teaches creative writing to sixth-, seventh-, and eighth-graders at Heritage Academy in Longmeadow. Her book *Just Enough Is Plenty* won the National Jewish Book Award.

Goldin says she feels very close to the Triangle Factory fire story. Her mother's family lived on the Lower East Side, and her grandfather was a garment worker at the time of the fire. In writing about these times, she hopes to pass on to young people a sense of what conditions were like for the workers and why unions were so important to them.

Activities

1. Have students write diary entries from Freyda's point of view. At least one entry should be written before the fire and one after the fire.

2. Have students compare *Fire! The Beginnings of the Labor Movement* with *Lyddie*. What were the similarities and differences? The students can list this information on charts to be hung in the classroom.

3. To learn more about labor reform and the Triangle Shirtwaist Company, have students read these books:

    Bader, Bonnie. *East Side Story.* Kaleidoscope, 1993.

    Wertheimer, Barbara Mayer. *We Were There: The Story of Working Women in America.* New York: Pantheon Books, 1977.

4. Encourage this group to do an oral presentation for the class with the group that read *East Side Story*, combining information on factory conditions gained from both books.

Discussion

Give the small group the following instruction: As your group reads this book, discuss the following questions.

1. Why does Rosie think her sister, Freyda, is lucky?

2. Why does Rosie have to hurry home?

3. What do young factory workers do when the inspector comes along?

4. Why does Freyda spend so much time at union meetings?

5. Why do you think Rosie didn't tell her parents where the fire was?

6. Discuss Rosie's feelings when she learned what building was on fire.

7. How did Freyda escape the burning factory?

8. Describe the factory conditions that led to the fire at the Triangle Shirtwaist Company.

9. How would unions help factory workers?

10. What was Rosie's plan to help the union?

11. What changes took place after the Triangle Shirtwaist Company fire?

Vocabulary

Sabbath (p1)
a day of the week set aside for rest and worship; Saturday is the Sabbath for Jews and some Christians, while Sunday is the Sabbath for most Christians

lye (p2)
a strong alkaline solution, usually sodium hydroxide, used for several purposes, including making soap and refining oil

challah (p8)
a white bread, often baked in the shape of a braid, traditionally served by Jews on the Sabbath

synagogue (p11)
a place of meeting for Jewish worship and religious instruction

feather boa (p12)
a long scarf made of feathers

shirtwaist (p13)
a tailored blouse that looks something like a shirt

kerchief (p24)
a piece of fabric, usually square, worn over the head or around the neck

grindstone (p27)
a flat, circular stone that is rotated and used for grinding and sharpening tools

banister (p35)
a post that supports a railing, such as along a staircase

sweatshop (p53)
    a place where workers labor under poor conditions, for very little pay, and for long hours

immigrant (p53)
    a person who comes into a country or region where he or she was not born with the intention of living there

garment (p53)
    an article of clothing

memoirs (p54)
    the story of a person's own life and experiences

cloak (p54)
    a loose outer garment, usually without sleeves

Small Group Reading

Ross, Pat. *Hannah's Fancy Notions: A Story of Industrial New England*. New York: Viking Kestrel, 1988.

This is the story of Hannah and her family in industrial New England. When Hannah sets out to make something special for her sister, who works to support the family, she doesn't suspect the consequences of her gift. Grades 3-6.

Author Information

Pat Ross was born February 4, 1943 in Baltimore, Maryland.

Ross began her publishing career as an assistant editor of *Humpty Dumpty's Magazine* in 1965 and quickly became the managing editor. She eventually became vice president and editor-in-chief of Pantheon and Knopf.

In the 1970s, Ross was one of the founding members of Feminists on Children's Media, a group dedicated to improving the portrayal of girls and women in books.

Ross's books include a beginning-to-read series of books, which features two best friends named Mandy and Mimi. Titles include *Meet M and M* and *M and M and the Santa Secrets*.

Ross continues to write for children but is no longer involved in editorial work.

Activities

1. Have students design and make their own bandboxes based on the descriptions in the text and the illustrations.

2. On a map of the United States, have students locate Lowell and Boston, Massachusetts.

3. Have students write an epilogue for *Hannah's Fancy Notions*. It should take place ten years after the story ends and tell how Hannah's, Rebecca's, and their fathers' lives have changed.

4. On a poster-size chart, have students compare and contrast Rebecca's life in the factories and after with that of Lyddie's in *Lyddie* by Katherine Paterson. The students can then present their findings to the class.

Discussion

Give the small group the following instruction: As your group reads this book, discuss the following questions.

1. Why has Hannah's sister, Rebecca, taken a factory job in Lowell?

2. How has life changed for Hannah since Rebecca went to work at the factory?

3. What did Hannah and her father make for Rebecca for her birthday?

4. How did Rebecca's gift make her feel better about going back to Lowell?

5. What reminds Hannah so much of her mother?

6. Why did Rebecca's birthday gift cause such excitement?

7. Why was Rebecca fired from her job at the factory?

8. How did Hannah's dreaming change her and her family's lives?

9. Do you have a dream for your future that you hope will come true?

Vocabulary

avalanche (p4)
a pile of something that falls

parlor (p12)
a room for receiving visitors or entertaining guests

satchel (p16)
a small bag or case

sweltering (p28)
extremely hot and humid

cobbler (p35)
a shoemaker

trellis (p36)
a structure made of crossed strips, such as of wood or metal, used as a screen or support for climbing plants

dismal (p43)
dark, gloomy, and depressing

homespun (p52)
cloth made of homespun yarn or a strong, loose fabric

scoff (p52)
to show scorn or mocking disbelief; to jeer

Bibliography

Individual Titles

Adler, David A. *Benjamin Franklin: Printer, Inventor, Statesman.* New York: Holiday House, 1992.
This biography follows the life of a well-known American who achieved greatness as a writer, scientist, inventor, and statesman. Grades 3-5.

———. *Thomas Alva Edison: Great Inventor.* New York: Holiday House, 1990.
This is a biography of the inventive genius who developed the electric lightbulb. Grades 3-5.

Bender, Lionel. *Eyewitness Books: Invention.* New York: Alfred A. Knopf, 1991.
Photographs and text explore such inventions as the wheel, gears, levers, clocks, telephones, and rocket engines. Grades 5 and up.

Clare, John D., ed. *Living History: Industrial Revolution.* San Diego, CA: Gulliver Books, 1994.
This book describes the dramatic technological, industrial, and social changes brought about by the Industrial Revolution in America and Europe. Grades 5 and up.

Clements, Gillian. *The Picture History of Great Inventors.* New York: Alfred A. Knopf, 1994.
This book contains an illustrated introduction to sixty major inventors, from the unknown inventor of the wheel to today's developers of virtual reality. Grades 4 and up.

Doherty, Berlie. *Granny Was a Buffer Girl.* New York: Orchard, 1986.
The night before Jess goes off to France for a university year abroad, her parents and grandparents gather to celebrate and share the stories of their lives. Winner of the 1986 Carnegie Medal. Grades 5 and up.

Dublin, Thomas. *Farm to Factory: Women's Letters, 1830–1860.* 2d ed. New York: Columbia University Press, 1993.
The letters included show how these young mill women contributed to the support of distant family members. The first edition of this book was published in 1981. Grades 7 and up.

———. *Transforming Women's Work: New England Lives in the Industrial Revolution.* Ithaca, NY: Cornell University Press, 1994.
Dublin explores the work and family lives of rural and urban New Englanders across the Industrial Revolution of the nineteenth century. This very thorough book would make an excellent research resource. Grades 7 and up.

———. *Women at Work: The Transformation of Work and Community in Lowell, Massachusetts, 1826–1860.* New York: Columbia University Press, 1979.
The rise of the cotton textile industry in New England drastically changed the lives of working women. Thousands of single women left their homes

to work in mill towns. This book details the lives of women factory workers in Lowell, Massachusetts in the mid-nineteenth century. Grades 8 and up.

Fisher, Leonard Everett. *The Unions*. New York: Holiday House, 1982.

Fisher traces the growth and development of the labor movement during the nineteenth century. Grades 4 and up.

Giblin, James Cross. *The Skyscraper Book*. New York: Thomas Y. Crowell, 1981.

The author describes the first skyscraper, built in Chicago in 1884, which triggered new architectural wonders around the world. Grades 4-8.

Green, Connie Jordan. *Emmy*. New York: Margaret K. McElderry, 1992.

When, in the 1920s, eleven-year-old Emmy's father is disabled in a coal mining accident, she and the others in her family do what they can to help; her fourteen-year-old brother takes Pa's place in the mines. Grades 5-8.

Hall, Donald. *Lucy's Christmas*. San Diego, CA: Browndeer Press, 1994.

In the fall of 1909, Lucy begins making Christmas presents to give to her family and friends at the church's Christmas program. Grades K-4.

——. *Lucy's Summer*. San Diego, CA: Browndeer Press, 1995.

For Lucy Wells, who lives on a farm in New Hampshire, the summer of 1910 is filled with helping her mother can fruits and vegetables, enjoying the Fourth of July celebration, and other activities. Grades K-4.

Josephson, Hannah. *The Golden Threads: New England's Mill Girls and Magnates*. New York: Duell, Sloan and Pearce, 1949.

In this book, Josephson describes the lives of the mill girls in Lowell, Massachusetts during the Industrial Revolution. Grades 7 and up.

Kraft, Betsy Harvey. *Mother Jones: One Woman's Fight for Labor*. New York: Clarion Books, 1995.

Mother Jones was one of America's most effective union organizers. This book tells of her fight for workers' rights. Grades 5 and up.

Langley, Andrew. *The Industrial Revolution*. New York: Viking, 1994.

The results of the Industrial Revolution are revealed in wonderful see-through cutaways. The text itself is excellent, and illustrations are numerous. Grades 3 and up.

Macaulay, David. *Mill*. Boston: Houghton Mifflin, 1983.

Through text and illustrations, Macaulay brings imaginary mills to life. Although imaginary, their planning, construction, and operation are typical of mills

in New England in the nineteenth century. Grades 4 and up.

——. *The Way Things Work*. Boston: Houghton Mifflin, 1988.

David Macaulay demonstrates, in four sections, the workings of hundreds of machines and devices. Explanations of the scientific principles behind each machine are included. The illustrations are wonderful, and the text is easy to understand. Grades 4 and up.

McKissack, Patricia, and Fredrick McKissack. *African-American Inventors*. Brookfield, CT: Millbrook Press, 1994.

This book presents the stories of some of the remarkable African-American men and women inventors. Grades 5 and up.

Mitchell, Barbara. *Click! A Story About George Eastman*. Minneapolis, MN: Carolrhoda Books, 1986.

Mitchell follows the life and career of the man who revolutionized photography by developing a camera simple enough for anyone to use. Grades 3-5.

Parker, Steve. *Random House Book of How Things Work*. New York: Random House, 1991.

This comprehensive, illustrated guide shows how more than 300 machines, mechanisms, and processes that affect our everyday lives work. Grades 3-7.

Platt, Richard. *Smithsonian Visual Timeline of Inventions*. New York: Dorling Kindersley, 1994.

This is a detailed time line of inventions, from the very first prehistoric tools to today's modern inventions. Many of the photographed objects are from the collections of the Smithsonian Institution's National Museum. More than 400 inventions are included. Grades 4 and up.

Rappaport, Doreen. *Trouble at the Mines*. New York: Thomas Y. Crowell, 1987.

This is a fictionalized account of actual events surrounding the 1898 coal miner strike in Arno, Pennsylvania. Eight-year-old Rosie joins Mother Jones in organizing workers. Grades 3-6.

Schwartz, Alvin. *When I Grew Up Long Ago*. New York: J. B. Lippincott, 1978.

This book is filled with recollections from a variety of people who were children at the turn of the century. They provide insights into family life, schools, recreational activities, holiday celebrations, and health. Grades 4-8.

Selden, Bernice. *The Mill Girls: Lucy Larcom, Harriet Hanson Robinson, Sarah G. Bagley*. New York: Atheneum, 1983.

Selden tells of the lives of three women in New England at the beginning of the Industrial Revolution, a time important in the history of both women and labor. Grades 5 and up.

Simonds, Christopher. *Samuel Slater's Mill and the Industrial Revolution*. Englewood Cliffs, NJ: Silver Burdett Press, 1990.

This is a biography of the Englishman who, concerned over the heavy human toll the Industrial Revolution was taking in England, left for America despite laws forbidding the emigration of textile workers. There, he established the American textile industry. Grades 5-8.

Walsh, Jill Paton. *A Chance Child*. New York: Farrar, Straus & Giroux, 1978.

Christopher is compelled to search for his half-brother Creep, whom some people insist is nonexistent. Creep had traveled back in time into England during the Industrial Revolution. Christopher locates Parliamentary Papers containing Nathaniel Creep's personal narrative of working conditions during the Industrial Revolution 100 years earlier. The personal narrative confirms that Nathaniel Creep was Christopher Creep's half-brother. Grades 5 and up.

Welch, Catherine A. *Danger at the Breaker*. Minneapolis, MN: Carolrhoda Books, 1992.

Eight-year-old Andrew, the son of a coal miner, leaves school in 1885 to work at the mines, where he learns the dangers of a coal mine on his first day on the job. Grades 2-4.

Theme Resources

Commercial Resources

Butts, Miriam, and Patricia Heard. *Jackdaw: The Early Industrialization of America: "From Wharf to Waterfall."* Amawalk, NY: Jackdaw Publications, 1993.

This portfolio of primary source materials includes a letter from Samuel Slater to his employer, William Almy, dated August 19, 1795; and maps showing the principal canals, railroad, and highways in 1840 and 1860 among other things. Use with students in grades 5 and up.

Cobblestone: The History Magazine for Young People. Peterborough, NH: Cobblestone.

The topic of the September 1981 issue for grades 4 and up is "America at Work: The Industrial Revolution." Articles include "Steps in Time: Revolutionary Ideas and Inventors" and "The Story of America's Industrial Revolution."

The June 1994 issue for grades 4 and up focuses on women inventors. Articles include "Early Women Inventors" and "Women Inventors of World War I."

Jefferies, David. *Thematic Unit: Industrial Revolution.* Huntington Beach, CA: Teacher Created Materials, 1993.

This resource for use with students in grades 5 and up includes a variety of activities for all curriculum areas related to the Industrial Revolution.

Kids Discover: Ben Franklin. New York: Kids Discover, November, 1994.

The focus of this issue for grades 4 and up is Ben Franklin. Articles include "Young Ben," "Printing and Publishing," and "Ben the Statesman." It includes a few simple experiments with electricity that students can do.

Martin, Rebecca. *Inquiring into the Theme of the Industrial Revolution: Based on Katherine Paterson's Lyddie.* Logan, IA: Perfection Learning, 1995.

This resource provides grades 6-8 activities for *Lyddie*, background information for the theme, and much more.

Computer Resources

Macaulay, David. *The Way Things Work.* [CD-ROM]. New York: Dorling Kindersley, 1994.

This CD-ROM is based on David Macaulay's book. It will make science and technology come alive for students.

Who Built America? From the Centennial Celebration of 1876 to the Great War of 1914. [CD-ROM]. New York: Voyager, 1994.

Students will be able to experience history by accessing some of the original source documents: audio, video, and text.

Videos

Trumpet Video Visits: Katherine Paterson. Holmes, PA: Trumpet Club, 1993. (20 minutes)

Students will learn what inspires Katherine Paterson's writing, as well as her approach to the writing process.

United States History Video Collection: Industrialization and Urbanization 1870–1910. Bala Cynwyd, PA: Schlessinger Video Productions, 1996. (35 minutes)

This video presents the rise of heavy industry and the birth of corporate America, mechanized farming and the agricultural revolution, immigration, the rise of industrial cities, and pollution and the birth of the conservation movement.

End-of-Unit Celebration

Industrial Revolution Research Project

Divide your class into groups of two or three to research the following topics. When students have completed their projects, hold a presentation day.

Child Labor During the Industrial Revolution

A Time Capsule for Future Generations (Children in 1900 would never have believed that in the future, people could . . .)

A Time Line of Inventions

Factory Conditions During the Industrial Revolution

Famous Inventors

The Labor Reform Movement

Samuel Slater

Technological Advances

The Event I Would Like to Have Witnessed and Why

Whom I Would Liked to Have Met and Why

Women and the Industrial Revolution

Industrial Revolution Vocabulary Activity

In addition to the research project, you might wish to celebrate the end of the unit by having students work in teams to complete the vocabulary activity presented in figure 7.1 (p. 169). This could be competitive or noncompetitive, with appropriate prizes awarded to all.

Fig. 7.1. **Industrial revolution vocabulary activity.**

Directions: Place the letter of the correct definition in the blank next to the vocabulary word.

1. servitude _____
2. garment _____
3. shirtwaist _____
4. blacklist _____
5. oppressive _____
6. diphtheria _____
7. sweatshop _____
8. porridge _____
9. overseer _____
10. tenement _____
11. strikebreaker _____
12. immigrant _____
13. apprentice _____
14. doffer _____
15. textile _____

a. a person who supervises laborers at their work

b. burdensome; harsh; cruel

c. a place where workers labor under poor conditions, for very little pay, and for long hours

d. slavery

e. a person who comes into a country or region where he or she was not born with the intention of living there

f. a list of persons or organizations regarded as bad or dangerous

g. of or having to do with weaving or woven fabrics

h. a worker in a cotton mill who removes the whirling bobbins when they are filled and replaces them with empty ones

i. a person who works for another to learn a trade or a business

j. a tailored blouse that looks something like a shirt

k. an article of clothing

l. a soft food made by boiling oatmeal or some other grain in water, milk, or other liquid

m. an apartment house that is poorly built or maintained, usually overcrowded, and often in a slum

n. a person who contributes to a strike's failure by taking a striker's job

o. a serious contagious disease of the throat, usually associated with a high fever

Chapter 8

World War I

Introduction

World War I began in Europe in July 1914. The causes of the war run from economics to the rivalry between the two triple alliances of the powers of Europe. The precipitation of the war is explained by the Serbian assassination of the Austro-Hungarian Archduke Franz Ferdinand in Sarajevo on June 28. Austria-Hungary moved to punish the Serbians. This move caused Tsarist Russia to mobilize against Austria-Hungary in defense of their ancient allies, the Serbian slavs. Germany then declared war on Russia to defend Austria-Hungary. The war was originally known as The Great War and The War to End All Wars and later was called The First World War and World War I. It was the first time war had been fought on a global scale, with battles being fought in the air as well as on land.

Fear and hatred drove both France and Germany into finding ways to strengthen themselves against each other. Alliances were formed. By the end of 1914, Great Britain had set up naval blockades in the Northern Atlantic, which intercepted supply ships bound for the Central Powers of Germany, Austria-Hungary, Turkey, and Bulgaria. In early May of 1915, German U-boats had set up their own blockade to prevent ships from reaching the Allied Powers of Great Britain, France, Russia, and after 1915, Italy.

Americans watched from a distance, glad to be on the far shore of the Atlantic. However, Americans were outraged when the U.S. passenger ship *Lusitania* was sunk by German U-boats in 1915. Finally, on April 2, 1917, President Woodrow Wilson declared war on Germany, and the United States joined the Allied Powers and was no longer an observer.

The books recommended in this chapter were chosen in an attempt to help students understand the horrors of World War I and its effects on Americans at home, as well as on those who fought.

Whole Group Reading

📖 Rostkowski, Margaret I. *After the Dancing Days*. New York: Harper & Row, 1986.

Annie is very happy when her father returns home at the end of World War I. Her father continues to work as a doctor in a veteran's hospital near their home. Annie visits the hospital and becomes friends with a young veteran named Andrew, who was badly burned in the war. Through their friendship, Annie comes to understand the devastation war can bring, and Andrew learns to accept his situation and continue on with his life. Grades 5 and up.

After the Dancing Days was chosen to be read with the whole class because of its emphasis on the feelings of people back home in the United States after the war ended and the need to educate people to diminish prejudice.

Author Information

Margaret Rostkowski was born January 12, 1945 in Little Rock, Arkansas. She has a bachelor of arts degree in History from Middlebury College and a master's degree in teaching from the University of Kansas. She is a high school teacher. Rostkowski has won many awards for *After the Dancing Days*, including the 1987 International Reading Association's Children's Book Award, the 1987 Jefferson Cup Award from the Virginia Library Association, and the 1986 Golden Kite Award for fiction. It was also named a 1986 "Notable Children's Trade Book in the Field of Social Studies" by the National Council for the Social Studies.

Activities

1. On a map of the United States, have students locate Colorado; Kansas City, Kansas; and Topeka, Kansas.

2. Have students write a letter from Annie to Andrew's father. They should attempt to convince him to visit Andrew at St. John's.

3. Choose a student or group of students to recite the speech on pages 210 and 211 for the rest of the class.

4. If possible, ask your school's music teacher to sing one or more of the following songs mentioned in the book with your class:
   "Over There"
   "It's a Long Way to Tipperary"
   "Smile, Smile, Smile"
   "Onward, Christian Soldiers"

5. Have students write letters to the editor of Annie's hometown newspaper. In their letters they should try to convince the townspeople that they should not forget the men who fought in World War I. They should use what they have learned from this novel, as well as other materials used in studying World War I, in writing their letters.

Discussion

Give the class the following instruction: As we read this book, we will be discussing the following questions. Write down your ideas about these questions and add to them as needed.

1. How does Annie feel while she waits at the train station for her father to arrive?

2. In 1918, what did telegrams mean to people who received them?

3. Why did Annie's mother appear frightened at the station?

4. What did Annie and her mother see at the station?

5. Why did Annie feel shy with her father on his first day home?

6. Why didn't Annie want her father to work at St. John's?

7. Discuss Annie's relationship with her Uncle Paul.

8. What made Annie want to visit St. John's?

9. Why did Annie defend her father to Emily and Miss Peterson?

10. How did Annie feel about her father riding her Uncle Paul's motorcycle?

11. What did Annie's mother do at St. John's that upset Annie?

12. Discuss Annie's mother's feelings about the war and the men at St. John's.

13. Why did Andrew receive the Purple Heart?

14. How is Annie important to Andrew?

15. Why didn't Andrew's father ever visit him?

16. Discuss your feelings when Timothy's bandages were removed.

17. Why do you think it is so hard for Annie's mother to understand her feelings?

18. Why did it upset Annie to find out how her Uncle Paul really died?

19. Why did Andrew's happiness make Annie feel sad?

20. Why did Annie's mother change her opinion about Andrew?

21. Describe the scene at the ceremony to dedicate the monument. Discuss the differences in feelings about the ceremony that people had.

22. How did you feel when Andrew asked Annie to keep his Purple Heart for him?

23. How did Annie change from the beginning of the novel?

Vocabulary

telegram (p3)
a message sent by telegraph; a device for sending and receiving messages by means of a series of electrical or electromagnetic pulses

customary (p12)
based on custom; usual

silhouette (p14)
the outline of a person or object seen against a light or a light background

phosphorus (p23)
a nonmetallic element that forms many compounds essential to life but in the elemental state is poisonous and ignites spontaneously in air

mortar (p23)
a short cannon, loaded through the muzzle and fired at a high angle

shrapnel (p23)
an artillery shell that explodes in the air and scatters a quantity of small metal balls

resolved (p24)
determined

earnest (p26)
very serious, determined, or sincere

chariot (p30)
a two-wheeled vehicle pulled by horses, used in ancient times for racing, in war, and in processions

enlist (p31)
to join a branch of the armed forces voluntarily

tuberculosis (p32)
a disease, caused by certain bacteria and marked by the formation of tubercles (lesions) in various parts of the body, that mostly affects the lungs and is accompanied by a slow wasting away of strength and vitality

dreary (p36)
full of or causing sadness or gloom

chigger (p36)
the larva of certain mites, attaches itself to the skin and causes great itching

sober (p36)
modest and quiet, as in color or manner of dress

cathedral (p38)
the main church of a diocese of some Christian churches, containing the bishop's throne

solitary (p38)
secluded or lonely

convent (p39)
the house or building where a group of nuns live together, following set religious rules

cicada (p42)
a large insect with four transparent wings

veranda (p45)
a long, open, outdoor porch, usually roofed and running alongside a building

marquee (p53)
a canopy, usually made of metal, projecting over the entrance of a building such as a theater or hotel

treaty (p59)
a formal agreement between two or more nations in reference to peace, commerce, or other matters

attest (p66)
to state that something is true or genuine

humble (p66)
not proud or vain; modest; meek

autocrat (p66)
a ruler with absolute power

oppression (p66)
> the act of oppressing; to burden or keep down by unjust use of force or authority

hallowed (p66)
> made holy or sacred

truce (p97)
> a temporary stop in warfare or fighting by agreement of the warring factions

gallantry (p105)
> bravery; nobility

engross (p112)
> to occupy completely; take up the attention of

mustard gas (p117)
> a poisonous gas

peak (p140)
> the highest point or level

gingerly (p140)
> in a cautious, careful, or reluctant manner

platoon (p143)
> a subdivision of a company, troop, or other military unit, commanded by a lieutenant

prune (p153)
> to cut or trim unwanted branches or twigs from a tree, shrub, or other plant

jaunty (p182)
> having a lively or self-confident air or manner

sacred (p205)
> deserving of reverence, honor, or respect

armistice (p210)
> an agreement to stop fighting for a short time; a truce

patriotism (p210)
> love of one's country and loyal devotion to it

Small Group Reading

Foreman, Michael. *War Game*. New York: Arcade, 1994.

A British boy experiences trench warfare in World War I. On Christmas there is a break in the fighting, and the Germans and the British play soccer against each other. When fighting resumes, the British boy dies in a shell hole along with a German. This story is based on a true episode. Grades 2-6.

Author Information

Michael Foreman was born March 21, 1938 in Pakefield, Suffolk, England. Foreman is a graphic artist as well as a children's author. He has won numerous awards for his work. Foreman has written and illustrated many books, and has illustrated dozens of books by other authors.

Much of Foreman's inspiration for writing, as well as illustrating, comes from his travels around the world.

Activities

1. Have students write a letter from Freddie to his parents, telling them of his experiences in World War I. Students should share their letters with the rest of the class.

2. Have students choose five to ten vocabulary words they learned from reading the book and write them on 5-by-7-inch cards, along with the definitions and illustrations. Hang these on a classroom bulletin board.

3. Have students use shoe boxes to make dioramas from a scene in the book. They should include a short summary explaining the scene. Display the finished products in your classroom.

4. Have students research trench warfare during World War I and create a poster incorporating the information they learn along with an illustration.

Discussion

Give the small group the following instruction: As your group reads this book, discuss the following questions.

1. Why did the German emperor, Kaiser Wilhelm (William II) want to start a war?

2. Why did Freddie want to join the army?

3. How did Will feel when they reached France?

4. How did things change as the soldiers neared the battlefront?

5. What was Will's first reaction upon seeing the sky lit up from the fighting?

6. How were dogs sometimes used in World War I?

7. What did Freddie say was "less than a goal kick away"?

8. When were attacks most expected?

9. What did the old soldiers believe the sudden disappearance of rats meant?

10. Why did the soldiers fear flares lighting up the sky?

11. Why was there always mud in the trenches?

12. Describe Christmas Eve in the trenches.

13. What took place on Christmas? What did the soldiers do for fun?

14. Why were the officers worried after Christmas?

15. What happened to destroy the peace?

16. How did British Tommies get their name?

17. What became of Will?

Vocabulary

Note: the original book is not page numbered. The numbers in parenthesis indicate page number based on the first page of text and counting back from there.

archduke (p4)
a prince of the former ruling house of Austria

seize (p4)
to take possession of by force

recruit (p4)
to enlist soldiers for the armed services

vicar (p6)
a parish priest in the Church of England

pulpit (p6)
a raised platform or desk for a preacher in a church

squire (p6)
in England, a person who owns much land

converted (p11)
changed; transformed

vast (p14)
of very large size; enormous; huge

supply depot (p14)
a place for storing military equipment and supplies, or for receiving and training troops

shunted (p14)
moved to one side or out of the way

babel (p14)
noise and confusion, as when many people talk at once

salvage (p16)
to save, as from being wrecked, ruined, or burned

trench (p16)
a long ditch with earth piled up in front, used by soldiers in battle to protect themselves from enemy fire

brigade (p18)
a unit of troops smaller than a division but still rather large

slog (p20)
to move slowly and with difficulty

parapet (p20)
a low wall built by soldiers as a defense

sentry (p20)
a person, especially a soldier, assigned to guard an area against intruders and to look out for danger

bayonet (p26)
a daggerlike weapon that may be attached to the muzzle of a rifle

infested (p26)
   overrun or occupied in large numbers so as to be annoying and dangerous

corrugated (p26)
   having a ridged or wrinkled surface

imminent (p26)
   likely to happen soon

venture (p30)
   to expose to chance or risk; place in danger; hazard

illuminate (p30)
   to light up

eternity (p30)
   forever

sniper (p30)
   a person who shoots at an enemy from some hiding place

munitions (p32)
   materials and supplies for war, as ammunition and guns

regiment (p34)
   an army unit, larger than a battalion and smaller than a division, usually commanded by a colonel

primitive (p34)
   simple or crude, like that of early ages

grenade (p34)
   a small bomb thrown by hand or fired from a rifle

daft (p38)
   crazy or foolish

tunic (p51)
   a close-fitting jacket, often worn as part of a uniform

Tommies (p52)
   British soldiers

Small Group Reading

Kinsey-Warnock, Natalie. *The Night the Bells Rang*. New York: Cobblehill Books, 1991.
Mason is tormented by a bully in rural Vermont during World War I. Grades 4-7.

Author Information

Natalie Kinsey-Warnock was born November 2, 1956 in Newport, Vermont.

Along with her career as a writer, she has worked as an energy auditor, elderhostel director, and cross-country ski instructor.

Her writing has won her an American Library Association Notable Book citation in 1989, and New York Library's 100 Best Books citation in 1989, along with several other awards.

Kinsey-Warnock attributes her love of books and words to her mother, a former teacher. She says, "It is because of her that my brother Leland and I are writers."

Of her writing, she says, "I guess anything to do with history appeals to me. History teaches us who we are, and in all my talks with school groups I encourage every person to record their family histories and stories before they are lost forever."

Activities

1. Have students find out more information about glaciers, particularly the effect they had on your region of the United States.

2. Discuss with your students how maple syrup is made. Bring in some real maple syrup for students to taste following this discussion.

    The gathering of the maple sap that is used to make maple syrup takes place in March, April, September, and October. Tapholes are drilled into the trunks of maple trees and spouts are placed in the holes. Buckets are hung under the spouts to collect the sap. The sap is then cooked in a tank until it thickens and becomes syrup.

The following books are recommended for you to use with your students to explain the process of making maple syrup.

> Burns, Diane. *Sugaring Season: Making Maple Syrup.* Minneapolis, MN: Carolrhoda Books, 1990.
> This book describes through text and photographs, the making of maple syrup from tapping the tree and collecting sap to cooking and packaging. Grades 3 and up.

> Lasky, Kathryn. *Sugaring Time.* New York: Macmillan, 1983.
> Text and photographs show how a family taps the sap from maple trees and processes it into maple syrup. Grades 4 and up.

3. Have students locate the constellations Orion and Pleiades (the Seven Sisters) in resource material from your library.

4. Have students illustrate spring, as seen through Mason's description on pages 52 and 53.

5. Have students write letters from Mason to Aden after Aden went away to fight in World War I. They should tell Mason's feelings about their relationship and what has been happening at home while Aden has been away. Students can share these letters with the rest of the class.

Discussion

Give the small group the following instruction: As your group reads this book, discuss the following questions.

1. Why is school getting worse every day for Mason?

2. Discuss your feelings about what Mason's father said about why Aden Cutler behaves the way he does.

3. How does Mason's father feel about the war?

4. Why do you think Mason's stomach bothers him in the mornings?

5. What surprising thing did Aden do for Mason? Why do you think he did it?

6. How does Mason's mother make syrup and sugar?

7. What is sugar-on-snow?

8. How did Mason feel when he found out that Aden had joined the army?

9. How does Mason's father make apple cider?

10. What happened to Aden Cutler? How did Mason react to the news?

11. Why did Mason decide to be a better brother to Ira?

12. What did the town do to celebrate the end of World War I?

13. What did Mason say to Mrs. Cutler? What do you think it meant to her?

Vocabulary

constellation (p9)
a group of stars to which an official name has been assigned

foal (p10)
a young horse

rationing (p15)
limiting the amount of something that a person can have or use

bay mare (p18)
a reddish-brown female horse

sheath (p23)
any caselike covering

stern (p25)
harsh in nature or manner; strict; severe

glacier (p25)
a large mass or field of ice that moves very slowly down a mountain valley or across land until it either melts or breaks off in the sea to form icebergs

furrow (p26)
a long, deep trench made in land by a plow

killdeer (p26)
 a North American wading bird, having a loud cry

castor oil (p28)
 a thick, pale yellow oil extracted from the bean of a shrubby tropical tree

colander (p29)
 a kitchen utensil with holes, used for draining off liquids from foods

pewter (p32)
 a gray alloy of tin and other metals, chiefly lead and copper, used for pitchers, plates, and other tableware

iron spile (p39)
 a plug for a cask or barrel

resin (p41)
 a gummy, brown yellow substance given off by certain plants, especially fir and pine trees

turpentine (p41)
 an oily liquid obtained from various cone-bearing trees, especially pines

whetting (p46)
 sharpening a knife or tool by rubbing on or with something

envious (p50)
 full of envy; jealous

enlist (p50)
 to join or cause to join a branch of the armed forces voluntarily

Kaiser (p51)
 an emperor, especially an emperor of Austria or Germany before 1918

thicket (p54)
 a thick, dense growth, such as of trees and bushes

pomace (p61)
 the soft, usually edible part of certain fruits or vegetables; pulp

giddy (p72)
 silly

Small Group Reading

📖 Kudlinski, Kathleen V. *Hero Over Here*. New York: Viking, 1990.
 This story is set during the influenza epidemic of 1918. Ten-year-old Theodore takes care of his sick family while his father and older brother are off fighting in World War I. Grades 3-6.

Author Information

Kathleen V. Kudlinski lives in Guilford, Connecticut.

She is the author of biographies of Rachel Carson, Juliette Gordon Low, and Helen Keller for the Women of Our Time series.

Kudlinski heard about the Spanish flu from her two grandmothers. They told her about so many adults becoming sick that the children had to take charge. Kudlinski wanted children today to know that they could handle such responsibility, too, if they had to.

Activities

1. On a map of the United States, have students locate Montana and Trenton, New Jersey.

2. Have your school's music teacher teach the song "Over There" to the whole class.

3. Have students make mustard plasters. They could place them on their arms for a few minutes to see if they really give off heat. To make: Mix flour, water, and mustard and spread on two large squares of cloth.

4. Have students choose a scene from the book to act out. They can write a short script and perform it for the class.

Discussion

Give the small group the following instruction: As your group reads this book, discuss the following questions.

1. What did Theodore dream about?

2. What did Everett tell Theodore before he left to fight in World War I?

3. Why did the windows have to be closed even in summer?

4. Why does Theodore want to go to Montana?

5. Why did Theodore and George pick up coal by the railroad tracks?

6. Why did Dr. Meyers tell Theodore to go home?

7. What is Victory Bread, and why do Theodore and his family eat it?

8. Where is Theodore's father?

9. Discuss Theodore and Irene's relationship.

10. Why were the iceman and the grocery clerk so worried about the flu?

11. Discuss the changes in Theodore's life since his mother and sister became sick.

12. As Theodore walked home with George, how did he feel?

13. What did some people do to try to help their sick family members get better?

14. What did Theodore do to help the sick man he found on his way home from the hospital?

15. How did Theodore react to the news about his cousin Calvin?

16. What news did the policeman bring to Theodore?

17. Discuss the town's reaction to the end of the war. How did you feel when Theodore's father came home?

18. People treated Theodore like a hero—do you think he was one?

19. Why do you think Theodore decided to wait to go to Montana?

20. How did the "Spanish flu" epidemic of 1918 affect people's lives around the world? Why was it spoken of as a war?

21. Discuss why getting the flu today is not as big a worry as it was in 1918.

Vocabulary

shrill (p1)
having or making a high-pitched, piercing sound

flu (influenza) (p5)
a contagious viral disease causing inflammation of the nose, throat, and bronchial tubes, or of the intestines, and accompanied by fever, weakness, and discomfort

convalescent (p12)
a person recovering from illness

colt (p12)
a young horse or donkey

pinto horse (p13)
a horse with spots, usually of two or more colors

icebox (p14)
a cabinet kept cool by putting ice in it, used for storing food

roundup (p24)
a bringing together of cattle scattered over a range, such as for branding or inspection

hooligan (p25)
a person who goes about committing violent or destructive acts for little or no purpose

mustard plaster (p27)
a mustard preparation spread on cloth and applied to some part of the body for healing

camphor (p32)
a white, crystalline substance with a strong odor, used in medicine, plastics, lacquers, and mothballs

kerosene lamp (p32)
a lamp that burns a thin oil made from petroleum

tramp (p39)
a homeless person who wanders around and begs for a living

knickers (p41)
loose-fitting, short pants, gathered in below the knee

astonishment (p48)
amazement

Small Group Reading

📖 Skurzynski, Gloria. **Good-bye, Billy Radish**. New York: Bradbury Press, 1992.

In 1917, as the United States enters World War I, ten-year-old Hank sees change all around him in his western Pennsylvania steel mill town. He fears that his older Ukrainian friend Billy is drifting away from him. Grades 7 and up.

A word of caution: As with all books used in whole group and small group reading, it is recommended that the teacher read the book first. There are two scenes in this book for the teacher to pay particular attention to before asking students to read them. They are located on pages 105–8 and page 121. This is an excellent book; however, it is one you should think about carefully before using in terms of the maturity of your students. An alternative would be to use this book with your whole class as a read-aloud and simply skip over these two scenes.

Author Information

Gloria Skurzynski was born July 6, 1930 in Duquesne, Pennsylvania. She has five grown daughters. She lives in Salt Lake City, Utah.

Skurzynski's writing includes picture books, folktales, middle-grade adventure stories, novels, and young adult nonfiction titles. She has received special acclaim for her historical fiction.

The Tempering, which is about the same family featured in *Good-bye, Billy Radish*, received a Golden Kite Award and was named a Best Book for Young Adults by the American Library Association and a Best Book of the Year by *School Library Journal*.

Activities

1. Have students illustrate the street scene on the Fourth of July, 1917, which is described on pages 31 and 32.

2. Have students do research to learn more about the history of Ukrainian Easter eggs.

3. This story describes how waste was dumped from the steel mill into a nearby river. Have students write persuasive essays about why this is a dangerous practice and how important clean water is to everyone.

4. On a map of the United States, have students locate Pennsylvania, New Jersey, Wyoming, and the Monongahela River, which begins in West Virginia.

5. Have students write character sketches of Hank, Billy, and Karl, then present them orally to the rest of the class.

Discussion

Give the small group the following instruction: As your group reads this book, discuss the following questions.

1. Why does Karl feel his job in the steel mill is as important to the war effort as being a soldier?

2. On what date did America declare war on Germany?

3. How old did a boy have to be before he could wear long pants?

4. How did Hank and Billy meet?

5. Why is Hank afraid of the steel mill?

6. How does Hank feel about his brother Karl?

7. What happened when Hank took Karl's dinner pail to him? Why did Hank feel he was to blame?

8. Describe July 4, 1917.

9. Why didn't Hank want to watch the fireworks at the park?

10. What made Hank so excited about talking to Francis X Culley at Karl's wedding?

11. Why did Mrs. Bonner lose her teaching job when she got married?

12. What makes Billy Radish's fourteenth birthday so important?

13. How did the war change the type of jobs boys ages fourteen and fifteen were given in the steel mill?

14. Why did officers want to get the greatest number of immigrants naturalized as quickly as possible?

15. What are the three branches of the United States government?

16. What secret did Karl share with Hank after telling him about the death of Francis X?

17. Where did Billy and Hank spend Hank's twelfth birthday?

18. On what day was the armistice signed, which ended World War I?

19. What made Hank decide that he wanted to be a doctor?

20. How did Hank feel about what happened to Billy?

Vocabulary

democracy (p3)
a form of government in which the people rule, either by voting directly or by electing representatives to run the government and make the laws

rigid (p3)
fixed; unmoving

knickers (p3)
loose-fitting, short trousers, gathered in below the knee

dank (p4)
unpleasantly cold and wet

ingot (p14)
a mass of metal cast into the shape of a bar or block

idle (p14)
not operating

molten steel (p14)
steel made into a liquid, as by great heat

stature (p23)
the natural height of a person

serge (p25)
a strong, woven fabric, usually of wool, having slanting lines or ridges on its surface and used for clothing such as coats and suits

genuflect (p25)
to bend one knee, as in worship

platoon (p32)
a subdivision of a company, troop, or other military unit, commanded by a lieutenant

recruits (p32)
newly enlisted members of the armed forces

inconspicuous (p34)
not very noticeable; not attracting attention

greenhorn (p35)
an inexperienced person; a beginner

stamina (p36)
strength; endurance

calliope (p40)
a musical instrument consisting of a series of steam whistles played by means of a keyboard

horde (p40)
a great crowd

parasol (p40)
a small, light umbrella carried to protect oneself from the sun

ridicule (p46)
words or actions intended to make another person or thing seem foolish; mockery

deference (p47)
respect and consideration for the wishes and opinions of another

bayonet (p47)
a daggerlike weapon that may be attached to the muzzle of a rifle

indignant (p52)
angry because of something that is not right, just, or fair

amends (p55)
   something done or given to make up for a
   wrong, a loss, or an injury

reverent (p58)
   feeling or showing great respect

immigrant (p61)
   a person who comes into a country or region
   where he or she was not born with the intention
   of living there

cantor (p63)
   the chief singer in a synagogue

aghast (p63)
   shocked or horrified

veranda (p64)
   a long, open outdoor porch, usually roofed,
   running alongside a building

coiffure (p66)
   a hairstyle

idolize (p67)
   to love or admire blindly or too much

privy (p69)
   an outdoor toilet; an outhouse

jovial (p71)
   possessing or showing good nature; jolly; happy

parlor (p72)
   a room for receiving visitors or entertaining
   guests

dignitary (p73)
   a person having a high position, as in a government, church, or university

boisterous (p76)
   noisy and wild

paregoric (p77)
   a solution of camphor and a small amount of
   opium in alcohol, used to relieve pain, cough-
   ing, and other symptoms

naturalization (p83)
   the process of being made into or accepted as a
   citizen

expedite (p83)
   to make go faster or more easily; to speed up

bailiff (p83)
   a court officer

renounce (p85)
   to give up, especially by formal statement

abjure (p85)
   to take an oath publicly to give up, such as a
   religion or a belief

allegiance (p85)
   loyalty to a government or ruler

fidelity (p85)
   faithfulness in carrying out one's duties or
   responsibilities; loyalty

discretion (p88)
   good judgment

telegraph (p90)
   a device for sending and receiving messages
   by means of a series of electrical or
   electromagnetic pulses

duplex (p91)
   a house having separate dwelling units for two
   families

patriotic (p94)
   having or showing love, loyalty, and devotion
   toward one's country

decorum (p103)
   something proper, such as behavior, speech, or
   dress

armistice (p111)
   an agreement to stop fighting for a short time; a
   truce

influenza (p112)
   a contagious viral disease causing inflammation of the nose, throat, and bronchial tubes, or
   of the intestines, and accompanied by fever,
   weakness, and discomfort

aura (p118)
   a special air or quality that seems to surround
   or come from a particular source

perpetual (p118)
   continuing indefinitely

catechism (p122)
   a short book written in the form of questions
   and answers for teaching the principles of
   religion

valid (p135)
   truthful, acceptable, or reasonable

Small Group Reading

Tomlinson, Theresa. ***Riding the Waves***. New York: Macmillan, 1993.
   Matt is given a class assignment to interview an older person to find out what it was like growing
up after World War I. He talks to Florrie, an elderly neighbor. She ends up helping him go after his
dreams and come to terms with being adopted. Grades 4-8.

Author Information

Theresa Tomlinson grew up in Northern England. Her grandparents lived in the seaside town of Saltburn, where the setting of *Riding the Waves* is based. Tomlinson currently lives in Sheffield, England with her husband and children.

Riding the Waves is Tomlinson's second book to be published in the United States. *Summer Witches* was her first.

Activities

1. On a world map, have students locate the following:
   Cleveland, England
   Dunkirk, France
   Holland
   London, England

2. Have students write a journal entry from Matt's point of view. It should be written after Matt's first time surfing and should include his feelings about the experience.

3. Have students write persuasive essays about why it is important to form relationships with older people. They should discuss how beneficial it can be to both the child or young adult and the elder. The students can share their essays aloud with the rest of the class.

Discussion

Give the small group the following instruction: As your group reads this book, discuss the following questions.

1. Why was Matt visiting Aunt Florrie?

2. What did Aunt Florrie want from Matt?

3. What was the history homework that Matt had to do?

4. Why did Matt decide to interview Aunt Florrie after all?

5. Why did Aunt Florrie's house remind Matt of his grandmother's house?

6. Discuss Matt's reaction when his teacher said that he had done an excellent piece of work. Share any similar experiences in your group.

7. What was a bathing machine?

8. How have Matt's feelings about Florrie changed?

9. Discuss the effect Matt's father not having a job had on their family.

10. How did the surfers know Aunt Florrie?

11. What did Aunt Florrie do to help make Matt's dream come true?

12. When Aunt Florrie said that the war stopped everything, what did she mean?

13. How did Aunt Florrie help Matt to understand more about his own adoption?

14. What was the special gift that Florrie wanted to give to Matt? Why did he refuse it?

15. How did things finally seem to turn around for Matt's dad?

16. Miss Teesdale felt that a visit from Matt was what Florrie needed. Do you agree? Explain your answer.

17. What did Matt say to Florrie in the hospital to motivate her to get better?

18. Discuss Matt and Florrie's relationship and how they each benefited from it.

Vocabulary

promenade (p7)
a walk for amusement or exercise; a stroll

vicar (p11)
in the Church of England, a parish priest who receives a salary but no tithes

derelict (p16)
a poor, homeless person

posh (p16)
luxurious or elegant

hydrangeas (p17)
shrubs with large clusters of white, blue, or pink flowers

contingent (p20)
likely, but not certain, to happen; possible

brocade (p24)
a fabric woven with a raised design, often in gold or silver threads

antimacassar (p24)
a piece of material placed over the arms and the upper back of a chair as protection against wear and dirt

diphtheria (p26)
a serious contagious disease of the throat, usually associated with high fever, that blocks air passages and makes breathing difficult

coronation (p27)
the crowning of a king or queen

ebony (p28)
a hard, heavy wood, usually black

tunic (p28)
a close-fitting jacket, often worn as part of a uniform

pram (p94)
a baby carriage

queue (p119)
to form a line, such as one of persons or cars, waiting for something

Bibliography

Individual Titles

Bosco, Peter I. *World War I: America at War.* New York: Facts on File, 1991.
Bosco tells why the United States abandoned its isolationism to participate in World War I, and the significance of that participation for the U.S. Grades 6 and up.

Clare, John D., ed. *Living History: First World War.* San Diego, CA: Harcourt Brace Jovanovich, 1995.
This is an excellent book about World War I, which includes numerous photographs and maps. Grades 5 and up.

Colby, C. B. *Fighting Gear of World War I: Equipment and Weapons of the American Doughboy.* New York: Coward-McCann, 1961.
This is a thorough presentation of the equipment, uniforms, and weapons of World War I. It is full of photographs. Grades 5 and up.

Houston, Gloria. *The Year of the Perfect Christmas Tree: An Appalachian Story.* New York: Dial Books for Young Readers, 1988.
Since Ruthie's father left the Appalachian area to go to war, Ruthie and her mother wonder how they will fulfill his obligation of getting the perfect Christmas tree to the town for the holiday celebration. Grades K-4.

Kent, Zachary. *World War I: "The War to End All Wars."* Hillside, NJ: Enslow, 1994.
Kent brings to life the stories of the patriotic Americans who fought in the trenches and from the home front during the First World War. The book includes maps and a chronology of major events and battles of the war. Grades 5 and up.

Marrin, Albert. *The Yanks Are Coming.* New York: Atheneum, 1986.
This is the exciting story of how the Yanks helped the Allies turn the tide of World War I in Europe. This is an excellent source for research. Grades 6 and up.

McGowen, Tom. *World War I.* New York: Franklin Watts, 1993.
This book provides an overview of the military battles and political changes that occurred during World War I. Grades 4 and up.

Parkinson, Roger. *The Origins of World War One.* New York: G. P. Putnam's Sons, 1970.
In this book, Parkinson discusses the causes of World War I. Grades 5 and up.

Rabin, Staton. *Casey Over There*. San Diego, CA: Harcourt Brace Jovanovich, 1994.

Aubrey misses his brother Casey, who is far away fighting for Uncle Sam in World War I. After weeks of no mail from Casey, Aubrey writes to Uncle Sam and asks if he is through with his brother. Grades K-3.

Snyder, Louis L. *World War I*. New York: Franklin Watts, 1981.

Snyder highlights the important events and people of World War I. Grades 4 and up.

Stewart, Gail B. *World War I*. San Diego, CA: Lucent Books, 1991.

This book examines the United States's role in World War I. It includes preparations for war, trench warfare, use of airplanes, major battles, and the results of the war. Grades 5 and up.

Theme Resources

Commercial Resources

Cobbletone: The History Magazine for Young People. Peterborough, NH: Cobblestone.

The focus of the June 1986 issue for grades 4 and up is the United States involvement in World War I. Articles include "World War I Time Line" and "World War I: The Trench War."

Cooper. *Connect/Social Studies: After the Dancing Days*. Littleton, MA: Sundance, 1992.

This resource contains a teacher's guide and reproducible activity sheets for students in grades 6 and up which reinforce map study, comprehension, vocabulary, and writing skills for *After the Dancing Days*.

Video

United States History Video Collection: The Great War. Bala Cynwyd, PA: Schlessinger Video Productions, 1996. (35 minutes)

This video covers American neutrality and the road to war; the Doughboys; the War Industries Board; the Great Migration; Espionage and the Sedition Acts; the American Expeditionary Force in Europe; Wilson's Fourteen Points; the Strikes of 1919; the Red Scare; and the Palmer Raids.

The Great War, 1918. Alexandria, VA: PBS Video, 1989. (58 minutes)

This video was originally broadcast on PBS as a segment of the television program *The American Experience*. It gives a history of the United States soldiers in the closing battle of World War I through letters and diaries. It also features interviews with French and American veterans and nurses.

Computer Resources

The Causes of WWI. [CD-ROM]. Chicago: Clearvue, 1994.

This CD-ROM explores the political, economical, and social factors and events that led to World War I. Students will compare the goals of major powers with the outcome of the war.

World War I. [CD-ROM]. Boston: Flagtower Multimedia, 1995.

World War I is illustrated with twenty minutes of film, more than 500 photographs, sixty battle maps, and a series of interviews.

End-of-Unit Celebration

World War I Research Project

Divide your class into groups of two or three to research the following topics. When the projects are completed, hold a presentation day.

American Doughboys	President Woodrow Wilson
Causes of World War I	The Sinking of the *Lusitania*
The Home Front	The Treaty of Versailles
Kaiser Wilhelm II, Emperor of Germany	Trench Warfare
The League of Nations	

Chapter 9

World War II

Introduction

The peace treaty that ended World War I came at a heavy price for Germany. The Germans could not rebuild their army and navy. Germans were forced to pay high fines for the damage caused by starting World War I. Many men were out of work, and money became worthless. Adolf Hitler sought to restore the pride of the German people by promising to bring Germany out of poverty and by building the country into a mighty empire. He built new factories and constructed new roads. His promises made Hitler popular with the German people. On January 30, 1933, Hitler became Germany's leader. Soon many of the rights of the German people were taken away. However, few cared because men were working again and families had food and clothing. Thus, in the 1930s, Hitler's Germany became the greatest threat to world peace and stability.

Before World War II even started, persecution of Jews began in Germany. The result was the inconceivable death of 6 million Jews by the end of World War II.

By the middle of 1941, the Axis powers—Germany, Italy, and Japan—were at war with the Allies—led by Great Britain, France, Russia, and China. The United States stayed out of the war until December 7, 1941, when Japan made a surprise attack on the U.S. forces stationed at Pearl Harbor.

World War II was the most destructive war in history. The result was millions of lives lost and the destruction of entire cities. It is important that students learn about the horrors that took place during World War II so that they might never happen again. The trade books selected here offer much opportunity for discussion and development of a more personal level of understanding.

Whole Group Reading

Lowry, Lois. *Number the Stars*. Boston: Houghton Mifflin, 1989.

Annemarie, a ten-year-old girl in Nazi-occupied Copenhagen, finds the courage to help her Jewish friends escape danger in this exciting adventure story. Winner of the 1990 Newbery Medal. Grades 4-8.

Although there is much excellent literature available on the subject of World War II, *Number the Stars* stands out from the rest. This novel provides readers with insight into the courage of people who helped Jews escape the Nazis, as well as revealing the absolute horror of the war. For these reasons, *Number the Stars* was chosen to be read with the whole class.

Author Information

Lois Lowry was born March 20, 1937 in Honolulu, Hawaii. Her father was a career army officer, and as a result, her family moved many times as she was growing up. At age seventeen Lowry went to Brown University to study writing. She left school when she was nineteen and proceeded to have four children, all of whom provided her with much material to use in her writing.

Activities

1. On world map, have students locate the following:

Baltic Sea	France	Norway
Belgium	Holland	Ryvangen
Copenhagen	Nørrebro	Sweden
Denmark	North Sea	Tivoli, Italy

2. Have students write a letter to Ellen from Annemarie after the war ended and Denmark was free.

3. Have students write three journal entries as if they were Ellen Rosen. The entries should take place at the following points in the novel: Ellen's first night in hiding with Annemarie and her family; Ellen's reunion with her parents; and following the Rosens' trip to Sweden and freedom.

4. Have students write a speech that could have been given along with a medal for bravery to the people who helped Jews escape the horrors of the concentration camps.

Discussion

Give the class the following instruction: As we read this book, we will be discussing the following questions. Write down your ideas about these questions and add to them as needed.

1. Why did Annemarie feel contempt toward the German soldiers?

2. How and why did Kirsti feel differently about the German soldiers than the other girls?

3. Why do you think Mrs. Rosen told the girls not to give the soldiers any reason to remember their faces?

4. How had life changed for Annemarie and her family since the occupation of the Germans?

5. Why did the Germans close down the Hirsches' button shop?

6. Why did Annemarie's parents want her to keep an eye on her friend Ellen?

7. Kirsti thought there had been fireworks for her birthday. What had really happened?

8. Why did Ellen come to stay with Annemarie?

9. Discuss Annemarie's and Ellen's feelings as the German soldiers search the Johansens' apartment.

10. Why couldn't Ellen wear the necklace that her father had given her?

11. Why do you think Annemarie's mother took the children to visit her brother?

12. What did Uncle Henrik mean when he said, "It is much easier to be brave if you do not know everything"?

13. Discuss possible reasons why Uncle Henrik and Annemarie's mother made up the death of a fictitious great-aunt Birte.

14. What had been hidden in the casket?

15. Do you think Ellen and Annemarie will ever see each other again?

16. What could be in the package that Mr. Rosen was supposed to give to Henrik?

17. How could a handkerchief be so important to the people who were helping the Jews escape?

18. How did Annemarie's sister, Lise, died?

Vocabulary

lanky (p1)
> ungracefully tall and thin

obstinate (p4)
> stubbornly holding to one's opinions or purposes

sabotage (p8)
> the destruction of a country's property, resources, or productive capacity by enemy agents in wartime

trousseau (p14)
> a bride's wardrobe, including clothing and household linens

ration (p18)
> to limit the amount of something scarce that a person can have or use

kroner (p20)
> a basic unit of currency in Denmark

swastika (p21)
> an ancient symbol of a cross with arms bent at right angles, a form adopted by the Nazis

curfew (p22)
> a rule or law requiring certain persons to keep off the streets after a certain hour

exasperated (p28)
> annoyed or irritated almost to the point of anger

synagogue (p33)
> a place of meeting for Jewish worship and religious instruction

staccato (p83)
> cut short; disconnected

condescending (p83)
> patronizing

typhus (p84)
> an acute contagious disease, caused by a germ carried by certain body lice or fleas, that is marked by high fever, skin eruptions, and extreme physical weakness

tantalize (p111)
> to torment by making something that one desires almost but never quite available

permeate (p136)
> to spread itself or spread through

Small Group Reading

Adler, David A. *Hilde and Eli: Children of the Holocaust*. New York: Holiday House, 1994.

In this extremely powerful book, Adler tells the stories of Hilde Rosenzweig from Germany and Eli Lax from Czechoslovakia. Both were children during the early years of Nazi rule in Germany. They were among the 1.5 million Jewish children who were victims of the Holocaust. Illustrations by Karen Ritz are engaging and an integral part of the book. Grades 3 and up.

Author Information

David A. Adler was born April 10, 1947. He was a math teacher from 1968 to 1977 in New York City, and has been writing children's books since 1972. Adler is also a professional artist. His drawings and cartoons have appeared in magazines and newspapers.

Adler is a prolific writer, having written more than 100 books, including the popular Cam Jansen series, and many picture book biographies.

Adler has won numerous awards for his books, including: an Outstanding Science Trade Book for Children citation and several Social Studies Trade Book for Children citations.

Activities

1. On a world map, have students locate the following:

Austria	France	Italy
Belgium	Germany	Norway
Bulgaria	Greece	Poland
Czechoslovakia	Holland	Romania
Denmark	Hungary	Yugoslavia

2. Have students write reactions to the book in their journals as they read.

3. As a group, have students write memorial tributes for Eli and Hilde. These tributes should include how their lives changed and how it is important for people to read stories such as this to understand what took place so that it might never happen again. These tributes should be shared with the class. Students can illustrate these tributes as well.

Discussion

Give the small group the following instruction: As your group reads this book, discuss the following questions.

1. Where was Hilde from?

2. Why was 1923, when Hilde was born, a difficult year for Germany?

3. What did Adolf Hitler do in 1923?

4. As a young girl, what did Hilde like to do?

5. How did things change for Hilde and her family in 1932?

6. What did Adolf Hitler promise the German people?

7. Whom did Hitler believe was to blame for all of Germany's problems?

8. How did the Nazis celebrate Hitler being named chancellor?

9. In what ways did the Nazis show their hatred for Jews?

10. What laws were passed in Germany in 1935?

11. What took place on November 9, 1938 that brought terror to Hilde's life? What did that night become known as?

12. Where was Eli from?

13. As young children, how were Eli's and Hilde's lives similar?

14. What happened to begin the start of World War II?

15. What was the Nazi "Final Solution"?

16. Who were the Nazi allies in World War II?

17. What happened to Hilde and her mother? Discuss your feelings about this.

18. What were Eli, his brother, and his father told before they were killed?

19. By May 8, 1945, the day the war in Europe ended, approximately 6 million Jews had been murdered by the Nazis. When you think about this horrible fact, what goes through your mind?

Vocabulary

Note—This book is not page numbered. Numbers inside the parentheses indicate the page from the first page of text.

Holocaust (p1)
defined as huge destruction by fire, it refers to the murder of Jews by the Nazis

revolt (p2)
an uprising against authority; a rebellion or mutiny

Hanukkah (p3)
a Jewish festival lasting eight days, commemorating the rededication of the Temple in Jerusalem in 165 B.C.

Protestant (p5)
a member of one of the following Christian churches split off or derived from the Roman Catholic Church since the Reformation: Baptists, Presbyterians, Lutherans, and Protestants

Lebensraum (p6)
living space

Reich chancellor (p7)
prime minister

citizen (p10)
> a person who is born in or officially made a member or a country or nation

visa (p11)
> a mark of approval made on a passport by an official of a foreign country, giving permission to visit that country

diabetes (p11)
> a disease in which carbohydrates that have been eaten cannot be absorbed into the system because of too little natural insulin

looting (p12)
> robbing

synagogue (p12)
> a place of meeting for Jewish worship and religious instruction

concentration camp (p12)
> a fenced and guarded camp for confining political enemies or prisoners of war

Kristallnacht (p13)
> The Night of Broken Glass was a savage attack against Jews in Germany on November 9, 1938, which resulted in the destruction of Jewish homes, businesses, and synagogues; the bill for broken glass alone was 5 million deutschmarks; as many Jews as could be accommodated in the prisons were arrested and all Jews were forced to pay for their property losses by turning over their insurance claims to the government

ghetto (p20)
> the section of some cities or towns where Jews were forced to live

persecute (p32)
> to mistreat or oppress because of religion

liberated (p32)
> freed; released

Small Group Reading

Ayer, Eleanor H. *Parallel Journeys*. New York: Atheneum, 1995.

Parallel Journeys is an overwhelming account of the nightmare that was World War II. It is told in alternating fashion from Alfons Heck's and Helen Waterford's perspectives. Alfons Heck was a patriotic young German who rose to high rank in the Hitler Youth, while Helen Waterford, a young Jewish girl, was forced to flee her homeland for Holland. She was captured by the Gestapo and shipped to the Auschwitz death camp in Poland. Close to forty years later, Alfons and Helen met and found they shared a common purpose: to show young people that if peace is possible between a Jew and a former Nazi, then it is also attainable on a larger scale. Grades 8 and up.

Special Note: Throughout the writing of this book, I was able to read some of the very best historical literature (fiction and nonfiction) for children and young adults. Of these, *Parallel Journeys* had the most profound effect on me. The message it gives readers is tremendously important. I feel that as teachers, this is a book that we must share with older middle or high school students. Not to do so would be a disservice to them. If this book is not appropriate for students at your grade level, please suggest it to a colleague who teaches older students.

Author Information

Eleanor Ayer is a freelance writer with a master's degree in journalism. Her specialty is writing books for young adults and teenagers, many of which deal with World War II, Germany, and the Holocaust.

Ayer lives in Colorado with her husband and two sons. She and her husband also operate a small book publishing company.

Ayer met Alfons Heck and Helen Waterford in 1983 when they gave a lecture at the University of Northern Colorado. The Ayers published their biographies, and Eleanor Ayer convinced them to let her write their joint story for young adults. The result is *Parallel Journeys*.

Activities

1. After students have completed this book, allow them time to absorb its powerful effect. Some may want to write their feelings down in a journal, others may want to sit quietly and think, and still others may feel the need to sit and talk about it with a friend. After you have read this book, you will understand why this unstructured time needs to occur.

2. On a world map, have students locate the following:

Argentina	England	Luxembourg
Austria	Finland	North Sea
Baltic Sea	France	Poland
Belgium	Germany	Rhine River
Czechoslovakia	Lithuania	Russia
Egypt		

3. Have students illustrate Kristallnacht, which is described on pages 27 through 30.

4. Have students illustrate the liberation of Paris, France, on August 25, 1944.

5. Encourage students to think of creative ways to help spread Alfons's and Helen's message to others. Challenge them to produce these creations and present them to the class. Some suggestions could include posters, audiotapes, videotapes, and short skits.

6. Encourage students who wish to read further accounts of the Holocaust to read *We Are Witnesses: Five Diaries of Teenagers Who Died in the Holocaust* by Jacob Boas. Ask them to compare these accounts to Helen's in *Parallel Journeys*.

Discussion

Give the small group the following instruction: As your group reads this book, discuss the following questions.

1. In the introduction, what does the author mean when she says, "Truth can be stranger than fiction"?

2. What does the author believe needs to take place for people to be able to live together peacefully? Do you agree?

3. What was Germany like for non-Jewish teenagers in the 1930s? What did Adolf Hitler promise them?

4. How was life so very different for Jewish, Communist, and other teenagers who were considered low-class citizens by the Nazis?

5. Why did Rhineland Germans hate their French neighbors?

6. Why did German money become worthless after World War I?

7. Whom did Hitler blame Germany's defeat on in World War I?

8. What did Hitler promise the German people?

9. How was Hitler able to build such a strong following?

10. What rumor did Hitler spread among the people that resulted in many important rights being lost?

11. How did Alfons Heck's view of the Nazis differ from that of his twin brother, and why?

12. How were Alfons and other German children taught to hate Jews in school?

13. What two points were stressed to non-Jewish youth?

14. Why didn't Siegfried's parents want him to marry Helen?

15. How did the German government make it difficult for Jews to leave the country?

16. Discuss the Nuremberg Racial Laws that were passed in Germany in September 1935.

17. Discuss your feelings surrounding Alfons's friendship with Heinz Ermann and the ending of that friendship.

18. What happened during Kristallnacht?

19. What countries offered German Jews the best chance for escape?

20. How were Fred and Helen's parents able to emigrate to the United States?

21. When the Nazis did things with which people disagreed, why did they hide their feelings?

22. What event signaled the beginning of World War II?

23. Why did Helen and Siegfried feel they needed to give up their daughter?

24. How did their friend Ab Resusink help Helen and Siegfried?

25. How was Auschwitz different from many concentration camps?

26. What did Alfons and many other Germans believe about Auschwitz?

27. What was Hitler's "Final Solution"?

28. What was the "Night and Fog Decree"?

29. Discuss Japan's surprise attack on Pearl Harbor and how this event launched the United States into World War II.

30. With the formation of Judenrats (Jewish Councils), how did the Nazis plant the seeds of mistrust and hatred of the Jews towards each other?

31. How did Righteous Gentiles help the Jews? How have they been honored since?

32. Imagine living in hiding for a year in a closed room. Discuss your feelings.

33. D-Day, June 6, 1944, marked an important victory for the Allied forces. What took place on that day?

34. Discuss Alfons's feelings upon meeting Adolf Hitler. If you had been in his shoes, how would you have felt?

35. Why was Helen's life spared at the first "selection" at the concentration camp?

36. Why was it so important for prisoners to go unnoticed by the guards?

37. How did Alfons end up in charge of some 6,000 troops at the age of sixteen?

38. How must Helen have felt when she arrived at Camp Kratzau in Czechoslovakia?

39. Why did Helen believe that prisoners had more to fear from each other than from the Germans?

40. How did being able to speak English save Alfons's life?

41. After being set free, what did Helen do?

42. How did Alfons react to the fact that millions of Jews had been murdered?

43. Discuss Helen's reunion with Doris and why they went to the United States.

44. Why did Alfons go the Nuremberg trials? What were the Nuremberg trials?

45. What is Helen's goal in life now?

46. Why do Helen and Alfons believe it is so important for all to understand the horror of the Holocaust? What are your feelings?

Vocabulary

charismatic (pvii)
having or showing a personal quality that attracts many devoted followers

shroud (pviii)
anything that wraps up or conceals

Holocaust (pviii)
defined as huge destruction by fire, it refers to the murder of Jews by the Nazis

genocide (pviii)
the intentional murder of an entire race of people

prejudice (pviii)
hatred of or dislike for a particular group, race, or religion

bigotry (pviii)
an attitude, belief, or action of a person who has narrow-minded and intolerant attitudes, especially as they relate to religion, politics, or race

anti-Semitism (pviii)
hostility, discrimination, or prejudice against Jews

Volksschule (p1)
   an elementary school in Germany

patriotic (p1)
   having or showing love, loyalty, and devotion
   toward one's country

Aryan (p1)
   non-Jewish

Hitlerjugend (p1)
   Hitler Youth, the Nazi national organization for
   young Germans

Untermenschen (p2)
   low-class citizens

Treaty of Versailles (p3)
   the agreement that ended World War I

pogroms (p11)
   massacres of Jews

boycott (p13)
   to unite in refusing to buy from, sell to, use, or
   deal or associate with

swastika (p14)
   an ancient symbol of a cross with arms bent at
   right angles, one form of which was adopted by
   the Nazis as their emblem

neutral (p17)
   not interfering or taking sides, as in a dispute,
   contest, or war

platoon (p22)
   a subdivision of a company, troop, or other
   military unit, commanded by a lieutenant

Kristallnacht (p27)
   The Night of Broken Glass was a savage attack
   against Jews in Germany on November 9, 1938,
   which resulted in the destruction of Jewish
   homes, businesses, and synagogues; the bill for
   broken glass alone was 5 million deutschmarks;
   as many Jews as could be accommodated in the
   prisons were arrested and all Jews were forced
   to pay for their property losses by turning over
   their insurance claims to the government

concentration camps (p28)
   special prisons set up by the Nazis

plight (p32)
   a condition or situation, usually bad

diphtheria (p34)
   a serious contagious disease of the throat,
   usually associated with high fever, that blocks
   air passages and makes breathing difficult

devout (p38)
   religious

Blitzkrieg (p39)
   lightning war; a war conduced with speed and
   surprise

parliament (p40)
   an assembly whose function is to make the
   laws of a country

propaganda (p42)
   ideas, facts, or allegations spread in an effort to
   influence public opinion

pessimist (p47)
   a person who tends to expect failure or
   disappointment

terrorist (p49)
   a person who uses violence and threats to frighten
   people or a government into submission

wrath (p49)
   great or violent anger; rage

neutrality (p67)
   a neutral condition or attitude, especially of a
   nation in time of war

barbaric (p68)
   uncivilized

prestigious (p72)
   having or giving prestige; fame, importance, or
   respect based on a person's reputation, power,
   or past achievements

elite (p72)
   the social or professional group considered to
   be the best

Gestapo (p80)
   the Nazi secret state police

gentiles (p81)
   non-Jews

sarcasm (p86)
   a cutting, unpleasant remark that mocks or
   makes fun of something or someone

tedious (p102)
   long, dull, and tiresome

treason (p119)
   an act of betrayal, treachery, or breach of
   allegiance to one's country

ravine (p134)
   a long, narrow, deep depression in the earth
   that has steep sides

refugee (p140)
   a person who flees from persecution or danger

liberate (p150)
   to set free; to release

traitor (p160)
   a person who betrays friends, a cause, or an obligation, especially a person who betrays a
   country

desolate (p172)
   dreary; barren

deportation (p175)
  the expulsion of a person from a country

penitentiary (p182)
  a prison, especially one run by a state or federal government

atrocities (p200)
  terribly wicked, criminal, vile, or cruel acts

vengeance (p200)
  punishment inflicted in return for a wrong done; revenge

Yom Kippur (p209)
  a Jewish holiday marked by prayer and fasting for twenty-four hours; Day of Atonement

Small Group Reading

Colman, Penny. *Rosie the Riveter*. New York: Crown, 1995.

This is the story of the millions of women in the United States who worked hard to fill the civilian and defense positions left vacant when men went off to war. It also looks at the many other ways in which women contributed to World War II. Grades 6 and up.

Author Information

Penny Colman lives in Englewood, New Jersey.

Colman is a historian as well as an author. She has written numerous books for young readers, articles, and essays focusing on social history, women's lives, education, and parenting. Her books include *Women and the Civil War*, *Fanny Lou Hamer and the Fight for the Vote*, and *Mother Jones and the March of the Mill Children*.

Colman is a graduate of the University of Michigan and the Johns Hopkins University. She is a frequent guest speaker and presents programs for children and adults.

Activities

1. On a world map, have students locate the following:

Austria	Germany	Japan
Belgium	Guadalcanal	Luxembourg
Canada	Hiroshima, Japan	Nagasaki, Japan
Czechoslovakia	Holland	Norway
Denmark	Ireland	Pearl Harbor, Hawaii
England	Italy	Russia

2. Dot recalled seeing photographs of World War II in *Life* magazine and reading newspaper accounts. Have students visit your local library to search for copies of these issues. Articles about women who worked to help the war effort appear in: *Reader's Digest* (November 1942) and *National Geographic* (August 1944).

3. Have students write an essay on how their lives would be affected by a shortage of coffee beans, rubber, certain metals, sugar, gasoline, and heating oil.

4. Have students write their own *Magazine War Guide* (see pages 50-51 of the Crown edition of *Rosie the Riveter*).

5. Have students design their own posters to persuade women to join the workforce and help in the war effort.

6. Short advertisement films seeking women workers were shown in movie theaters in 1943 and 1944. Have students write and act out their own advertisement for the rest of the class.

Discussion

Give the small group the following instruction: As your group reads this book, discuss the following questions.

1. How did Dot Chastney first learn that there was trouble in Europe?

2. What event signaled the beginning of World War II?

3. What reasons did the United States have for being reluctant to become involved in World War II?

4. What happened that resulted in the United States involvement in the war?

5. What change in the United States did Dot first notice?

6. What items were rationed in the United States during World War II?

7. What items normally considered waste were Americans asked to save and salvage, and why?

8. How did Dot help the war effort?

9. Why were women joining the workforce by the millions during the war? What new work opportunities were they given?

10. What became of the majority of the women in the workforce after the war was over?

11. Why were many women, particularly married women, refused jobs after World War II ended?

12. What were the Jim Crow laws?

13. Discuss the treatment of black Americans during the war.

14. How did an executive order by Franklin Delano Roosevelt banning discrimination provide opportunities for people of color?

15. Discuss Executive Order 9066, an unprecedented violation of the civil rights of American citizens, because of which Japanese Americans from the West Coast were confined in camps.

16. What factories were converted to making wartime products?

17. Why were older people and those with various disabilities given jobs during the war?

18. How did helping the war effort make Dot and her friends feel better?

19. During the war, why did the population grow so much in such places as Detroit, Michigan?

20. What problems did the fast growth of cities create?

21. Why did some employers refuse to hire women, especially when they were needed so badly? Discuss your feelings about this.

22. How do you feel about the suspension of the Child Labor Laws during the war, allowing children as young as twelve years old to work?

23. What happened on June 6, 1944?

24. What dangers did women working in factories face?

25. How did some of the women workers feel about the jobs they were doing?

26. What events finally led to the Japanese surrender?

27. Discuss V-J Day (Victory over Japan Day). How do you think people must have felt on that day?

28. How did advertising campaigns change after World War II?

29. How have many women remembered their wartime job opportunities?

30. Discuss job opportunities for women today. How have they changed and improved? Is there still discrimination in the job market?

Vocabulary

Gestapo (p2)
the Nazi secret police

furtive (p12)
sly or sneaky

patriotism (p14)
love for one's country and loyal devotion to it

arsenal (p24)
a public building used for making or keeping such supplies as guns and ammunition

discrimination (p24)
the practice of thinking about or acting differently toward certain people or groups based on prejudice

prejudice (p24)
hatred of or dislike for a particular group, race, or religion

segregation (p26)
the practice of separating a racial or religious group from the rest of society, as in schools, housing, or parks

tenant farmer (p26)
a farmer who lives on and farms land owned by someone else and pays rent either in cash or in farm produce

coalition (p28)
a temporary alliance of leaders, parties, or nations

domestic (p29)
of or having to do with the home or family

armament (p34)
the military equipment, such as guns, ships, and bombs, used in war

propaganda (p49)
ideas, facts, or allegation spread in an effort to influence public opinion

deferment (p51)
a putting off, especially of induction into military service

migrate (p55)
to move from one country or region to settle in another

prefabricate (p57)
to manufacture in standard sections that can be rapidly set up and put together

influx (p57)
a continuous flowing or coming in, as of people or things

recruit (p58)
to cause to join a group or organization

acute (p58)
reaching a crisis quickly; severe

fuselage (p63)
the body of an airplane, excluding the wings and tail

liberty (p66)
freedom from control by others

lathe (p70)
a machine that holds and turns an article against the edge of a cutting tool so as to shape it

apprentice (p70)
a person who works for another to learn a trade or business

status (p72)
position or rank

telegraph (p72)
a device for sending and receiving messages by means of a series of electrical or electromagnetic pulses

bastion (p74)
a stronghold

stamina (p75)
vitality; vigor; strength; endurance

temperament (p75)
the nature or emotional makeup of a person; disposition

intricate (p82)
complicated or involved

greenhorn (p82)
an inexperienced person; a beginner

vital (p85)
having great importance

foundry (p93)
a place where molten metal is shaped in molds

inkling (p95)
a slight suggestion or hint

Small Group Reading

📖 Matas, Carol. *Lisa's War*. New York: Charles Scribner's Sons, 1987.
During the Nazi occupation of Denmark, Lisa and other teenage Jews become involved in an underground resistance movement and eventually must flee for their lives. Grades 7 and up.

Author Information

Carol Matas lives in Winnipeg, Canada. She has a degree in English literature from the University of Western Ontario. She is the author of *The D.N.A. Dimension*, *The Fusion Factor*, *Kris's War*, and *Daniel's Story*, among others.
Matas writes full-time and visits schools to conduct workshops and do readings.
While writing *Lisa's War*, Matas drew on the experiences of family and friends in wartime Denmark.

Activities

1. On a world map, have students locate the following:
   Austria   Copenhagen, Denmark   Germany

2. Have students research Winston Churchill and present their findings to the class.

3. As a demonstration for the whole class, have the group simulate a blackout in the classroom. They should cover all windows as completely as possible. Then light some candles to illustrate what Lisa's family did when blackout curtains were necessary.

4. Encourage students to read *Kris's War* and *Daniel's Story*, both by Carol Matas.

Discussion

Give the small group the following instruction: As your group reads this book, discuss the following questions.

1. What did Lisa wake up to that she had thought was a dream?

2. How does Stefan feel about Denmark surrendering to the Germans?

3. Why did Lisa's family put black blinds on their windows?

4. Why can't Lisa and her family believe what is written in the newspapers anymore?

5. What did Lisa suggest that would help her father?

6. How does Lisa think she can help the resistance?

7. What has Stefan arranged for Lisa to do to help?

8. What happened to Susanne?

9. Why did Susanne finally begin to talk again?

10. Discuss how Susanne's and Lisa's lives have changed since the German occupation of Denmark.

11. Why is Lisa's family sending Susanne away?

12. Why can't people talk freely to each other in Denmark during the occupation?

13. Why doesn't Erik believe Lisa when she tells him the Germans will be rounding up the Jews to take them to concentration camps?

14. If you were Lisa, would you stay behind and help Stefan and the resistance and go to Sweden later?

15. Who warned the Jewish people of Denmark of the roundup, saving thousands of lives in the process?

Vocabulary

warmonger (p5)
a person who advocates or tries to bring about war

sarcasm (p5)
a cutting, unpleasant remark that mocks or makes fun of something or someone

synagogue (p6)
a place of meeting for Jewish worship and religious instruction

Nazi (p7)
a member of the fascist political party that controlled Germany from 1933 to 1945 under Adolf Hitler

Passover (p10)
a holiday beginning on the 14th of Nisan (the seventh month of the year in the Jewish calendar) and traditionally continuing for eight days, commemorating the exodus of the Jews from Egypt

matzoh (p10)
a flat piece of unleavened bread eaten during Passover

leavening (p10)
a substance, such as yeast, that when added to dough or butter helps it to rise and become light and fluffy

Seder (p11)
in Judaism, the feast in remembrance of the departure of the Israelites from Egypt, celebrated on the eve of the first day of Passover

Exodus (p11)
the second book of the Old Testament, describing the departure of the Israelites from Egypt

propaganda (p12)
ideas, facts, or allegations spread in an effort to influence public opinion

saboteur (p15)
a person who engages in sabotage

Gestapo (p17)
the secret police in Germany under the Nazis

benevolent (p21)
desiring or showing the desire to do good

alibi (p27)
the fact or the defense that a person suspected of a crime was in another place when it was committed

retaliate (p52)
to do something to get even, such as for an injury or wrong

martial law (p54)
temporary rule by the military instead of by civilian authorities, such as during a war or crisis

sabotage (p54)
the destruction of a country's property, resources, or productive capacity by enemy agents in wartime

remorse (p54)
great regret or anguish for something one has done

reverie (p56)
distant and pleasant thoughts; daydreaming

Rosh Hashanah (p61)
the Jewish New Year, celebrated in late September or early October

bat mitzvah (p84)
a Jewish religious ceremony in which a thirteen-year-old girl is recognized as having reached the age of religious responsibility

convoy (p86)
a group, as of ships or trucks, traveling with an escort

refugee (p89)
a person who flees from persecution or danger

comrade (p95)
a close companion or friend

gentile (p111)
a person who is not Jewish

Small Group Reading

📖 McSwigan, Marie. *Snow Treasure*. New York: E. P. Dutton, 1942.

Children help a small Norwegian village save millions of dollars worth of gold bullion from the clutches of the Nazis during World War II by smuggling out gold bars on their sleds. Although many believe this incident to be true, no proof exists that it really happened. Grades 5 and up.

Author Information

Marie McSwigan was born May 22, 1907 in Pittsburgh, Pennsylvania.

McSwigan worked as a reporter and as an author. Her family background influenced significantly her career. Her father had been a city editor, her uncle an editor, and her sister a woman's-page editor.

Snow Treasure won Marie McSwigan national acclaim and is still in print after more than fifty years. She died in 1962 at the age of fifty-five.

Activities

1. On a world map, have students locate the following:

Arctic Circle	Holland	Poland
Belgium	Minnesota	Oslo
England	New York	Pittsburgh, PA
Finland	Norway	Rumania
France		

2. Have students write a letter from Peter to his mother and father after reaching the United States, telling them of his journey and what took place before he left Norway.

3. Have students write newspaper articles with the heading, "Norwegian Children Save Norway's Gold for the Germans." They can share these articles with the rest of the class.

4. Have students illustrate their favorite scenes from the novel, then display them when students share their newspaper accounts with the class.

Discussion

Give the small group the following instruction: As your group reads this book, discuss the following questions.

1. What is the climate like where Peter, Michael, and the other children live?

2. Why do you think Peter's Uncle Victor has returned before the ice is gone?

3. Why are Peter's father and his Uncle Victor worried about the gold?

4. What were Uncle Victor and some other men building in town, and why?

5. How does Mr. Anders, the schoolmaster, feel about Norway becoming involved in the war?

6. What is an air-raid drill?

7. To what position did Uncle Victor appoint Peter?

8. Why are Peter's father and his Uncle Victor willing to guard Norway's gold with their lives?

9. Where are the gold bullion bricks being stored?

10. Why does Uncle Victor want the Germans to see the children sledding right away?

11. Why does Uncle Victor insist that the children not speak a word to any strangers?

12. How does Peter feel about the job the children are going to do?

13. How has the cave been hidden?

14. Describe Peter's first encounter with Germans.

15. How did the children feel when they completed their first trip with the gold?

16. What did Herr Holm say that worried Peter?

17. How did the April blizzard bring hope?

18. What precautions have been taken to keep the Germans from finding the gold?

19. What did Dr. Aker do to keep the school from being opened?

20. How did many of the first Germans come into Norway without being noticed?

21. Why do Peter and his mother need to find Uncle Victor's ship?

22. Why did Uncle Victor name his ship the *Cleng Peerson*?

23. Where does Uncle Victor plan to take the gold?

24. What reason did Jan Lasek give Uncle Victor for following the children? Do you believe what he told them?

25. According to Jan Lasek, how did Jan come to be with the Germans?

26. Discuss the difference in the treatment of the people of Norway and the people of Poland by the Germans.

27. Why was Peter taken as a prisoner by the Germans? What do you think will happen to him?

28. Who came to help Peter?

29. How do you think Peter feels about going to the United States?

30. What promise did Peter's mother want him to make?

Vocabulary

accustomed (p2)
used to

fjord (p2)
in Norway, a long, narrow inlet of the sea between high cliffs or banks

harbor (p2)
a place or port where ships can anchor or gain protection in a storm

idle (p6)
not busy

assailant (p6)
an attacker

defiant (p6)
full of defiance; boldly opposed to power or authority

tribute (p6)
something, such as a speech, compliment, or gift, given to show admiration, gratitude, or respect

Nazis (p9)
members of the fascist political party that controlled Germany from 1933 to 1945

bullion (p10)
bars of gold or silver, often later made into coins

kroner (p10)
a basic unit of currency in Denmark

scheme (p14)
a plan or plot, often secretly and slyly made

navigator (p14)
a person trained in charting the position and course of a ship

precaution (p17)
something done to avoid a possible danger or evil

lieutenant (p17)
a military rank

grave (p20)
solemn and dignified; sober; serious

invasion (p21)
the act of entering by force with the purpose of conquering

impending (p29)
likely to happen soon; imminent

regiment (p29)
an army unit, larger than a battalion and smaller than a division

void (p31)
not occupied; empty; vacant

meekly (p33)
patiently; gently

welfare (p35)
the condition of being healthy, prosperous, and happy; well-being

sepulchers (p44)
tombs

sentry (p47)
a person, especially a soldier, assigned to guard an area against intruders and to look out for danger

infantry (p51)
soldiers, or a branch of the army, trained and equipped to fight on foot

tarpaulin (p53)
a piece of canvas or other material that has been made waterproof and is used to cover exposed objects

famished (p59)
extremely hungry

turmoil (p62)
>a condition of great confusion or agitation; disturbance

disposition (p66)
>a person's usual mood or spirit; nature; temperament

rebuked (p66)
>reprimanded

rheumatism (p67)
>a painful inflammation and stiffness of the joints

cataract (p69)
>a very large waterfall

calamity (p70)
>a disaster

stupor (p70)
>a dazed state in which the power to feel, think, or act is lost or greatly lessened

barometer (p74)
>an instrument for measuring air pressure, used for such purposes as forecasting weather and determining height above sea level

stealthy (p76)
>secretive, furtive, or underhanded

resolute (p82)
>determined or bold

consternation (p83)
>great fear or dismay that makes one feel helpless

epidemic (p87)
>the sudden spread of a disease among many people

diphtheria (p88)
>a serious contagious disease of the throat, usually associated with high fever, that blocks air passages and makes breathing difficult

scarlet fever (p88)
>a contagious disease chiefly affecting young people, marked by a sore throat, fever, and a scarlet rash

quarantine (p88)
>the keeping of persons or things that have been infected by or exposed to contagious diseases away from other people or things

debate (p96)
>to discuss or argue for or against, especially in a formal way between persons taking opposite sides of an issue

exalt (p103)
>to praise or honor

boor (p106)
>a crude, ill-mannered person

disclaim (p114)
>to deny any knowledge of or connection with

menace (p115)
>to threaten with evil or harm

insignia (p120)
>a badge or emblem used as a special mark of membership, office, or honor

armistice (p124)
>an agreement to stop fighting for a short time; a truce

Gestapo (p126)
>the secret police in Germany under the Nazis

patriot (p127)
>a person who loves his or her country and loyally defends and supports it

Fuehrer (p128)
>a German word meaning "leader"

ballast (p156)
>anything heavy, such as sand, stone, or water, carried in a ship, balloon, or other container to steady it

Small Group Reading

📖 Yolen, Jane. *The Devil's Arithmetic*. New York: Viking Kestrel, 1988.
>This story answers those who question why the Holocaust should be remembered. It is a time-warp story that transports a young girl back to Poland in the 1940s. Grades 4-8.

Author Information

Jane Yolen was born February 11, 1937 in New York, New York.

Yolen has been a professional writer since 1965. She has worked at various positions in the publishing world, including production assistant, assistant editor, associate editor, and assistant juvenile editor. She has been the editor of the imprint Jane Yolen Books for Harcourt Brace Jovanovich since 1988.

Yolen has won numerous awards and honors, including the Caldecott Medal in 1988 for *Owl Moon* and the Regina Medal for a body of writing in children's literature, 1992.

Jane Yolen has written dozens of books for a variety of age groups in various genre: young adult fiction, adult fiction, adult nonfiction, juvenile fiction, juvenile nonfiction, and juvenile poetry. She has also contributed articles, reviews, and short stories to publications such as *The Writer*, *The New York Times*, *The Los Angeles Times*, *Parents' Choice*, and *The Horn Book*.

Activities

1. Have students research any of the following Nazi concentration camps, then share the information orally with the class.

Auschwitz	Chelmno
Bergen-Belsen	Dachau
Birkenau	Mauthausen
Buchenwald	Ravensbruck

2. After students have finished reading *The Devil's Arithmetic*, have them write letters to the Nazis telling them their feelings about what took place in concentration camps. They should reinforce their opinions with facts they have learned. Have students share their letters with the rest of the class.

3. Throughout their reading of *The Devil's Arithmetic*, have students write journal entries from Hannah's point of view.

4. Have students in the group prepare a book talk to give to another class or to the whole school during morning announcements. They should explain why it is so important for people today to understand the horrors that the Jews faced at the hands of the Nazis.

Discussion

Give the small group the following instruction: As your group reads this book, discuss the following questions.

1. Why doesn't Hannah want to go to her grandparents' house?

2. Why was Hannah's grandfather so upset when Hannah and her family arrived?

3. What happened when Hannah opened the door for the prophet Elijah?

4. When Hannah tried to explain to Shmuel that she was not Chaya, what did he think?

5. When Hannah tells Rachel and the other girls that her best friend is Catholic, what is their reaction?

6. Why were the girls shocked when Rachel told them she went to school?

7. Why did Hannah ask what year it was when they got to the bride's village?

8. How could Hannah's memories serve as a warning?

9. What were Hannah, the wedding party, and all the wedding guests told by the Nazis about why they were being taken away in the trucks?

10. What were the people arguing about in the boxcars?

11. What is the most important word the Jews were told to learn?

12. What happened to Rachel?

13. How does the information that Hannah has from the future frighten her even more?

14. What happened to Hannah as her hair was being cut off?

15. Discuss what is happening to Hannah and the rest of the Jews in the barracks. Think about what you have to be thankful for in your life and compare it to their life in the barracks.

16. Why did Rivka tell Hannah that the bowls they were given were called "Every Bowls."

17. What did Rivka mean about the stories being such brutal arithmetic?

18. Describe what takes place when there is a Choosing?

19. What happened when Hannah and the others tried to escape?

20. Why did Hannah take Rivka's place with the guard and tell her to run and remember?

21. What was the surprise Hannah received when she was mysteriously transported back to her own time?

22. According to Jane Yolen, what were the victories of the death camps?

Vocabulary

Passover (p3)
a Jewish feast commemorating the night when God, killing the firstborn children of the Egyptians, "passed over" the houses of the Hebrews

Seder (p4)
in Judaism, the feast in remembrance of the departure of the Israelites from Egypt, celebrated on the eve of the first day of Passover

steerage (p10)
the part of a passenger ship, it offered little or no comfort or privacy, that was open to passengers paying the lowest fares

exodus (p13)
a departure or going away

fast (p36)
to go without food or avoid certain foods, such as for religious reasons

cossack (p46)
one of a people of southern Russia noted as horsemen and soldiers

clique (p51)
a small group whose members stick together and shut out outsiders

synagogue (p62)
a place of meeting for Jewish worship and religious instruction

Nazi (p64)
a member of the fascist political party that controlled Germany from 1933 to 1945 under Adolf Hitler

desecrate (p69)
to treat something sacred without reverence, or use it in an unworthy way

Holocaust (p72)
defined as a huge destruction by fire, it refers to the murder of Jews by the Nazis

crematoria (p72)
furnaces or buildings containing such furnaces where dead bodies are burned to ashes

stench (p78)
a foul odor

peasant (p79)
in Europe, a country person of humble birth, such as a small farmer

hysteria (p80)
uncontrolled excitement or emotion

alienate (p81)
to make unfriendly; to lose the friendship of

kosher (p82)
clean or proper, according to Jewish religious laws

impudent (p82)
offensively bold; rude; insolent

stark (p88)
barren; bleak

schnell (p89)
German word for "fast" or "quickly"

ritual (p90)
a body or system of rites and ceremonies

affirmation (p101)
a validation; a positive assertion

ominous (p102)
threatening or foreboding

arbitrary (p108)
based only on one's own will, feelings, or notions

elusive (p109)
hard to understand, remember, or recognize

raucous (p110)
rough in sound; hoarse; harsh

cholera (p120)
an infectious bacterial disease that attacks the intestines, often causing death

portent (p146)
a warning or sign of what is to come

Bibliography

Individual Titles

Abels, Chana Byers. *The Children We Remember.* New York: Greenwillow Books, 1986.

Using simple language, this book makes it painfully clear and understandable for children today what happened to Jewish children when the Nazis came to power. Grades 4-6.

Avi. *Who Was That Masked Man, Anyway?* New York: Orchard, 1992.

In a story told through dialogue, sixth-grader Frankie lives through World War II by immersing himself in his beloved radio serials. Grades 5-7.

Bachrach, Susan D. *Tell Them We Remember: The Story of the Holocaust.* Boston: Little, Brown, 1994.

The author uses text and photographs to convey the powerful stories and images of the Holocaust. She draws on artifacts, photographs, maps, and taped oral and video histories from the United States Holocaust Memorial Museum to tell the story of the Holocaust and how it affected the lives of innocent people throughout Europe. Grades 5 and up.

Boas, Jacob. *We Are Witnesses: Five Diaries of Teenagers Who Died in the Holocaust.* New York: Henry Holt, 1995.

Boas, a survivor of a Nazi concentration camp himself, gives personal diary accounts of five Jewish teenagers who died in concentration camps during the Holocaust. Grades 8 and up.

Coerr, Eleanor. *Sadako and the Thousand Paper Cranes.* New York: G. P. Putnam's Sons, 1977.

This is a biography about Sadako Sasaki, a Japanese girl who died of leukemia ten years after the bombing of Hiroshima as a result of radiation exposure. Grades 2-5.

Davies, Andrew. *Conrad's War.* New York: Crown, 1980.

Conrad has daydreams about war that become terrifyingly real when he wakes up a prisoner in Nazi Germany. Grades 4-8.

Frank, Anne. *Anne Frank, The Diary of a Young Girl.* Revised edition. New York: Doubleday, 1967.

This is the diary of a young girl who was forced by the encroaching Nazi regime to live in enforced seclusion with family and friends. Grades 7 and up.

Garrigue, Sheila. *The Eternal Spring of Mr. Ito.* New York: Bradbury Press, 1985.

During World War II, Sara is evacuated to live with her aunt and uncle in Vancouver. Mr. Ito, the family's gardener, becomes a special friend to Sara. After the Japanese attack Pearl Harbor and Hong Kong, Japanese-Canadians are persecuted, but Sara manages to maintain her relationship with the Itos. Grades 4 and up.

Gehrts, Barbara. *Don't Say a Word.* New York: Margaret K. McElderry, 1986.

Anna's father is a Luftwaffe colonel who secretly opposes the Nazis. His two children learn how essential silence is, as they must appear to be loyal members of the Hitler Youth. Grades 7 and up.

Green, Connie Jordan. *The War at Home.* New York: Margaret K. McElderry, 1989.

During World War II, thirteen-year-old Mattie and her family move to Oak Ridge, Tennessee, where her father has a secret job. Grades 5-8.

Greene, Bette. *The Summer of My German Soldier.* New York: Bantam Books, 1974.

A mistreated Jewish girl befriends an escaped German prisoner of war because he is kind to her. Grades 6-9.

Greenfeld, Howard. *The Hidden Children.* New York: Ticknor & Fields, 1993.

Stories of thirteen survivors create a portrait of the Holocaust as lived by the hidden children. Grades 5 and up.

Hahn, Mary Downing. *Stepping on the Cracks.* New York: Clarion Books, 1991.

In 1944, while her brother is overseas fighting in World War II, eleven-year-old Margaret gets a new view of school bully Gordy when she finds him hiding his own brother, an army deserter, and decides to help. Grades 3-7.

Hall, Donald. *The Farm Summer 1942.* New York: Dial Books for Young Readers, 1994.

Peter spends the summer on his grandparents' farm in New Hampshire while his mother works in the war effort in New York and his father serves on a destroyer in the Pacific. Grades 2-4.

Hest, Amy. *Love You, Soldier.* New York: Four Winds Press, 1991.

When seven-year-old Katie says good-bye to her soldier father in 1942, her family seems to shrink unbearably. Over the long and difficult years of World War II, Katie's ideas of what a family are changed. Grades 2-5.

Hoestlandt, Jo. *Star of Fear, Star of Hope.* New York: Walker, 1995.

Nine-year-old Helen is confused by the disappearance of her Jewish friend during the German occupation of Paris. Grades 2-5.

Holm, Anne. *North to Freedom*. San Diego, CA: Harcourt Brace Jovanovich, 1963.

A boy who has never known anything except life in a concentration camp makes his way across Europe alone and escapes to freedom. Grades 6-8.

Hotze, Sollace. *Summer Endings*. New York: Clarion Books, 1991.

Twelve-year-old Christine is a Polish immigrant whose father is trapped in Poland as a result of the Nazi invasion. During the summer of 1945 many things happen, including the end of the war and the finding of Christine's father. Grades 5 and up.

Houston, Gloria. *But No Candy*. New York: Philomel, 1992.

While her Uncle Ted is off fighting in World War II, Lee watches the candy gradually disappear from the shelves of her family's store and realizes that her entire world has changed. Grades 1-4.

Hurwitz, Johanna. *Anne Frank: Life in Hiding*. The Jewish Publication Society, 1988.

Hurwitz's easy-to-read story of Anne Frank's life allows young readers to share Anne's childhood dreams and to feel the tension of the years that follow. Grades 2-5.

Innocenti, Roberto, and Christophe Gallaz. *Rose Blanche*. Mankato, MN: Creative Education, 1985.

A German girl discovers a concentration camp near her home during World War II, brings food to the children there, and is later killed in cross fire. The illustrations are wonderful. Grades 4-7.

Krull, Kathleen. *V Is for Victory*. New York: Alfred A. Knopf, 1995.

This book describes life in the United States during World War II, discussing such activities as civil defense, the Japanese relocation, rationing, propaganda, and censorship. Grades 4 and up.

Kudlinski, Kathleen V. *Pearl Harbor Is Burning! A Story of World War II*. New York: Viking, 1991.

Historic events are brought into perspective in a fictional framework as Frank, a newcomer to Hawaii, must learn to adjust to island living. Grades 4-6.

Levitin, Sonia. *Journey to America*. New York: Atheneum, 1993.

Lisa and her family try to escape from Nazi Germany to join her father in the United States. Grades 3-6.

Little, Jean. *Listen for the Singing*. New York: HarperCollins, 1991.

As the world braces itself for World War II, a young Canadian girl with impaired vision prepares to begin public high school. Grades 4-7.

Lowry, Lois. *Autumn Street*. Boston: Houghton Mifflin, 1980.

Six-year-old Elizabeth, her sister, and her mother go to live with her grandmother in Pennsylvania during World War II. Grades 6-9.

Marko, Katherine McGlade. *Hang Out the Flag*. New York: Macmillan, 1992.

In 1943, sixth-grader Leslie tries to come up with a welcome-home present for her soldier father. Her surprise, a giant American flag painted on a water tower, turns out to be the perfect gift. Grades 3-7.

Marrin, Albert. *Victory in the Pacific*. New York: Atheneum, 1983.

Beginning with the attack on Pearl Harbor, this book tells what happened at such little-known places as Midway, Betio, and Guadalcanal that had a great effect on the war. Grades 6 and up.

Marx, Trish. *Echoes of World War II*. Minneapolis, MN: Lerner, 1994.

Marx presents the stories of six people from different parts of the world whose childhoods were shaped by their experiences during World War II. Grades 5 and up.

Matas, Carol. *Daniel's Story*. New York: Scholastic, 1993.

Through real and mental pictures, a Jewish man recalls his childhood during the Nazi Holocaust. Grades 4-8.

———. *Kris's War*. New York: Scholastic, 1989.

After the Nazi occupation of Denmark forces his Jewish friends to flee the country, seventeen-year-old Jesper continues his work in the underground resistance movement. This sequel to *Lisa's War* was formerly titled *Code Name Kris*. Grades 7 and up.

Mazer, Harry. *The Last Mission*. New York: Delacorte Press, 1979.

This novel is about a young American Jewish boy who lied his way into military service in World War II. Grades 6 and up.

Mochizuki, Ken. *Baseball Saved Us*. New York: Lee & Low Books, 1993.

A Japanese-American boy learns to play baseball when he and his family are forced to live in an internment camp during World War II, and his ability to play helps after the war is over. Grades 2-5.

Pfeifer, Kathryn Browne. *The 761st Tank Battalion*. New York: Twenty-First Century Books, 1994.

The 761st Tank Battalion was the first black armored unit to be committed to combat in World War II. These soldiers were called the "Black Panthers." Their 183 continuous days in combat are chronicled in text and photographs. Grades 5 and up.

Poynter, Margaret. *A Time Too Swift*. New York: Atheneum, 1990.

This novel about fifteen-year-old Marjorie is complete with songs and expressions from 1940s

America. Marjorie has romantic daydreams about the war, which become colored by what happens to people she loves and cares for. Grades 5 and up.

Ray, Deborah Kogan. *My Daddy Was a Soldier: A World War II Story*. New York: Holiday House, 1990.
Young Jeannie tells how she felt when her father first left to fight in the war and relates her fears of bombs and her father coming home wounded or not at all. Grades 1-5.

Raymond, Patrick. *Daniel and Esther*. New York: Margaret K. McElderry, 1990.
Daniel, an unruly, intelligent teenager in a progressive English school, tells the story of gifted youths under the threat of war during the years 1936 to 1939. Grades 7 and up.

Reiss, Johanna. *The Upstairs Room*. New York: Thomas Y. Crowell, 1972.
Two young Jewish girls hide for more than two years in the home of a simple Dutch peasant during the German occupation. Grades 5-8.

Rosenberg, Maxine B. *Hiding to Survive: Stories of Jewish Children Rescued from the Holocaust*. New York: Clarion Books, 1994.
Fourteen men and women tell about their childhood, the horrors they witnessed, the courage of their rescuers, and their will to survive. Grades 6 and up.

Roth-Hano, Renée. *Touch Wood: A Girlhood in Occupied France*. New York: Four Winds Press, 1988.
This is an autobiographical novel set in Nazi-occupied France. Renée, a young Jewish girl, and her family flee their home in Alsace and live a precarious existence in Paris until Renée and her sister escape to the shelter of a Catholic women's residence in Normandy. Grades 5-9.

Schellie, Don. *Shadow and the Gunner*. New York: Four Winds Press, 1982.
This is a remembrance of World War II—of friendship, parting, and death. Grades 4-6.

Serraillier, Ian. *Escape from Warsaw*. New York: Scholastic, 1990.
Three Polish children try to escape from their war-ravaged home during World War II. Grades 7 and up.

Stanley, Jerry. *I Am an American: A True Story of Japanese Internment*. New York: Crown, 1994.
Shi Nomur, a high school senior, and his family witness the typical conditions that American citizens of Japanese origin had to endure during World War II. Many photographs are included. Grades 5 and up.

Sullivan, George. *Strange but True Stories of World War II*. New York: Walker, 1983.
This book features eleven very strange, true incidents that took place during World War II. Grades 5 and up.

Todd, Leonard. *The Best Kept Secret of the War*. New York: Alfred A. Knopf, 1984.
This is the story of a young boy growing up in North Carolina during World War II. Grades 5-7.

Tripp, Valerie. *Happy Birthday Molly!* Middleton, WI: Pleasant, 1987.
When an English girl comes to stay at Molly's during World War II, she and Molly learn to bridge their differences and ultimately enjoy a wonderful, mutual birthday party. Grades 4-6.

———. *Meet Molly: An American Girl*. Middleton, WI: Pleasant, 1986.
Molly grows up in the United States during World War II without a father. Grades 3-5.

———. *Molly's Surprise: A Christmas Story*. Middleton, WI: Pleasant, 1986.
Molly's father finds a way to make Christmas special even though he is away serving in an English hospital during World War II. Grades 4-6.

Uchida, Yoshiko. *Journey Home*. New York: Atheneum, 1978.
Twelve-year-old Yuki and her Japanese-American family face many problems getting their lives back together in California after leaving Topaz, a World War II concentration camp in Utah. Contrast this book with *Introducing Shirley Braverman* by Hilma Wolitzer. Grades 5-7.

van der Rol, Ruud, and Rian Verhoeven. *Anne Frank: Beyond the Diary*. New York: Viking, 1993.
Photographs, illustrations, and maps accompany historical essays, diary excerpts, and interviews, providing an insightful look at Anne Frank and the tremendous upheaval that tore her world apart. Many of the photographs of Anne and her family had never been published previously. Grades 5 and up.

Vos, Ida. *Anna Is Still Here*. Boston: Houghton Mifflin, 1993.
This is a story of a survivor of the Holocaust and her adjustment to freedom after years of solitude and terror. Grades 4-8.

———. *Hide and Seek*. Boston: Houghton Mifflin, 1991.
This is a first-person narrative of a Jewish girl in Holland during the Nazi occupation. Grades 4-8.

Weatherford, Doris. *American Women and World War II*. New York: Facts on File, 1990.
World War II was the beginning of a permanent role for women in the military. Besides their active military service, women also worked as nurses, airplane builders, and civil volunteers. Grades 8 and up.

Westall, Robert. *The Machine Gunners*. New York: Greenwillow Books, 1976.

A group of teenagers plan to use a scavenged Nazi machine gun to launch a counterattack on invading Germans in this novel, based on a true World War II incident. Grades 5 and up.

Wolitzer, Hilma. *Introducing Shirley Braverman*. New York: Farrar, Straus & Giroux, 1975.

This novel tells of twelve-year-old Shirley Braverman's experiences growing up in Brooklyn during the last year of World War II. Contrast this book with *Journey Home* by Yoshiko Uchida. Grades 8 and up.

Theme Resources

Commercial Resources

Cobblestone: The History Magazine for Young People. Peterborough, NH: Cobblestone.

The subject of the January 1993 issue for grades 4 and up is "World War II: Americans in Europe." Articles include "Chronology of the War in Europe" and "Wartime Food."

The subject of the January 1994 issue for grades 4 and up is "World War II: Americans in the Pacific." Articles include "War in the Pacific: The Big Picture" and "They're Bombing Pearl Harbor!"

Gilbert, Martin, compiler. *Jackdaw: The Coming of War 1939*. Amawalk, NY: Jackdaw Publications, 1995.

This portfolio of primary source materials contains eleven reproductions of historical documents. They include a booklet of pictures and quotations illustrating the spread of fascism and Hitler's rise to power and the front page of the *New York Daily Herald*, September 4, 1939, announcing the outbreak of war. This booklet includes comprehensive notes on the documents, along with a reading list and critical thinking questions for students in grades 5 and up.

Klimowski, Bob, and Mary Gillaspy. *Anne Frank: The Diary of a Young Girl*. Logan, IA: Perfection Form, 1988.

This reproducible activity book contains activity sheets, an author biography, and writing activities for students in grades 6-12.

Myers, Kathleen, ed. *Inquiring into the Theme of World War II, The Resistance: Based on Louis Lowry's Number the Stars*. Logan, IA: Perfection Learning, 1994.

This resource includes activities for *Number the Stars*, and background information for the theme. Use with students in grades 6-8.

Phillips, William. *Jackdaw: The Holocaust*. Amawalk, NY: Jackdaw Publications, 1992.

This portfolio of primary source material contains twelve reproductions of historical documents. They include A Chronology of the Holocaust, 1933–1945; newspaper accounts of Nazi terror, 1938–1942; and a collection of photographs on the horrors of the Holocaust. The portfolio also includes notes on the documents, a reading list, and critical thinking questions for students in grades 5 and up.

Reeves, Barbara. *Novel Ties: Number the Stars*. New Hyde Park, NY: Learning Links, 1991.

This resource contains pre-reading and post-reading activities, vocabulary skills, comprehension questions, and writing activities in a chapter-by-chapter format for *Number the Stars*. Use booklet with students in grades 4-8.

Strathman, Julie R. *Thematic Unit: World War II*. Huntington Beach, CA: Teacher Created Materials, 1994.

This resource book for use with students in grades 5 and up includes a variety of theme-based activities for all curriculum areas.

Tretler, Marcia. *Novel Ties: Anne Frank: The Diary of a Young Girl*. New Hyde Park, NY: Learning Links, 1991.

This resource contains pre-reading and post-reading activities, vocabulary skills, comprehension questions, and writing activities in a chapter-by-chapter format for *Anne Frank: The Diary of a Young Girl*. Use with students in grades 7 and up.

Computer Resources

The Causes of WWII. [CD-ROM]. Chicago: Clearvue, 1994.

This interactive CD-ROM explores how the events and consequences of World War I sowed the seeds for a new conflict. It chronicles the rise to power of new totalitarian regimes and the events that led to global conflict.

War in the Pacific. [CD-ROM]. Boston: Flagtower Multimedia, 1995.

War in the Pacific tells the story of what took place in the Pacific during World War II through film footage, commentary, maps, and historical photographs.

World War II. [CD-ROM]. Boston: Flagtower Multimedia, 1995.

This CD-ROM provides forty minutes of film footage, two hours of commentary, more than 100 maps, and more than 2,000 photographs. Key themes examined include Hitler, the Holocaust, and the civilians' war.

Videos

The Diary of Anne Frank. Beverly Hills, CA: CBS/Fox Video, 1984. (151 minutes)

This video is based on the diary that Anne Frank kept while in forced seclusion during the Holocaust.

The Holocaust: In Memory of Millions. Bethesda, MD: Discovery Channel, 1994. (60 minutes)

Journalist Walter Cronkite tells the story of the Holocaust—from the rise of the Nazis and their plan to exterminate the Jewish people, to tales of incredible bravery among Holocaust survivors and those who liberated the concentration camps.

Summer of My German Soldier. New York: Simon & Schuster Video, 1986. (98 minutes)

Sheltering an escaped German prisoner of war marks the beginning of some shattering experiences for a twelve-year-old Jewish girl in Arkansas.

End-of-Unit Celebration

World War II Research Project

Individually or in groups of two, have your students research the following topics. When completed, hold a presentation day.

Auschwitz

Bergen-Belsen

Bombing of Hiroshima

Bombing of Nagasaki

Bombing of Pearl Harbor

Chelmo—in Poland

D-Day

Dachau

General Dwight D. Eisenhower

Japanese-American Internment Camps

Life in the United States During World War II

President Franklin D. Roosevelt

Sobibor

Soviet Leader Joseph Stalin

Theresienstadt

Treblinka

Winston Churchill

Women's Roles in the United States to Help the War Effort

Chapter 10

Supplemental U.S. History Resources

Aten, Jerry. *Challenge Through American History.* Carthage, IL: Good Apple, 1992.

Explore American History with students in grades 4-8 through 1,440 questions on 360 durable game cards.

Cobblestone: The History Magazine for Young People. Peterborough, NH: Cobblestone.

The focus of the January 1990 issue for grades 4 and up is "What Is History?" Articles include "We Cannot Escape History," "History for the Future," and "Living History."

The January 1995 issue contains articles on the U.S. Constitution of the United States, Abraham Lincoln, and World War II.

Cohn, Amy L., compiler. *From Sea to Shining Sea: A Treasury of American Folklore and Folk Songs.* New York: Scholastic, 1993.

This is an anthology of more than 140 American folktales, songs, poems, and essays arranged in fifteen thematic, chronological sections. Use this book with students in grades 4 and up to trace America's history from pre-Columbian time to today.

Fischer, Max W. *American History Simulations.* Huntington Beach, CA: Teacher Created Materials, 1993.

Simulations, problem-solving dilemmas, and games related to important events in American history will excite your students in grades 4-8.

Garraty, John A. *1,001 Things Everyone Should Know About American History.* New York: Doubleday, 1989.

This book presents short entries about people, places, ideas, politics, and events from America's past in an entertaining manner. Use with students in grades 7 and up.

Gordon, Patricia, and Reed C. Snow. *Kids Learn America! Bringing Geography to Life with People, Places and History.* Charlotte, VT: Williamson, 1992.

This book provides information on geography, history, and culture of the states and territories of the United States. Can be used with students in grades 4-8.

Hopkins, Lee Bennett, collector. *Hand in Hand: An American History Through Poetry.* New York: Simon & Schuster, 1994.

This collection of poems and lyrics from several songs provides students in grades 3 and up with a look at our country, from colonial times to the present.

Kalman, Bobbie. *Historic Communities: 18th Century Clothing.* New York: Crabtree, 1993.

Kalman examines the clothing styles, accessories, and hygiene habits of men, women, and children in eighteenth-century North America. Use with students in grades 4-7.

———. *Historic Communities: 19th Century Clothing.* New York: Crabtree, 1993.

Kalman examines the clothes and accessories worn by nineteenth-century men, women, and children in North America. Use with students in grades 4-7.

Laughlin, Mildred Knight, Peggy Tubbs Black, and Margery Kirby Loberg. *Social Studies Readers Theatre for Children.* Englewood, CO: Teacher Ideas Press, 1991.

This volume includes fourteen tall-tale scripts, as well as a section using eight books by Laura Ingalls Wilder in a readers theatre program. Also included are sixty suggested scripts for students to write based on passages from books about colonial America and the Revolutionary War, the Civil War, the settling of the West, and twentieth-century America. Use with students in grades 4 and up.

Lloyd, Ruth, and Norman Lloyd, compilers. *The American Heritage Songbook.* New York: American Heritage, 1969.

This book contains many songs about United States history for use with students in grades 5 and up.

Panzer, Nora, ed. *Celebrate America in Poetry and Art.* New York: Hyperion Books for Children, 1994.

Panzer includes a collection of American poetry that celebrates more than 200 years of American life and history as illustrated by art from the collection of the National Museum of Modern Art. Use this book with students in grades 3 and up.

Perl, Lila. *It Happened in America: True Stories from the Fifty States.* New York: Henry Holt, 1992.

This book, suitable for students in grades 4-8, contains historical anecdotes from each of the fifty states. It emphasizes women and ethnic minorities.

Philip, Neil, selector. *Singing America.* New York: Viking, 1995.

This is a wonderful volume of American poetry, appropriate for use with students in grades 5 and up.

Pillar, Arlene M., Ph.D. *Reading Books for Social Studies: A Study Guide.* New Hyde Park, NY: Learning Links, 1991.

This resource describes how social studies trade books should be used as a part of the instructional program. Includes reproducible student pages for use with students in grades 2-5.

Rubel, David. *Scholastic Timelines: The United States in the 20th Century.* New York: Scholastic, 1995.

Through the use of time lines and many photographs and illustrations, students in grades 4 and up can discovers a treasure of information on the twentieth century.

Ryan, Concetta Doti. *Learning Through Literature: Social Studies.* Huntington Beach, CA: Teacher Created Materials, 1994.

This book includes book summaries, connecting activities, reproducible student pages, and more on topics such as American Symbols and Monuments, Our Nation's Heroes, Life in the Past, and Immigration. Use with intermediate-level students.

———. *Learning Through Literature: U.S. History.* Huntington Beach, CA: Teacher Created Materials, 1994.

This resource includes book summaries, activities, and reproducible student pages for Discovery of the Americas, Colonization, Westward Expansion, the American Revolution, Civil War, World War I, World War II, and the Vietnam War. Use with intermediate-level students.

Computer Resources

Eyewitness History of the World. [CD-ROM]. New York: Dorling Kindersley Multimedia, 1995.

This CD-ROM provides a wealth of information about the history of the world, including U.S. history.

Mario Is Missing! A Multimedia Geography Adventure. [CD-ROM]. Novato, CA: Software Toolworks, 1992–1994.

Although students will have fun learning about geography, they will also discover historical information.

Time Table of History. [CD-ROM]. Novato, CA: Software Toolworks, 1991.

This is a CD-ROM for the Macintosh. More than 6,000 stories and thousands of graphics trace the history of man. It includes a time line of major historic events through which students can select a range of years to explore.

Total History. [CD-ROM]. Parsippany, NJ: Bureau of Electronic Publishing, 1994.

This three-disc CD-ROM set contains information on the history of the world, countries of the world, and U.S. history.

U.S. History and Geography. [CD-ROM]. Bloomington, MN: Dinosoft, 1995.

Students learn about U.S. history through time lines on explorers, presidents, and states.

Videos

School House Rock: History Rock! Racine, WI: American Broadcasting, 1987. (32 minutes)

This animated video contains songs and sketches that make it fun to learn about history.

(Figures 10.1, 10.2, and 10.3 follow on pages 210–12.)

Fig. 10.1. **Literature response guide.***

The use of literature response journals is an excellent way to guide students' reading of individual trade books. Literature response journals can be used as part of independent reading at home or at school.

Each student will need a notebook of some type for responding to their reading. The following is a guide to help lead students in responding to literature. Each student should have a copy of this guide stapled to the inside of his or her notebook. Although you may have more specific events you would like students to respond to in certain books, this general guide is very helpful. I have seen it used with upper elementary students and the results have been wonderful! In a short span of three months, growth in their responses was remarkable. Students put a lot more thought into their reading and their written responses.

LITERATURE RESPONSE GUIDE

1. **Pointing Response**

    What did you like about what you read?

    What does the author make you see or feel?

    Use quotes from the book to point out things you liked.

2. **Questioning Response**

    What questions do you have about the reading?

    What would you like to find out more about?

    I wonder . . .

3. **Memory Response**

    What do things or events in the book make you think of?

    Does the reading remind you of something you read in another book? Explain.

    Does a character remind you of a person you know in your life or a character you met in another story?

4. **Prediction Response**

    What do you think will happen next and why?

5. **Information Response**

    What did you learn from the book?

    What do you want to learn more about?

6. **Vocabulary Response**

    Make a note of any vocabulary words you do not know, look up the words, and write down the definitions

7. **Feeling Response**

    How are you feeling about events or characters? Have your feelings changed while reading? How and why have they changed?

8. **Summary Response**

    Write a three- or four-sentence summary of the chapter or what you have read so far. Remember to only include the most important events of the chapter.

*Written by Leslie Wood.

Fig. 10.2. **Research guide.**

Student Name _____

Topic _____

OUTLINE

I. Introduction of Topic:

II. Notes (Important facts from library sources; use notebook paper for additional space)**:**

III. Conclusion:

IV. Bibliography (Be sure to write down all necessary information for each source used. This includes: author, title, publisher, copyright date. Also, if you are using a magazine article, include the name of the article and page numbers)**:**

Fig. 10.3. **Social studies/language arts integrated project.**

GRADING SHEET

Student Name_____

Topic _____

Graded by Social Studies teacher: _____

   Grade for historical facts present in the paper _____
   Comments:

Graded by English teacher: _____

   Grade for written presentation _____
   Comments:

Overall Project Grade: _____

Index

About
the Author

Wanda Miller received her bachelor's degree in psychology and her master's degree in reading from Nazareth College of Rochester in Pittsford, New York. Besides being certified to teach reading, she also holds New York State certification in elementary education and special education.

Wanda has worked as a freelance writer and editor for Perma-Bound, and has had eight teacher guides published. She also wrote a short story titled "Mom, I'm a Reader!" which was published in the Our Own Stories section of the October 1996 issue of *The Reading Teacher*, a journal of the International Reading Association.

Wanda teaches remedial reading in grades three through five in Williamson Elementary and Middle Schools in Williamson, New York. She served on the Board of Directors for the Rochester Area Reading Council from 1994 to 1997.

Wanda lives in Marion, New York with her husband, Randy, and their two children, Randy and Kari.

More Social Studies Fun

from **Teacher Ideas Press**

TEACHING U.S. HISTORY THROUGH CHILDREN'S LITERATURE: Post World War II
Wanda J. Miller

This book contains more great resources to help you combine recommended children's literature with actual events in U.S. History, from World War II to the present. The perfect companion to *U.S. History Through Children's Literature*! **Grades 4–8.**
xiii, 229p. 81/2x11 paper ISBN 1-56308-581-X

EXTRAORDINARY PEOPLE IN EXTRAORDINARY TIMES: Heroes, Sheroes, and Villains
Patrick M. Mendoza

Stories about dozens of unsung heros, from the first woman to receive the Congressional Medal of Honor to the African American man who broke precedence to fire a gun during the attack on Pearl Harbor, will spark student curiosity in American history. **Grades 4–9.**
x, 142p. 6x9 paper ISBN 1-56308-611-5

FOUR GREAT RIVERS TO CROSS: Cheyenne History, Culture, and Traditions
Patrick M. Mendoza, Ann Strange Owl-Raben, and Nico Strange Owl

Selected as an Honor Anthology of the Storytelling World Awards, this book presents the story of the Cheyenne people and chronicles their history and culture. Short stories focus on everything from creation accounts and the introduction of horses to society to tales of the present day. **Grades 3–8.**
x, 131p. 8½x11 paper ISBN 1-56308-471-6

NATIVE AMERICANS TODAY: Resources and Activities for Educators, Grades 4–8
Arlene Hirschfelder and Yvonne Beamer

Reproducible activities, biographies of real people, and accurate background information help you present a realistic and diverse picture of American Indians in the twentieth century. Each lesson has everything you need to plan and carry out the enriching projects. **Grades 4–8.**
xix, 243p. 8½x11 paper ISBN 1-56308-694-8

TEACHING WITH FOLK STORIES OF THE HMONG: An Activity Book
Dia Cha and Norma J. Livo

Teach students about Hmong culture, build appreciation of diversity, and extend learning across the curriculum with engaging activities based on Hmong folktales and traditions. **All Levels**.
ca.110p. 8½x11 paper ISBN 1-56308-668-9

JURY TRIALS IN THE CLASSROOM
Betty M. See

Court is in session! Use these mock trials to help students participate in the dynamics of the judicial and criminal systems. As students prepare and conduct cases as in real life, they learn what makes the bureaucracy function. Detailed instructions are included. **Grades 5–8.**
xiv, 163p. paper ISBN 1-56308-561-5

For a free catalog or to place an order, please contact: Teacher Ideas Press/Libraries Unlimited
• **Call: 1-800-237-6124**
• **Fax: 303-220-8843**
• **E-mail: lu-books@lu.com**
• **Mail to: Dept. B022 • P.O. Box 6633**
   Englewood, CO 80155-6633